The Arnold and Caroline Rose Monograph Series
of the American Sociological Association

Cities with little crime

The case of Switzerland

Other books in the series

J. Milton Yinger, Kiyoshi Ikeda, Frank Laycock, and Stephen J. Cutler: *Middle Start: An Experiment in the Educational Enrichment of Young Adolescents*

James A. Geschwender: *Class, Race, and Worker Insurgency: The League of Revolutionary Black Workers*

Paul Ritterband: *Education, Employment, and Migration: Israel in Comparative Perspective*

John Low-Beer: *Protest and Participation: The New Working Class in Italy*

Rita James Simon: *Continuity and Change: A Study of Two Ethnic Communities in Israel*

Orrin E. Klapp: *Opening and Closing: Strategies of Information Adaptation in Society*

Volumes previously published by the American Sociological Association

Michael Schwartz and Sheldon Stryker: *Deviance, Selves and Others*

Robert M. Hauser: *Socioeconomic Background and Educational Performance*

Morris Rosenberg and Roberta G. Simmons: *Black and White Self-Esteem: The Urban School Child*

Chad Gordon: *Looking Ahead: Self-Conceptions: Race and Family as Determinants of Adolescent Orientation to Achievement*

Anthony M. Orum: *Black Students in Protest: A Study of the Origins of the Black Student Movement*

Ruth M. Gasson, Archibald O. Haller, and William H. Sewell: *Attitudes and Facilitation in the Attainment of Status*

Sheila R. Klatzky: *Patterns of Contact with Relatives*

Herman Turk: *Interorganizational Activation in Urban Communities: Deductions from the Concept of System*

John DeLamater: *The Study of Political Commitment*

Alan C. Kerckhoff: *Ambition and Attainment: A Study of Four Samples of American Boys*

Scott McNall: *The Greek Peasant*

Lowell L. Hargens: *Patterns of Scientific Research: A Comparative Analysis of Research in Three Scientific Fields*

Charles Hirschman: *Ethnic Stratification in Peninsular Malaysia*

Cities with little crime

The case of Switzerland

Marshall B. Clinard

Professor of Sociology
The University of Wisconsin – Madison

Cambridge University Press

Cambridge

London   New York   Melbourne

Published by the Syndics of the Cambridge University Press
The Pitt Building, Trumpington Street, Cambridge CB2 1RP
Bentley House, 200 Euston Road, London NW1 2DB
32 East 57th Street, New York, NY 10022, USA
296 Beaconsfield Parade, Middle Park, Melbourne 3206, Australia

© Cambridge University Press 1978

First published 1978

Printed in the United States of America

Typeset by Telecki Publishing Services, Yonkers, New York
Printed and bound by the Murray Printing Company, Westford, Massachusetts

Library of Congress Cataloging in Publication Data

Clinard, Marshall Barron, 1911–
Cities with little crime.
(The Arnold and Caroline Rose monograph series)
Includes bibliographical references and index.
1. Crime and criminals – Switzerland. 2. Criminal
justice, Administration of – Switzerland. I. Title.
II. Series: The Arnold and Caroline Rose monograph
series in sociology.
HV7053.C58   364'.9494   77–88672
ISBN 0 521 21960 4   hard covers
ISBN 0 521 29327 8   paperback

To Ruth
Companion on many travels
Who gave up her career to help with mine

Contents

Tables

Preface

This study attempts to analyze the unique crime situation in Switzerland and to compare it with that of other European countries and the United States. It might be presumed that Switzerland, as one of the world's most highly developed, affluent, industrialized, and urbanized countries, like the United States, Sweden, and the Federal German Republic, would also have a high and a rapidly increasing rate of crime. In the light of this study, however, it appears that Switzerland represents an important exception. For those countries that are faced with high and continually rising rates of crime, the findings have practical, as well as theoretical implications.

In carrying out this pioneer study of Swiss crime, I have tried to make a contribution to comparative criminology and, in particular, to methodology. In order to determine whether crime constitutes a problem to the Swiss, I have used a number of unusual research methods and sources in addition to official crime data. I have, for example, studied parliamentary debates, examined press coverage of crime news, carried out a crime victimization survey in Zürich, and considered theft insurance rates and trends. The crime victimization survey in Zürich is among the first to be conducted outside the United States. Throughout, I have tried to make the study comparative in nature, with frequent use of material from Sweden, the United States, and the Federal German Republic. In the end I have tried to offer some explanations or hypotheses for the relatively minor nature of crime in Switzerland, particularly as compared to Sweden. In addition, I have discussed the practical implications of the study for the United States and similar countries. I hope that these hypotheses will stimulate further studies of this type in Switzerland and elsewhere.

Comparative sociology and criminology have long been major interests of mine. I believe, like Durkheim, that we must test findings derived in one type of society on both similar and dissimilar societies. Some years ago I began my comparative research with a study of the relation

xi

of urbanization to the high crime rate of Sweden. Later I spent three years in India as a consultant with the Ford Foundation, looking into the problem of slums; in this endeavor I became familiar with the crime problem of Indian cities. (The results of this work in India were later published as *Slums and Community Development* [New York: The Free Press, 1966].) This stimulated my interest in crime in developing countries, and in 1968—69 I carried out, with Daniel Abbott, a comprehensive study of crime in Uganda. This research, carried out under a Rockefeller teaching and research grant, was the first systematic test in a developing country of a number of hypotheses derived in more affluent, developed countries. Together with extensive research in a number of other developing countries, it resulted in *Crime in Developing Countries* (with Daniel Abbott [New York: Wiley, 1973]). I then returned to my original interest in the highly developed countries, stimulated by my earlier work in Sweden.

For some time I had heard reports about the low crime profile in Switzerland, but all of them lacked adequate evidence. Moreover, I had had a number of personal experiences related to crime in Switzerland that had intrigued me. Years ago, while traveling in Italy, my wife and I were faced each night with the problem of protecting our car and its contents from theft. One night, when we could find no accommodation in the Lake Como area, we drove across the Swiss border to find a hotel. In reply to my inquiry about the safest place to leave the car and whether or not all contents should be removed, the proprietress said, "Sir, this is not Italy, this is Italian Switzerland." Later, at a dinner party in Stockholm, I was seated next to a man who had been a member of the Swiss parliament for fifteen years, and he astonished me by stating that he could not recall a single question about crime ever having been raised in Parliament while he was a member. My last personal experience was in Davos, Switzerland, in 1971, when I dropped my wallet on the streets. The concierge at my hotel assured me that I need not worry about its return. He said that if I called at the City Hall it would be there, in the Lost and Found office. It was!

I finally decided to apply for a grant to study crime in Switzerland. The research was carried out in 1973, supported primarily by a grant from the National Science Foundation that enabled me to live in Switzerland for eight months to gather data and to analyze them on my return. Other support has come from the University of Wisconsin Research Committee. Despite financial support from these sources, a cross-national survey of this type could not have been carried out without the full cooperation and assistance of many persons in Switzerland. In particular, I should like to acknowledge the continuing interest and help of Dr. Hans Schultz, Professor of Criminal Law at the University of Bern, who was my chief sponsor in the research. He helped to clarify issues and to make research arrangements with persons both in universities and in the government. In addition, he read the entire manuscript, caught errors, and made many helpful suggestions. (He is not, of course, responsible for what I did with them.) Three Swiss doctoral candidates served as my research assistants. They helped to gather the data, most of which were in German, and they continually offered suggestions and enthusiastic support for what turned out to be a far more difficult study than had been anticipated. Martin Killias, a student of law at the University of Zürich, did the work on the survey of the Zürich Canton Parliament and city council and the collection of data on insurance, on police and prisons, and on a variety of other subjects. Thomas Held of the Sociological Institute of the University of Zürich advised me on the victimization survey, translated the interview questionnaires, surveyed the crime content of newspapers, and, above all, furnished me with many sociological materials, insights, and suggestions about the nature of Swiss society. Klaus Biedermann, a law student at the University of Bern, conducted the study of crime questions in the Federal Parliament and helped to translate portions of several doctoral dissertations. Other academic persons who assisted me in various ways included Professor Peter Heintz, Director of the Sociological Institute of the University of Zürich, which sponsored the crime victimization survey, several professors of criminal law, Peter Noll, Günther Stratenwerth, Philip Graven, Karl Bader, and Jörg Rehberg, and also Professors Jacques Bernheim, Michel Bassand, and Kurt Mayer. Several journalists in the area of criminal justice, Alfred Messerli, Erick Meier, and Dr. Erich A. Fivian, were helpful in numerous ways. Our Swiss friends, Paul and Margaret Auberson, helped us to understand many aspects of Swiss society.

Many federal, cantonal, and city police officials and prosecutors, particularly in the cantons of Zürich, Bern, Basel-Stadt, and Geneva and in the cities of Zürich, Bern and Basel, went out of their way to give me their impressions of cime in Switzerland and to provide statistical data, some of which were especially prepared for this project. Police officials included Robert Schönbächler, Hans Hollinger, Werner Hofmann, Dr.

J. Meier, Wachtmeister Keller, Fritz Fassbind, Jean-Robert Warynski, and Hans Furrer. Prosecutors included Dr. H. Weiland, Dr. Stefan Trechsel, Dr. Harald Siegrist, Axel Tuchschmid, Dr. Heidi Burkhard, Dr. Walter Lehman, Dr. Rober Hänni, Dr. W. Brandenberger, Dr. L. Guidici, and Mario Luvini. Dr. Ulrich Zwingli and Dr. Zdenek Lomecky, both of the Zürich City Statistical Bureau, helped furnish data for the crime victimization sample. Dr. Rolf Hinterman, Director of Publitest, one of the country's largest opinion-survey organizations, carried out the actual crime victimization and attitude survey in Zürich. He took great pains to see that the survey was properly conducted.

In my search for criminological data with which to compare those of Switzerland, I had the assistance and the cooperation of many persons. Most important was Professor Günther Kaiser, Director of the Criminological Institute of the University of Freiburg. His decision to replicate in Stuttgart the Zürich crime victimization and attitude survey provided valuable comparable statistics. In addition, he furnished a set of his unpublished lectures in which he had compared Swiss crime data with those of other countries, particularly the Federal German Republic. Anthony G. Turner played a leading role in the development of contemporary U.S. crime victimization surveys of the National Institute of Law Enforcement and Criminal Justice and the Bureau of the Census. He offered several suggestions for the Zürich crime victimization survey, which was largely a replication of U.S. surveys. Much of the comparative Swedish data were provided by Göran Crona, Chief of Statistics, Social Administration, and Gunnar Andersson, Research Director, National Correctional Administration. Leif Persson helped to obtain comparative theft insurance data for Sweden. He, as well as Professor Knut Sveri, Professor Carl-Gunnar Janson, Sven Rengby, and Börje Alpsten were particularly helpful in supplementing my information about the contemporary Swedish crime situation. Richard Sparks of the Cambridge University Institute of Criminology provided the preliminary manuscript of the pioneer crime victimization survey that he recently conducted in three London areas. Professor Preben Wolf of the Criminological Institute, University of Copenhagen, furnished useful data from his recent victimization surveys of crimes of violence in Scandinavia and property crime in Copenhagen.

My research assistant at the University of Wisconsin, John Juettner, worked long hours getting the statistical data ready for the computers, seeing the runs through to completion, and preparing other statistical analyses. This arduous work he performed without complaint, and his competence in German was a great asset in the translation of data and other information gathered in Switzerland. My colleague, Professor Halliman Winsborough, suggested the statistical measures for the trend analyses.

It goes without saying, of course, that none of the persons who helped and offered suggestions is responsible in any way for what I have done with the information. My use of the data and the advice taken has had to be my own responsibility.

Finally, and perhaps most important of all, again I acknowledge the help of my wife, Ruth Blackburn Clinard, who has worked closely with me in research and writing both in Switzerland and in other countries where I have done research of a comparative nature. She has typed my illegible manuscripts, edited out the usual sociological verbiage, and corrected major grammatical flaws. Most of all, she has been a good hard-headed critic in helping me to come to the point by the shortest possible written route.

M.B.C.

Madison, Wisconsin
January 1978

1. Crime and Switzerland

Switzerland represents an exception to the general rule that a high crime rate accompanies a high degree of affluence, industrialization, and urbanization. Even in the largest Swiss cities crime is not a major problem. The incidence of criminal homicide and robbery is low, despite the fact that firearms are readily available in most households, owing to the nature of the country's military system. The low incidence of crime in Switzerland is even more intriguing, in view of the fact that the criminal justice system is neither harsh nor repressive. In German-speaking Switzerland, constituting nearly three-fourths of the country, persons are generally not arrested and booked for a crime but are given a citation; if they are prosecuted there is no plea bargaining. Sentences are generally short, even for the serious crimes, with the exception of murder. They rarely exceed a year, and most convicted offenders sentenced to prison are given suspended sentences. For the most part, those who do go to prison receive short sentences, and a large proportion of them are released prior to the expiration of the sentence.

Naturally, a country with this crime picture becomes of special interest because it appears to be an exception. Generally, crime is greatly increasing in the developing, as well as in the developed countries.[1] Moreover, countries in which the process of industrialization and urbanization is continuing — a situation that exists at present in most of, if not all, the countries of the world — must expect further increases in their crime rates.[2] Even if allowances are made for inadequacies in official crime data, it appears that the developed countries are far more vulnerable than the developing countries, precisely because they are developed. The United States, in particular, has not been able to cope effectively with crime as a problem.[3] As a country develops economically, and as this development is reflected in growing urbanization, crime generally increases rapidly. Despite some uncertainties surrounding statistical reports gathered from the developing countries, the findings have almost unanimously supported the generalization that crime, and in

1

particular property crime, is increasing rapidly and has become a major problem in the total developmental process.[4]

Any country that represents an exception to this general trend becomes of paramount significance, particularly when it ranks among the four most affluent industrialized nations in the world: Switzerland, Sweden, the Federal German Republic (Federal Republic of Germany), and the United States. In contrast to Switzerland's low rate of ordinary crime, however, is its high rate of alcoholism and suicide.[5] In total per capita consumption of absolute alcohol from 1966 to 1970 Switzerland ranked fourth behind France, Italy, and the Federal German Republic and far ahead of the United States and Sweden.[6] In 1971 it ranked tenth among thirty-eight countries in suicide: lower than Sweden, higher than France or Japan, and considerably higher than the United States, Canada, the Netherlands, and England and Wales.[7]

For some time, foreign criminologists, journalists, and visitors have believed that Switzerland has no crime problem comparable to that of other European countries.[8] Until the present study, there had been no attempt to examine crime in Switzerland in a comprehensive manner. Compared to other countries, there has been practically no sociological interest in criminology, there is no criminological institute, and the work that has been done has come primarily from law schools and has consisted mostly of articles on criminal law and a number of Ph.D. dissertations in criminology. This relative lack of attention is in sharp contrast to the great interest in the United States and in most European countries. For example, surveys of research in criminology conducted by the Council of Europe, of which Switzerland is a member, showed comparatively little research emanating from Switzerland, in sharp contrast to the large amount of research work that is carried out in Sweden, a country of similar size.[9]

Europeans have generally believed that Switzerland has a low crime rate, but the evidence to support this belief has been limited to analyses of trends in criminal convictions. Trend analyses have shown a general stability in crime rates, or even a decrease, over the past twenty-five years; one study, for example, concluded that as general affluence became more prevalent in the country, crime rates remained about the same, or even decreased.[10] Hans Schultz has analyzed criminal convictions published by the federal government from 1929 to 1962 and annually since then, and he has consistently found a general decrease, or at most a slight increase, in criminality over the years.[11]

This trend in Swiss conviction statistics impressed the President's Commission on Law Enforcement and Administration of Justice, appointed in 1965 by President Johnson to assess the problems of crime in the United States. The commission noted that since 1955 property crime rates have

increased more than 200 percent in West Germany, the Netherlands, Sweden, and Finland, and over 100 percent in France, England and Wales, and Norway. Of the countries studied, property crime rates in Denmark, Belgium, and Switzerland remained relatively stable. Crimes of violence could be studied in only a few countries. Rates declined in Belgium, Denmark, Norway and Switzerland, but rose more than 150 percent in England and Wales between 1955 and 1964.[12]

Conviction statistics, however, are not generally considered to be the most reliable indicators of crime trends. They are too far removed from the actual incidence of crime, such as is reflected in part in an index based on crimes reported to the police or arrest data. Conviction statistics are much too subject to variations involved in criminal justice administration. In Switzerland, however, these had been the only statistics available on a national basis until extensive criminological data were collected by the author in an independent research study conducted under the auspices of the National Science Foundation. It was carried out during an eight-months' residence in Switzerland in 1973. The study involved the collection of various data from the cantons and cities and employed several rather unusual methods of ascertaining the true crime situation in the country. For example, a crime victimization survey was designed to discover the amount of crime and how much of it goes unreported to the police. A systematic analysis was made of the extent to which crime is regarded as a problem of public concern. This effort included an attitude survey designed to determine to what extent the public is concerned about crime, how many questions about crime were raised in Parliament over a ten-year period, and to what extent and in what fashion crime is presented in the Swiss newspapers. An analysis was made of burglary, theft, and auto insurance rates and trends to see what these data might reveal about the extent of crime in the country. Surveys of this nature have not previously been made, not only because Swiss sociologists and other social scientists have not been interested in the problem of crime but also because criminal-law professors have not had the training necessary for the scientific study of these criminological problems. With the incorporation of the data available through governmental sources, together with a limited number of other Swiss studies and those conducted in this research, it appears that Switzerland does represent an exception to the generally high crime rates among the highly affluent urbanized countries.

Switzerland has all of the attributes of a country that one might anticipate would make it susceptible to a high crime rate: It is highly affluent, extremely developed, and very urbanized. It had a gross national product of $40 billion (throughout this book, American billions apply) in 1976. When this study was conducted in 1973, Switzerland ranked third in the world in per capita income, behind the United States and Sweden and second among European countries following Sweden.[13] According to the Population Reference Bureau and *The World Bank Atlas,* in 1975 Switzerland was in first place in per capita GNP among the industrialized nations ($7,870), with Sweden in second place ($7,240), and the United States in third place ($6,670).[14] Its wealth is largely derived from production and export of machinery and other metal goods, chemicals and drugs, clocks and watches, textiles and apparel, and food products. According to one correspondent,

They process relatively low-cost raw materials — the bulk of them imported — into carefully crafted high-priced goods. This way a few tiny strips of metal become an expensive watch, raw silk becomes the chiffon, satin, crepe de chine, faille, and other fabrics sought after by the couturiers of Paris. And relatively inexpensive milk becomes "luxury" cheese and confectionery items.[15]

Switzerland's engineering industry employs the largest percentage of the industrial labor force and exports two-thirds of its production of turbines (one in three diesel-powered ships on the high seas is driven by a Swiss-designed engine) and electrical equipment, machine tools, and precision instruments. Exports total annually well over $7 billion, which as a percent of gross national product is considerably higher than that of the United States, the Federal German Republic, or Great Britain. Swiss assets and investments abroad total about $52 billion. In 1975 Switzerland's monetary reserves exceeded those of Great Britain, Italy, and Canada, almost equaling those of France. While no autos are produced in the country, there is an extremely high number of passenger vehicles and telephones per 1,000 population; in 1972 the ratio of 244 passenger vehicles per 1,000 persons was not much lower than the 301 in Sweden. In 1976, Switzerland had nearly 2 million private motor cars. Telephone connections and television sets in Switzerland were

336 and 241, respectively, per 1,000 population, while the Swedish rates were 591 and 332, respectively.

In addition to these indexes of wealth, one must add two important items. Situated as it is in the heart of the Alps and easily accessible in the middle of Europe, Switzerland has become one of the world's leading centers of tourism, which provides a large proportion of the national income. Over the years, the leading city, Zürich, has become one of the world's chief international centers for banking, securities, and investments. Walter Sorell writes,

Since 1515, when Swiss policy turned to perpetual neutrality, guaranteed by all great powers again in 1815, its neutrality has been − figuratively speaking − its hottest export item. In a war-torn world, Switzerland became a storehouse for treasure and fortunes. By the grace of neutrality and the greed of the wealthy of the world, the vaults of the Swiss banks grew to mighty money mountains.[16]

Switzerland has become increasingly urbanized, with high population density. More than half of the country's inhabitants live in places of 10,000 or more population, an increase of approximately one-third since 1950. In fact, the population is largely concentrated in a limited area, with three-fourths of the people living in the central lowlands between the Alps and the Jura mountains. Nine Swiss cities had more than 50,000 inhabitants in 1973, the five largest being Lausanne (141,000), Bern (159,000), Geneva (171,000), Basel (205,000), and Zürich (420,000). Switzerland would not rank high among the most industrialized nations in the percentages of persons living in nucleus cities of 100,000 or more, but in this respect it still ranks higher than Sweden, with which it will be frequently compared in this research.[17] It must be kept in mind, however, that the metropolitan areas are densely populated. The 1969 metropolitan area populations of the largest cities were: Zürich, 671,500; Basel, 364,800; Geneva, 307,500; Bern, 258,000; and Lausanne, 214,900.[18]

The figures on affluence, industrialization, and urbanization give only a partial picture of the country. Switzerland now has over 6.2 million inhabitants, of whom approximately 1 million were foreign workers at the time of this study in 1973, a number now declining. It is only 209 miles from east to west and 117 miles from north to south, about the size of Massachusetts and New Hampshire combined. Geographically, it is locked in by the Rhine and two mountain chains, the Jura and the Alps, and is bordered by Germany, Austria, France, and Italy. Politically, it had its origin in a league formed in 1291 by three small states, now called cantons, at the foot of the Gotthard Pass. Established primarily to oppose the domination by the Habsburg dynasty, whose dominions then included Switzerland, the league turned into a permanent confederation of various cantons. The members increased from the original three, to number thirteen cantons in 1513, and important regions (e.g., the present Italian- and much of the French-speaking part of the country) became dependent on the confederation or on certain cantons. Other cantons were admitted to membership within the confederation, which largely attained its present size in the sixteenth century. The last canton admissions, in 1815, were the French-speaking cantons of Geneva, Valais, and Neuchâtel, making a total of 22 cantons, or 25 federated states (three of the cantons are subdivided). In 1848, the confederation became the Federal State of Switzerland, with a constitution and Bern as the capital. The official name of the country is Confoederatio Helvetica (Swiss Confederation), and the abbreviation "CH" is used on the international plaque of Swiss autos. The country's present name, Schweiz, is taken from one of the three original cantons, Schwyz.

Individual Swiss cantons have surrendered only certain aspects of their independent authority to the Federal Constitution. Although they range greatly in population from 14,000 to over a million — with an average population of 250,791 — and maintain individual cultural and historical features, they are politically similar. Each has its own legislative, executive, and judicial branches. The cantonal councils make decisions on education, cantonal taxes, and other functions not reserved to the federal government. They also administer justice, including the cantonal police forces. Each of the cantons is divided into a number of political communes, totaling 3,095.[19] These communes, some of which have fewer than 100 persons, have various semiautonomous functions, including, in some cases, the administration of the school system and any local communal police forces, maintenance of public buildings and water supplies, and the basic collection of taxes, a share of which is sent to the cantonal and federal governments. In former days, when the communes were more powerful than they now are, citizens carried a communal, rather than a cantonal passport.

Federal sovereignty is exercised by the Federal Assembly or Parliament (Bundesversammlung) and the Federal Council (Bundesrat). The Federal Assembly consists of two chambers of equal rights: the National Council (Nationalrat) and the Council of States (Ständerat). The Swiss people are represented in the National Council by two hundred elected deputies; each canton, or half-canton, is guaranteed at least one representative. The Council of States consists of two representatives from each canton, or forty-four state councillors. The seven members of the Federal Council are elected for four years by the Assembly, and they serve as Cabinet ministers. The president of the Federal Council is elected for one year, and he is prevented from being reelected immediately. On the whole, as it has historically, governmental power still rests predominantly at the cantonal and communal levels, even though the federal government is increasingly being entrusted with matters formerly considered to be cantonal. For example, until 1942, when a Swiss Uniform Criminal Code went into effect (enacted in 1937), each of the cantons had its own system of criminal law. This resulted in great variations among them, and several still had capital punishment. Even now the administration of the criminal law is left to each canton.

Nowhere in Western Europe is there such diversity in a small country comparable to that encountered in Switzerland. The powerful central theme throughout Swiss history has been a quest for unity of the nearly sovereign cantons and communes, an effort that is vastly complicated by the great diversity in language, culture, and religion among them. The German-speaking population far exceeds the others, with 65 percent of the Swiss people primarily speaking this language, 18 percent speaking French, 12 percent Italian, and only 0.8 percent speaking Romansh. Of the cantons, seventeen are considered German-speaking: There are nineteen such cantons if one includes those two cantons where the German-speaking population exceeds the French-speaking. Two others are mixed but are predominantly French-speaking — making a total of four mixed cantons. Three cantons are French-speaking, and one is Italian-speaking. In addition to the overall language diversity, each region has its own dialect, so that it is possible to distinguish between persons from Basel, Bern, or the Grisons on the basis of dialect. Political diversities also exist; there are nine political parties in the Federal Parliament, although three are numerically much larger than the others.

The success of the Swiss political and social system rests on "amicable or consensus agreement," rather than on majority rule. Swiss political history indicates that majority rule is not the only form of democracy; if it were, the German-speaking population, the larger cantons, or the three large political parties could easily dominate the country. The low level of hostility among Swiss subcultures is due, it is said, to the practice of amicable agreement among all parties to a discussion, rather than one of majority rule.[20] For example, it is customary to have the three main language groups, German, French, and Italian, represented on the Federal Council according to their proportions in the population at large, even though nineteen of the cantons have a German-speaking majority. Moreover, custom indicates that the two largest German cantons, Zürich and Bern, and the largest French canton, Vaud, are always represented.

Switzerland has been slow to develop political equality between men and women. While males have long had the right to vote at the age of 20, voting privileges have come slowly and only recently to women. Beginning in 1959, Swiss women have gradually won the right to vote in cantonal or local elections. Women were not permitted to vote, and consequently not to hold political office, in federal elections until 1971, but in the first election eight women were elected to Parliament. In a few places today, however, cantonal and communal affairs continue to be decided exclusively by the male inhabitants.

As interesting as its political development has been this country's economic growth. Largely mountainous and land-locked, Switzerland is probably one of the poorest countries in Europe in terms of natural resources. Mineral resources are extremely limited, and originally it had no more than the basic means to provide a meager pastoral economy; in fact, the survival of the Swiss depended upon the export of military service to various countries, even to the Vatican. Between the fifteenth and nineteenth centuries some 2 million Swiss soldiers fought in foreign armies, constituting some of the best forces in Europe. Often they returned to their mountain homes with foreign capital and a broad knowledge of the world that soon transformed them into merchants. Even today the Swiss export manpower, but today it is civilian and mostly highly skilled. Approximately 330,000 Swiss live abroad — about 200,000 in European countries and 80,000 in the United States alone.

Gradually, the Swiss gave up exporting soldiers and began to develop their own special resources. As they developed electrical power for industry and railroads (now they produce 31 billion kilowatts per hour), they also imported raw materials for their developing industries. With their capital investment, highly developed skills, and intense work ethic, they have made Switzerland one of the most industrialized countries of the world, certainly the country with the hardest currency — entirely covered by gold — and the Swiss standard of living one of the highest in the world. They also give work to a large number of foreign workers. As a result of this intense industrialization, however, the farming population has declined from a high of 90 percent in 1800 to less than 8 percent at present. In 1975 Switzerland had a total of only 133,126 farm holdings, a decline of 35.4 percent from 1955, and two-thirds of the country's food supply must now be imported. The shortage of solid fuel has been met by developing the country's immense water power, now generated by over four hundred hydroelectric plants. The manufacturing plants depend greatly on foreign raw materials or semifurnished goods, a high degree of specialization in products, and broad foreign market outlets. Because of the widespread rapid development, the real income of workers has risen faster than have prices, until fairly recent times when problems of inflation have arisen. However, this inflation rate has now declined to the lowest level of all the industrialized Western countries, being only 1.8 percent in 1975 and 1.7 percent in 1976. More important, they have never had the marked disparities in distribution of wealth that characterize many other European countries, even though there have been certain inequalities, particularly in terms of property ownership. The position of the Swiss worker today is generally more favorable than that of workers in most other countries (but not as high as in Sweden), mainly as a result of high pay scales, the presence of foreign workers, who do most of the less skilled work, and the five-day work week.

Sweden: an affluent country with a high crime rate

Since comparisons will be made throughout between Switzerland and Sweden, it is important to indicate some of the similarities and differences other than the fact that the former appears to have a low crime rate whereas the latter has a high one.[21] Sweden is not a great deal more populous than Switzerland, with 8,115,000 inhabitants in 1971, compared to Switzerland's 6,200,000. In physical size, however, the difference is great. One of the largest European countries, Sweden is twice as large as Great Britain — nearly 1,000 miles long and 250 miles wide, although 90 percent of the population is concentrated in the lower half of the country. As a consequence of this size differential, Switzerland has 365 inhabitants per square mile, whereas Sweden has only 44. Both countries have a large foreign worker population; in 1971, the alien population of Sweden was 416,567, or 5 percent, as compared with Switzerland's 17 percent. Both countries have avoided wars for more than a century and a half, a fact that has undoubtedly contributed to their affluence. Both are neutral nations, but Switzerland is more neutral, as it does not belong to the United Nations although it did join the European Free Trade Association in 1960 and the Council of Europe in 1963.

Economically, Sweden is highly affluent, with the second highest per capita income in the world, both currently and at the time of the study, and with one of the strongest currencies in the world. It is also extremely industrialized, with little agriculture, relying upon heavy exports, such as ball bearings, heavy electrical equipment, telecommunications, autos, and shipbuilding for income. Chemical industries are also well developed, and, unlike Switzerland, Sweden derives substantial income from timber and wood products, as well as from fisheries. Both countries have enormous quantities of electricity from water power, but Sweden has iron ore, one great national resource not available in Switzerland. The high standard of living in Sweden is reflected in its consumption of goods and services. It has, for example, the highest ratio of autos, telephones, and television to population of any country in Europe.

While these similarities between the two countries are striking, so, too, are the differences. In sharp contrast to the Swiss diversity, Swedes are remarkably homogeneous as a people, with a common language and state religion (although few participate in religious activities and constitutional religious freedom was extended in 1952) and a common cultural background. Sweden has somewhat more urbanization, with 56.5 percent of the people living in urban places of 10,000 or more, as compared with 51.3 percent in Switzerland. In general, Swedish cities are larger, with greater concentrations in population: Thirty-four percent live in the twenty cities with 50,000 or more inhabitants. In 1971 the largest city, Stockholm, had 723,688 inhabitants, and the next largest cities were Göteborg, with 450,419, and Malmö, with 263,829. These cities have very large populations in their metropolitan areas: Stockholm's being 1,352,359; Göteborg's 685,992; and Malmö's 449,296.

The two countries are quite different with respect to political structure, even though both are strong democracies. Sweden has had a strong central government throughout most of its history, whether it was a monarchy or a parliamentary system. Since the early sixteenth century the country has been ruled by various royal dynasties, some far more powerful than others. Only in the latter part of the nineteenth century has this power declined. Today, Sweden is a consitutional monarchy with a strong elected Parliament (Riksdag). Political participation was low until well after the turn of the twentieth century. As late as 1905 only 8 percent of the population could vote, and in 1911 this privilege was given to only 19 percent. Sweden did not become fully democratic until immediately after World War I, under the impact of the Russian and German revolutions. Universal suffrage for both men and women was then introduced, the powers of the king were partially annulled (almost completely in the 1970s), and complete parliamentary rule was established.

The government was under the control of the Social Democrats from 1932 to 1976, and they continuously offered programs of strong centralized leadership, including extensive social welfare measures. Today the Swedish people have state-provided medical care, high retirement pensions, month-long vacations with pay, and an almost endless stream of social subsidies catering to almost every financial need. If a Swedish housewife wants to work outside the home the government will help train her for a job. There is little political decentralization, however. The central government appoints the governor (Landhövding), who heads the administrative board in each of the twenty-four counties. Local, self-governing units are run by popularly elected county councils and rural or district councils, and they are responsible for the local administration of the various central governmental services.

The Swedish government has been characterized by strong central government initiative; Switzerland has had a much weaker central government and strong local government. The strong sense of local responsibility has greatly affected the degree to which Swiss citizens participate at this level. It would appear, as will be pointed out later, that this has had an important bearing on the strikingly different crime problems of the two countries.

2. Swiss concern about crime

In a true democracy citizens tend to act both individually and jointly to express opinions and concerns about their society. Thus, it is to be expected that Swiss citizens would voice any apprehensions they might have about crime problems. In addition to reporting any crimes to the police, the Swiss citizens' concerns about crime could be reflected in several ways. First of all, they would be reflected in government reports and in special committees being appointed to investigate the problems. Second, the actions of elected representatives in the federal and cantonal parliaments, as well as in local city councils, would reflect, in all probability, any major fears of constituents about crime. Third, citizen concern for their own safety, or that of their possessions, would be shown in a survey of a representative sample of Swiss households of their attitudes toward crime, as well as their fears. Fourth, professionally trained persons in fields related to crime matters would provide information regarding the extent and the gravity of Swiss public concern about the problem. Fifth, citizens' concern about problems related to crime would be reflected in newspaper articles dealing with crime, as well as in letters to the newspapers. Each of these possible measures will be examined here, on the supposition that they indicate whether or not crime is extensive and if it is increasing in Switzerland.

Crime and the government

The Federal Council is the highest governmental authority in Switzerland. This seven-member body is elected by Parliament and is presided over by one of the members on an annually rotating basis. Each year the Council prepares a report on the chief problems faced by the nation for the consideration of Parliament.[1] In an effort to determine whether the Federal Council regarded crime as an important national problem, all council reports from 1962 to 1972 were carefully examined. No mention of crime was found in the reports from 1962 to 1969. The 1970 report revealed a concern about the use of drugs by juveniles, the increased sale of drugs (primarily hashish), and the apparent involvement of international gangs in the distribution of drugs in the country. In 1971, *for the first time*, the Federal Council reported that the police and the judiciary were becoming alarmed about increases in crime among juveniles, particularly in property and drug offenses. Prior to 1971 the chief topics of national concern mentioned in the 1969–71 reports were education, including greater coordination among cantons and long-term plans, economic problems, environmental pollution, and social security insurance. These problems, rather than crime, are still the chief concerns.

In addition to its annual reports, the Federal Council has recently been submitting a report every three years on what the council members see as future problems for the country. Only two such reports have been made, covering the periods 1968–71 and 1971–74, and crime was not mentioned in either of these reports.[2] The main topics presented were economics, education, science and research, national planning, pollution, social security, and regional development.

With the exception of the recent special committee on drug usage, no special investigative committees about crime have been appointed at the Federal level during the past thirty years. This is in marked contrast to the large number of commissions appointed to investigate the problem of crime in the United States, in Sweden, and elsewhere during the past one or two decades. On two occasions special committees have been named in Switzerland to work on changes in criminal law procedures, but this addresses an entirely different question. In 1937 the Swiss Parliament adopted a uniform criminal code, which came into effect in 1942; in 1950 and 1971 some additional changes were made in the code.[3] A commission of experts was appointed in 1971 to examine further changes in the Criminal Code.[4] Likewise, there have been changes in parts of the Swiss criminal code that regulate the criminality and the delinquency of youth, changes primarily made to modernize them.[5]

Concern in the Federal Parliament

The Federal Assembly, or Parliament, consists of two chambers, the National Council (Nationalrat) of two hundred elected members, which is roughly equivalent to the United States House of Representatives, and the Council of State, comprising representatives of the cantons and equivalent to the United States Senate. As is true of many European countries, Swiss parliamentary procedures provide a certain format for parliamentary discussions. Primarily, they are carried out through a question directed at government, by a motion raised by a member, or by the government's bringing an issue to the attention of the Federal Parliament (National Assembly). Any member may raise issues through a motion, a postulate, an interpellation, or a *kleine Anfrage* ("short question"). All four types are given in writing. Answers by the government (Bundesrat) or Federal Council to a motion and to a postulate must be given orally in the National Assembly as well. Answers to interpellations and *kleine Anfrage* may be given only in writing.[6] A specific example of the procedure is the following motion raised by a member about the use of weapons in crimes of violence.

Nature of Motion: There has been a considerable increase of crimes involving violence and crimes committed by the use of weapons. The Bundesrat (Government) is requested to:
  (1) establish federal control of dealing with weapons.
  (2) provide more severe punishment for unlicensed weapon carrying.
  (3) provide more severe punishment for crimes committed by the use of weapons and to integrate these regulations into the Criminal Code.
Answer of the Government: A request for federal control of weapons has often been made. This is not a matter that belongs to federal authority, however, but to cantonal authority. An amendment to the federal constitution to give authority to the Federation was rejected by the cantons. Since there exists an agreement between a considerable number of cantons to unify the legal regulations on dealing with weapons and carrying weapons and since in the near future all cantons will be members of this agreement, the Bundesrat does not consider interference by the federal authority as being necessary. It should be pointed out also that it is easier for local authorities to effect sufficient control. Inasmuch as the questioner suggests that the criminal code be changed with reference to the use of weapons, the government will submit the problem to the commission of experts engaged in working out the revision of the Criminal Code.

A thorough effort was made to locate all questions about crime raised by National Assembly members from 1950 to 1972 to ascertain the extent of concern about it among the elected members. Official reports of the Secretary of the Parliament did not list all motions and questions raised by the members prior to 1971, so data were obtained from the card file kept by the Secretary. Motions and questions were indexed under heads such as "criminal nature" and other categories. All questions indexed under "criminal nature" were included. In addition, a thorough research was made to locate all other questions, even those only remotely related to crime, because crime-related questions might have been listed under other categories. Once the motions and questions were located, the original parliamentary records, many of which were available in typed form only, were consulted. Between 1950 and 1960, questions were recorded only by general nature, whereas other motions and questions since 1960 were recorded on cards. In cases of particular interest the exact statement of the question and the answer of the government were recorded.

At the federal parliamentary level little concern was found: in fact, an analysis of questions addressed to the government during the twenty-three-year period from 1950 to 1972 showed that only 52 of them involved crime. In the Swiss National Assembly the average yearly number from 1950 to 1960 was 1.5; for the period 1961 to 1970 the average was 1.7; and for the year from 1971 to 1972 the number was 9. For the entire period analyzed an average of 2.3 crime questions per year was asked.[7] Although the total number of all questions raised during these various periods is not known, during the period from 1970 to 1972 nearly a thousand (996) of all types were raised in the National Assembly. Only nine of them dealt with crime, or 0.9 percent of the total.

Between 1950 and 1972, 54 percent of the crime questions in the Swiss National Assembly involved general crime matters; revisions of the Federal Criminal Code involved 19 percent; the police, 13 percent; problems associated with corrections, 8 percent; and the relation of such factors as alcoholism, the cinema, and youth to crime, 6 percent. Great variety was found in the "general questions" about crime. Few of them actually dealt with ordinary crime; more revealed concern about white-collar crime. Of the total for the twenty-three years, only four dealt with violent crime, and three of them were raised during the 1950 to 1960 period. The matter of sexual offenses was raised in five cases, drug offense issues involved nine, and the remainder were such problems of federal or national importance as security of certain employees, use of explosives, burglary of army depots, smuggling of gold, and subversive activities.

It thus appears that public concern about crime in Switzerland — at least as it is reflected in its federal government and by its public representatives — is not great. Nor does it appear to be increasing significantly. In this respect Switzerland differs markedly from Sweden. A great difference exists, for example, between the numbers of crime-related questions raised in the Swiss National Assembly and those raised in the Swedish Parliament (Riksdag). During the period 1965—72, for example, an average of thirty-five questions relating directly to crime were raised each year in the Riksdag, about fifteen times the number raised in the Swiss National Assembly.[8] Sweden's government is, however, highly centralized, whereas Switzerland's is extremely decentralized. In contrast to slogans of "law and order" that have played important roles in recent political campaigns in Sweden and the United States, this had not been an issue in Swiss elections through 1973, the period of this study. In the Swedish national elections of 1973, for example, problems of crime, law, and public order became extremely significant issues. It was pointed out that "many Swedes are clearly more concerned about their own welfare than that of criminals. They are worried about the violence in their midst. So much so, that the opposition Conservative Party has done very well so far by taking up law and order as its particular cause."[9] This was thought to be the one most significant factor in the considerable loss of parliamentary seats then suffered by the incumbent Social Democratic party, which was subsequently voted out of office in 1976. Even prior to the 1973 elections, however, the government tried to take certain measures to stem the increasing crime rate, as well as to counteract some of the charges. In this connection the Swedish Information Service reported:

The government is signaling vigorous measures against an increasing rate of violent crimes. At a cabinet meeting in early January it was decided to appoint immediately a parliamentary commission to suggest such measures. The commission is expected to present its report this spring.

At a press conference after the meeting, Prime Minister Olof Palme said that even though there have been distorted pictures of the situation and some people tend to be overly nervous, it cannot be denied that the increasing number of robberies is a very serious trend. "We are also experiencing an increasing rate of international crime that must be curbed," he added.

In the instructions for the commission four areas were especially stressed: Measures to prevent robberies of banks, post offices and stores; measures against sex clubs (not illegal as such), illegal gambling and liquor sales, and other operations with high crime risks; measures to improve security in the streets, on subways and trains; measures to improve the relations between the police force and the public.

It was pointed out that an increase in the rates of robberies and other violent crimes has been reported from many countries, which may indicate that this is not only a temporary phenomenon. This, the government adds, means that society must make a strong effort to eliminate violence.[10]

Crime concern in the Zürich Canton Parliament and the Zürich City Council

In view of Switzerland's highly decentralized form of government, it is quite possible, of course, that crime issues are raised more at the cantonal or city level than at the federal level. A test of such an hypothesis was made in the Zürich Parliament and the Zürich City Council. Included in the survey were all parliamentary decisions and questions concerning problems of criminality in general, special types of offenses, criminal law enforcement, augmentation of criminal justice agencies, and the enlargement of services dealing with delinquent youth. Excluded were certain issues dealing with hijacking, student rioting, and humanitarian, technical, and budgetary matters involving the administration of justice where there appeared to have been no relation to a concern about an increase in crime. Under the Swiss system, canton parliaments serve as "supervisors of justice," and occasionally they are asked to decide on individual cases involving commutation of sentences, the behavior of the police or the prosecuting attorney toward the defendant, and sometimes even the length of the sentence. Issues of this type are fairly numerous, due to the quasi-judicial nature of cantonal parliamentary responsibilities, but this type of query was not included in this particular survey.

The conclusion was negative: There were few questions either in the Zürich Canton Parliament or in the Zürich City Council. During the twelve-year period 1960—71 an average of only 2.2 questions or decisions relating directly to crime problems was raised in the 180-member Zürich Canton Parliament (Kantonsrat), which represents 1.2 million people. Although the total number raised during this period is not known, for the period 1967—71, the average annual number was 178. During this same period the average number of questions about crime was 3.3, or 0.6 percent of the total. A slight increase was shown in the number raised and the discussions during the 1960—71 period.

Most queries indicated little real concern about an increase in crime. During this twelve-year period, 38 percent of the dicussions and issues involved general crime, 35 percent involved police, prosecution, and the courts, 19 percent concerned corrections, and 8 percent related to other crime matters. None was raised about crimes of violence in general, but two members did raise the issue of the carrying of spring knives by foreign workers and regulations needed to prevent it.

On several occasions during this twelve-year period, parliamentary members in Zürich canton introduced motions or raised questions about the need to provide more police, district attorneys, or district court staffs, and positive action was taken on a number of these issues. It might be presumed that these actions were due to greater concern about crime in the canton. In general, however, the reasons for the additional staff were, in order of importance, suburban population growth, heavier road traffic and traffic accidents, larger numbers of civil law suits, and, last of all, an increase in criminal offenses, particularly white-collar offenses. It was on this basis, and for the reasons in this order, for example, that the Parliament decided in 1962 to increase the cantonal police force from 520 to 620, and from 620 to 800 in 1965. The number of district attorneys was increased by six in 1970, primarily due to heavier time demands on criminal investigations in the more complicated and time-consuming cases that have been resulting primarily from Zürich's position as an international financial and trade center.

The combined electoral districts (now twelve, formerly eleven) of the city of Zürich elect a total of 125 delegates to the Zürich City Council (Gemeinderat). A study was made of all decisions and parliamentary questions brought before this council that might indicate concern about an increase (or decrease) in crime during the 1962—70 period. The procedures for asking questions were similar to those in the federal or Zürich parliaments, although phrased in a somewhat different terminology. Official records give little detail with respect to the decisions of the council, and for this reason the decisions were further clarified by consulting the two main Zürich newspapers, the *Neue Zürcher Zeitung* and the *Tages Anzeiger*. This analysis revealed little concern; in fact, during this nine-year period the subject of crime had come up on only ten occasions. Such a comparative lack of concern is significant when one considers that Zürich, the country's largest city, might be expected to have a higher crime rate. Moreover, an informed observer and regular reader of all reports on the Zürich City Council sessions up to 1975 stated that "there has been absolutely no change in the interest in crime since 1970."[11] Even in the election campaign of 1974 no discussions of crime by the candidates were reported in the newspapers.

Public concern about crime in Zürich

A representative household sample of 517 persons in the city of Zürich was asked for opinions about the extent of crime in the country and in

Zürich and if they believed crime to be increasing in the city and in their own neighborhoods. (Chapter 5.)[12] In addition, they were asked if they were personally concerned about crime, if they felt unsafe in certain areas of the city, and if they had ever observed the commission of a crime during the preceding twelve-month period. Research of this type on a person's perception of crime and his apprehensions and fears about crime is subject to a variety of interpretations. The responses may be based on some personal experience or considered to be observation only. On the other hand, there are indications that fear of crime may be unrelated to personal experience in some cases. Women and elderly persons, for example, may report fears of going out at night, even if they seldom go out and may have no real reason for their concern. Other views may largely reflect opinions of relatives, friends, or neighbors. Still others may express opinions based only on crime reports in the mass media. Regardless of how they have come to feel as they do, people's attitudes about crime are "real" to them, and they may have considerable influence on public policy. Wherever possible, attempts were made to compare the attitudes of the Zürich respondents with respondents in Stuttgart, a city of 620,000 located in the southern part of the Federal German Republic and the capital of Baden-Württemberg, where the crime rates are generally much lower either than the country as a whole or the northern part of the Federal German Republic. This attitude study was replicated by the Criminological Institute of the University of Freiburg.[13]

Crime trend in Switzerland

When based on perceptions of their own local areas, the opinions that people hold about crime are probably more accurate than when reference is made to the country as a whole. Slightly more than two-thirds of the respondents (67 percent) felt that there had been an increase in crime, more than one-fourth (26 percent) felt it had remained constant, and about 4 percent of the sample expressed no opinions. Of those perceiving either an increase or a decrease throughout the country, 29 percent could not state what specific types of crime were involved. In Stuttgart, however, a much larger percentage (81 percent) felt that crime had been increasing in the Federal German Republic. Only minor differences were found by sex and age with reference to views about crime nationwide. The foreign-born were less likely to feel that crime had increased. (See Appendixes for all chi-squares.)

Crime trend in Zürich

A majority of the household residents interviewed, although by no means all of them, felt that crime in the major offense categories had been increasing in Zürich. (See Table 2.1.) The amount of this perceived increase, unfortunately, was not asked. With no indication of the amount, and with only two other response categories from which to choose ("a decrease" or "about the same"), the question naturally arises about the precise meaning of the "increase" to persons. Moreover, one must consider the crime level from which the increase was projected. Official statistics reveal few particularly significant increases (Chapter 3), reported crime victimization (Chapter 5) was not especially large in the city, and most persons appeared not to be concerned, personally, about crime in the city. Generally, women and older persons in Zürich perceived significantly more increases than did males and younger persons. The foreign-born workers, however, felt there had been less of an increase than did the Swiss. This might have been due to their inability

Table 2.1. *Percentage perceiving crime as increasing, remaining constant, or decreasing, Zürich and Stuttgart*

Crime	% increasing		% constant		% decreasing	
	Zürich	Stuttgart	Zürich	Stuttgart	Zürich	Stuttgart
Drug usage	95	71	5	18	1	11
Burglary	81	70	16	27	3	3
Shoplifting	81	87	17	12	2	2
General theft	78	80	20	18	2	2
Vehicle theft	68	75	30	20	2	5
Fraud	64	71	34	28	2	2
Assault/ Robbery	62	57	33	36	5	7
Vandalism	58	68	35	24	7	8
Rape/sexual offenses	58	48	36	42	6	10
Public fighting	34	43	49	39	17	17
Murder	24	34	64	49	12	17

to perceive changes over time in a country in which they have not lived for a long time, or perhaps they tend to compare Switzerland with their own countries — in which case the comparison would favor Switzerland.

In Zürich the greatest perceived increase in crime was in drug usage, burglary, and shoplifting; in Stuttgart it was in shoplifting, theft, and auto theft. In both cities a much smaller proportion thought that there had been increases in murder, assault, and robbery. Women viewed theft, assault, robbery, public fighting, and murder as increasing more often than did the men. With the exception of burglary there was no significant statistical difference by age group in the perception of increase or decrease in crime.

Trends in neighborhood crime

The Zürich household respondents felt that, in general, crime had not increased in their own neighborhoods. This is a highly significant finding, as the majority of them had said that they felt that crime in Zürich had increased. Only one in five (18 percent) in both Zürich and Stuttgart felt that it had increased in their own neighborhoods; nearly two-thirds (61 percent) in Zürich, slightly higher than in Stuttgart, felt that it had remained the same; the remainder felt that it had either remained the same or declined. In fact, 7 percent of them, considerably fewer than in Stuttgart (12 percent), felt that it had decreased. No significant statistical differences were found by sex, age, or by being foreign-born, nor was there a definite pattern by educational level. While there was no significant difference by type of area, in percentage terms the predominantly working class areas showed a tendency to believe that their neighborhoods had had an increase in crime. Of those who made references to specific crimes, 41 percent referred to an increase in burglary, 13 percent, theft, 6 percent, vandalism, 1 percent, auto theft, but only 9 percent, assault and robbery.

Approximately two-thirds of the respondents in both Zürich and Stuttgart felt that persons outside their neighborhoods were responsible for any neighborhood crimes. There was agreement by sex, but a significant difference by age group, the older age groups showing a tendency to attribute the crimes to outsiders. A significant statistical difference was also found between the Swiss and the foreign-born (nearly all of them foreign workers), with the former more likely to blame outsiders.

Crime as a major problem in Zürich

Crime was not one of the Zürich household respondents' major concerns, in contrast to United States cities where most opinion surveys have found it to be a major concern. In a national survey in 1973 of three hundred cities and communities of various sizes, for example, crime was found to be the leading urban problem.[14] When Zürich respondents were asked to name the five most important problems in the city, in order of importance to them, a *total* of only 9 percent in all rank order categories included crime — about the same percentage as had indicated the need for increased recreational facilities. The total mention of crime was much higher, one-third of the respondents, in Stuttgart. In Zürich, traffic was clearly the most important problem, three-fourths including it as one of the five most important concerns. Housing was second, followed by environmental, social, and youth education problems. No significantly different responses in Zürich were found by sex, age group, education, or marital status, and there was little difference by income group or between Swiss and foreign-born. For both males and females, only about one in eleven thought that crime was a serious problem.

Crime actually becomes a much less significant problem when the rank order of the five most important problems of concern to the Zürich respondents is considered. (See Table 2.2.) Whereas 44 percent regarded traffic as the most important problem, fewer than 1 percent considered crime as the most important. In Stuttgart the percentage rating crime as most important was 3 percent. Moreover, no significant differences were found among respondents in the designation of the most important problem, regardless of sex, age group, marital status, or income. More often it was viewed as a "fifth problem" because fewer respondents answered this question, and those who did answer replied as they did because they had already listed housing, traffic, and others as problems. Responses to rank order of the major problems generally did not differ significantly according to sex, age, marital status, and income. Even the Swiss and the foreign-born were in general agreement on how they would rank crime.

Personal concern about crime

Although a substantial majority of respondents felt crime to be increasing in Zürich, their opinions were not reflected in a marked personal

Table 2.2. *Five most important problems as perceived by citizen, respondents, Zürich and Stuttgart, in order of ranking*

Problem	First		Second		Third		Fourth		Fifth	
	Zürich	Stuttgart	Zürich	Stuttgart	Zürich	Stuttgart	Zürich	Stuttgart	Zürich	Stuttgart
Percentage of all persons responding	100	100	85	92	65	80	39	59	17	39
Traffic	44	38	22	13	12	9	7	7	4	6
Housing	17	11	24	15	19	16	10	10	6	7
Environment	10	12	18	13	14	9	15	11	8	10
Social	5	—	8	—	10	—	18	—	7	—
Youth, education	4	4	10	9	13	12	12	12	13	11
Finance	3	1	3	2	6	2	6	2	10	5
Labor	1	—	3	—	2	—	3	—	8	—
Energy	1	—	1	1	2	1	4	1	4	3
CRIME	1	3	2	5	4	5	4	9	12	10
Recreation	1	—	3	—	5	—	5	—	7	—
Others	7	4	7	4	15	4	18	4	20	10
No response	6	1	—	—	—	—	—	—	—	—

concern about their becoming victims of a robbery, burglary, theft, auto theft, or a break-in of their autos. Such concerns about crime were far greater in Stuttgart. If the replies of "very concerned" and "concerned" are combined, only one-fifth of the Zürich respondents, as compared with one-third in Stuttgart, felt this way about robbery; for burglary it was 18 percent, as compared with 26 percent in Stuttgart; for auto theft (for those who owned an auto) 16 percent, as compared with more than twice as large a percentage in Stuttgart; and breaking into the auto 17 percent, less than half that of those in Stuttgart. Slightly more than four out of five had little or no concern about these crimes: robbery, burglary, theft, auto theft, and breaking into the auto. This is undoubtedly the reverse of what one would expect to find in large cities in the United States and in most other European cities the size of Zürich, with some few exceptions, as indicated by the Stuttgart responses.[15] For example, those who were "very concerned" in Stuttgart about robbery, burglary, auto theft, and breaking into the auto were actually as numerous as those in Zürich who were "very concerned" and "somewhat concerned," combined.

The validity of responses indicating a lack of general concern about major crimes in Switzerland is strengthened by the uniformity in the replies by sex, age, or education, and between the Swiss and the foreign-born. (See Appendix E.) Analysis by sex, for example, showed no significant differences in amount of concern about burglary or theft, but significantly more females were concerned about robbery. No significant statistical differences by age were found with respect to robbery (it is of interest that 89 percent of those 65 and over felt little or no concern) or burglary and theft (80 percent or more of all age categories felt little or no concern). Moreover, an indication that the respondents' concern about crime reflects a low level of objective threat is the fact that the Swiss and the foreign-born were in general agreement about robbery, burglary, and theft. For example, four out of five of both groups expressed little or no concern about being victims of a robbery, a finding with added significance when one considers that most foreign workers, being single, are probably more often on the streets late at night, either in going to or coming from work or in pursuing recreational interests and are thus more vulnerable to robberies.

Neighborhood safety

Zürich residents reported that they generally feel safe when they are on foot and alone in their own neighborhoods at *night*.[16] Of the total respondents, 39 percent felt "very safe," 30 percent felt "somewhat safe," and 24 percent felt "somewhat unsafe." Only 6 percent reported feeling "very unsafe." In Stuttgart over three times as many felt very unsafe (21 percent) and only half as many (18 percent) felt very safe in their own neighborhoods, on foot and alone, at night. In a 1972 national survey done by the American Institute of Public Opinion, fear of walking alone in their own neighborhoods at night was expressed by 41 percent of those persons interviewed; for women it was 58 percent. In cities of 50,000 to 500,000, the category into which Zürich would fall, 49 percent of the interviewees said they would be afraid.[17] A 1974 opinion survey of New York City residents found that a high proportion of them, as well as New York State residents as a whole, feared walking alone on the streets at night.[18] The fear was far higher than that shown either in Zürich or in Stuttgart; approximately three-fourths of New York City residents, 45 percent of suburban residents and 43 percent of upstate New York residents, reported such fears.

No significant differences were found between a general feeling of nighttime safety in Zürich and in the neighborhoods in which the respondents lived. Older people generally showed a slight tendency to view the neighborhoods to be less safe, but no clear pattern was found in the responses by educational level. Both Swiss and foreign-born regarded their neighborhoods as generally quite safe. Pronounced differences were found by sex, with women more likely to regard their own neighborhoods in Zürich less safe at night than men, a finding that accounted for nearly all of the fears expressed. While the general difference between the male and female responses may be real, it is probably also associated with the generally sheltered, subordinate status of Swiss women.[19] Police statistics provide no evidence of a high rate of sexual or other molestation of Swiss women, and there were no reported cases in the criminal victimization survey.

Unsafe areas in Zürich

Although the Zürich household respondents generally considered their own neighborhoods quite safe, they did indicate that they would not feel safe on foot alone and at night in certain limited areas of the city. Three-fourths (72 percent, as compared with a larger figure of 88 percent in Stuttgart) acknowledged feeling unsafe in certain areas; one-fifth felt they would feel unsafe in no areas of the city, as compared with only 9 percent in Stuttgart. The fact that slightly more than one-fourth said that there were no such areas, or that they did not know of such, is highly significant for a city the size of Zürich. In Stuttgart, 8 percent felt that there were no unsafe areas. Of further significance, moreover, the fears in Zürich were of being "molested," and not of being robbed or having something stolen from them. Women were significantly more likely to feel unsafe than were men.

The respondents who did express fears for their safety in Zürich generally identified only three specific areas, as compared with seven areas identified in Stuttgart. In Zürich, regardless of the respondent's characteristics, the areas designated were the same: the "Old Town" (50 percent), the industrial quarter (19 percent), and Langstrasse (17 percent). Although the old part of the city does have apartments and houses, it primarily attracts tourists, foreign workers, young persons, and others in search of recreation. Numerous restaurants, bars, discotheques, tourist shops, and small movie houses line the narrow streets; it is the prostitutes' area, and numerous drunks wander along the streets. While many deviant acts can, and do, take place here, they are usually not of a serious nature. The industrial quarter is an isolated area with many factories and industrial complexes; due to zoning regulations almost no one lives here, and thus few people are around at night. Langstrasse, near the city center, is largely populated by resident foreign workers and transients. Two-thirds of the respondents who expressed fears about these particular, and quite unique, areas were afraid of being "molested" — for example, by a drunk or a prostitute: Only one-fifth feared personal assault, and less than 2 percent feared theft or robbery. In Stuttgart, on the other hand, 13 percent mentioned fear of being assaulted or robbed; 1 percent mentioned theft; 21 percent mentioned "asocial" people, and 18 percent mentioned risk of being molested or accosted by drunks. Negligible differences were found by sex or age groupings in Zürich. One significant finding was that none of the foreign-born, who were almost entirely foreign workers and were more likely to visit the Old Town, mentioned theft, and only 3 percent expressed a fear of personal assault: Their fears were almost entirely of being "molested."

Views of informed persons in Switzerland

The conclusions drawn from the Zürich attitude survey were supported in interviews about crime with thirty-five well-informed and important persons in Switzerland. Almost complete unanimity was expressed by these persons to the effect that the country has a considerably lower crime rate than almost any other European country, and particularly the neighboring nations of the Federal German Republic, France, and Italy. Almost identical opinions were expressed by professors of criminal law and of sociology, by prosecutors of youth and adult crimes, by police officials, and by journalists who specialize in crime reporting for some of the largest Swiss newspapers. The observations of these informed persons are particularly relevant, because those residing in Zürich, Basel, and Geneva — cities either on or not far from the border — were assumed to have based their conclusions on professional knowledge and experience.

A professor of law at the University of Zürich stated, for example, that the Swiss crime rate is decidedly lower than that of nearby Germany, and another professor of law said emphatically that crime is not a serious problem in Zürich. Still another criminal law professor believed that crime is far less prevalent in the large Swiss cities than in French or German cities of comparable size. A professor of sociology likened the crime rate in Zürich to that of a much smaller United States city, basing his opinion on his experiences in teaching at several American universities. A leading Zürich journalist stated that crime is much lower in Switzerland than in other countries and that there is no real organized crime.

The chief prosecutor in a large city located on the French and German borders stated that there is a lack of public concern about crime because there are few serious crimes, such as robbery. Another leading prosecutor stated that the lack of concern with crime in large cities is due to the fact that little violence is associated with those crimes that are committed. A prominent deputy prosecutor was of the opinion that Geneva has much less crime, and particularly less juvenile delinquency, than similar-sized cities in France. A professor of law asserted that both the city and the canton of Geneva have much less crime than do the bordering countries, that people are generally not overly concerned about auto theft, and that there is little organized crime. A Bern public prosecutor felt that crime is much less a problem in Switzerland than in other countries, that people are always safe on city streets, and that there is little youth violence. A prosecutor of youth cases in Bern stated that there was little concern about youth crime there. From interviews with well-informed persons in cities of Ticino, the Italian-speaking canton of Switzerland, it was evident that they do not regard crime as a serious problem and that it is much less a matter of concern than in the neighboring Italian area around Lake Como. They claimed that residents have far less fear about burglary, auto theft, or thefts from automobiles.

Emphasis on crime in Swiss-German newspapers

The daily Swiss-German newspapers reflect little concern by the public about crime, as measured by the extent, nature, and position of crime stories in the newspapers. Newspapers selected for the study of crime news coverage were chosen for the differences in general readership, in order to obtain as wide a coverage as possible of the general population. All of them were in Swiss-German, as the major emphasis of the research project was in this geographic area, particularly Zürich; resources were insufficient to make a study of newspapers in the French-speaking area.[20] Three newspapers were studied: *Tages Anzeiger,* a Zürich-based publication with a circulation of 220,000 and an estimated readership of 591,000 whose readers are more representative of the general population; *Neue Zürcher Zeitung,* with a much smaller daily circulation than either of the other two (93,000 circulation, estimated readership of 213,000) but regarded as comparable to *The New York Times* with respect to national and international, business, banking and other financial news coverage and read generally by a predominantly conservative, well-educated upper-class group; and *Blick,* whose coverage is the largest of the three. Its daily circulation is about 260,000, with a readership of 628,000 throughout all German-speaking Switzerland; it is considered a more "sensational" publication than the other two, and is read largely by working-class persons. Two periods in 1973 were chosen for analysis: the first in the summer (June 24–30), and the second in late fall (November 24–30), the two periods then being combined later to give a typical two-week period. Insufficient funds precluded a study of a more desirable longer time span. A card was prepared to tabulate various features on each crime story appearing during the period. In addition, all letters to the editor dealing with crime were studied for two one-month periods (June 1–30 and November 1–30), later being combined as a total typical two-month period. In the discussion that follows *Tages Anzeiger* and *Neue Zürcher Zeitung* will be referred to as "ordinary newspapers," and *Blick* as the "sensational" newspaper.

Extent of crime news

Regardless of the type of newspaper, the total space (exclusive of advertising) devoted to crime news was extremely small. Copies of each paper were measured in terms of average total inches and the average inch space devoted to crime news in the sample study. On an average day, 0.6 percent of total news space in the *Tages Anzeiger* was devoted to crime news; for *Neue Zürcher Zeitung* it was 0.4 percent, for *Blick*, 1.9 percent. While *Blick* devoted three to four times more total space to crime news than the others, it represented only a small percentage of total news coverage space. Moreover, from the limited comparative data available, it appears that Swiss newspapers carry a low percentage of total space on crime news. A 1971 study showed that the London *Daily Mirror,* the Paris *Le Soir,* the Stockholm *Expressen,* and the Vienna *Kurier* carried from 6.6 percent to 8.6 percent of total space devoted to crime news, exclusive of advertising.[21] A 1974 study of the proportion of crime news in two German newspapers found that the more popular *Bild's* proportion of crime news was 10 percent, while it was 6 percent for the more conservative Frankfurt *Allegemeine Zeitung.*[22] An even higher percentage has been found in United States newspapers. In 1973 *The New York Daily News* was found to have the highest concentration of any type of news in the crime category (18.5 percent); *The New York Times* had 16.6 percent. This particular study, however, made no distinction between ordinary conventional crime and government crime, an important consideration, because the crime news was greatly augmented during the period of the Watergate investigations.[23] A much earlier study of five large Ohio city newspapers had found great variation in space coverage devoted to crime news, from 7 to 11 percent of total inch space, exclusive of advertising space.[24] For individual New York City newspapers, crime news varied from a low 15 percent in *The New York Times* and 16 percent in *The New York Journal American* to 27 percent in *The New York Mirror.*

In all the Zürich newspapers only a small number of articles related to crime appeared each day, with a range from 2.1 to 3.1 in the ordinary newspapers to 2.6 in *Blick*. A fairly large proportion of the crimes reported, however, had taken place in foreign countries: seven percent in *Tages Anzeiger,* 16 percent in *Neue Zürcher Zeitung,* and a much larger percentage (36 percent) in the more sensational *Blick.*

Prominence of crime news

Newspapers in the German-speaking part of Switzerland generally do not emphasize crime news by placing it on the front page, where it is more readily seen by the reader. It is customary to use the front page for important national and international events, relegating news of a more local nature to the second and last pages. Consequently, none of the crime stories in the ordinary newspapers studied appeared on the front page, although 19 percent of those in *Blick* did. One-third of the crime news stories in *Tages Anzeiger* appeared on the second or last page, about a tenth of the *Neue Zürcher Zeitung* crime news stories were on either of these two pages, and four-fifths of the *Blick* crime stories appeared there.[25] Crime stories receiving more prominent placements — that is, on the first, second, or last pages — were practically all personal crimes such as murder, assault, robbery, or rape: They ranged from one-half to three-fourths, depending upon the newspaper. In contrast, crime articles in Swedish newspapers frequently appear on the front pages, and this is true in many European countries, as well as in the French-speaking area of Switzerland.

Newspapers emphasize crime stories not only through placement but also by means of the size of the type. About one-half of the crime stories in the ordinary newspapers were presented in large type. Stories can also be emphasized by the use of a picture, a heavy frame around a story, or both. None of the ordinary newspaper crime stories were emphasized in this fashion. The more sensational newspaper, *Blick,* tended to emphasize certain stories in this manner, although it was surprising to find relatively little emphasis of this type in crime stories, with only 3 percent being accompanied by a picture, or a picture and a frame, and 8 percent by a frame only.

Type of crime

Newspaper crime stories everywhere tend to emphasize personal violence, including robbery, even though the incidence of this type of crime is low in relation to total crime. Swiss newspapers were no exception. Of the crime stories in the two ordinary newspapers, crimes of violence ranged from 37 percent to 53 percent, and two-thirds of the more sensational *Blick* crime stories concerned violence. Studies of leading newspapers in four other European countries found a generally similar percentage of the crime news coverage related to crimes of violence. For the *London Daily Mirror* the percentage was 42.3; for *Le Soir* of Paris, 41.5; Stockholm's *Expressen*, 34.1; and the *Vienna Kurier*, 6.6[26] Only 9 percent of the stories about property crime appearing in the Swiss newspapers involved burglary, and only a few were about robbery; nearly all cases concerned fraud and theft.

Location of crime

A large proportion of the crime stories involved incidents that had occurred outside the Zürich area or even outside the country. For the two ordinary newspapers, either 53 percent (*Tages Anzeiger*) or 60 percent (*Neue Zürcher Zeitung*) of the stories on crime reported events that had occurred outside Zürich canton, and if the six cantons adjacent to Zürich were added, the percentages would be 65 and 79, respectively. Of even more significance, in view of the small number of crimes reported in the German-Swiss newspapers, one out of five stories was a report of a crime that had taken place outside the country: seven percent of those in *Tages Anzeiger*, 16 percent for *Neue Zürcher Zeitung*, and 36 percent for *Blick*. A large proportion of personal crimes reported had taken place outside of Switzerland, particularly the stories in *Blick*. Of all the personal crimes reported in the ordinary newspapers, 6 percent had occurred in a foreign country; such crime accounted for 26 percent of the *Blick* stories. With respect to accounts of property crimes occurring in foreign countries, the percentages were 6 for *Neue Zürcher Zeitung*, 10 for *Tages Anzeiger*, and 67 for *Blick*.

Letters to the editors concerning crime

All published letters to the editors during the months of June and November were studied to ascertain how they reflected concerns about crime and the nature of the issues involved. Although it was not possible to know the ratio of letters published to the total received, it was reported that *Neue Zürcher Zeitung* prints approximately one-half of the crime letters received, a ratio that is probably higher than for the other two newspapers, due to its more conservative editorial policies. In all, 33 letters about crime were published in the three newspapers. Although these letters revealed varied interests in crime, none of them reflected deep concern about increasing crime. One-third of them asked for more severe punishment for crimes committed and greater security and protection; eighteen percent asked for lighter sentences and more understanding of criminals. Letters advocating more punishment, protection, and security referred almost entirely to terror by extremists, violent political activities of youth, cruelty to children, or severe punishment for drug dealers; almost none of them dealt with ordinary crime. Actions of police or other officials were criticized in 9 percent of the published letters, the media were criticized for being too "soft" on crime in 12 percent, and a surprising 15 percent complained about cruelty to animals. One letter demanded more emphasis on white-collar crime, rather than on the "poor people's crimes."

Summary

Measured by government reports, questions and debates in the Federal Parliament (National Assembly), a survey of attitudes toward crime in Zürich, interviews with informed persons, and the extent and nature of crime news in the daily press, crime is not a major issue in Switzerland. The Swiss federal government has shown minimal concern about crime: Few discussions or questions about crime have taken place in the Federal Council; few special committees have been appointed to study the problem; few questions about crime have been asked in the National Assembly, the Zürich Canton Parliament, or in the Zürich City Council. Marked differences exist in concern about crime in Switzerland and in other countries, particularly in Sweden and in the United States, where governmental interest in rapidly rising crime rates has reached major proportions.

A survey of Zürich respondents revealed that crime is not regarded by them as a major problem. Nearly all of the attitudes expressed revealed much less fear of crime in Zürich than in Stuttgart. Crime was mentioned by only 9 percent of the respondents as a major problem in the city; even this mention of it was low in a rank order of chief issues. A substantial proportion of respondents believed that crime was increasing, both in the country and in Zürich city, but their beliefs did not appear to be strong enough to make them fear their own personal involvement in robbery, burglary, theft, auto theft, or breaking into their autos. They generally reported feeling safe at night, alone and on foot, in their own neighborhoods. Only three specific city areas were considered to be unsafe, and even in these areas they feared mainly the possibility of being molested.

Crime is not emphasized in Swiss-German newspapers. In terms of space devoted to crime stories, and the manner in which they are presented, one may conclude that crime is not regarded as a serious problem in the country. A large proportion of crime news stories referred to acts committed outside the country. This situation differs markedly from studies of crime news reported in other European countries and in the United States. Even the letters to the editors selected for publication revealed no great concern of an increase in ordinary crime. It is not possible to ascertain what proportion of this lack of newspaper emphasis actually reflects a low rate of crime and how much it reflects newspaper editorial policies. Overall, it might be said that even the most sensational type of newspaper in the Swiss-German area of the country does not present a picture of a city or a country ridden with ever-increasing crime.

3. Trends in official crime statistics

Only with great difficulty can the official crime statistics of one country be compared with those of another. In the case of Switzerland a major problem proved to be the serious lack of nationally collected official crime statistics. It is practically the only government in Europe that collects no statistics for crimes known to the police or for arrests on a national level. Data are collected nationally only on convictions. Specialists in the area of criminology ge1erally consider these data inadequate, as they are too far removed from the crime itself and largely reflect successes in apprehension and prosecution. This particular situation has developed from the unique nature of the Swiss system of government. The federal government is reluctant to collect these data, for fear of giving the impression that it is investigating the crime control activities of the cantonal or city police or that it might interfere in other ways with cantonal law enforcement. Furthermore, there has been no urgency for the national government to gather these data, because crime has not been considered a major national problem. Should crime become a more serious issue for the country, the collection of national crime data would undoubtedly be extended.

Some attempts, however, have been made to compare Switzerland's crime *rate* with that of other countries by estimating the number of crimes known to the police. Günther Kaiser attempted a rough overall comparison of the 1970 rates of crimes known to the police in Switzerland with the Federal German Republic.[1] He derived his estimate of the number of crimes known to the Swiss police from nationally collected conviction statistics, assuming convictions to be one-third to one-fourth of all crimes reported to the police, exclusive of traffic offenses. Kaiser based his assumption, which might be rather high, on an examination of the criminal justice administration data in several German-speaking Swiss cantons where crimes reported to the police were known and where there has generally been a rather high rate of prosecution and subsequent convictions for those arrested. He estimated crimes known

34

to the police in Switzerland in 1970, exclusive of traffic offenses, to be between 180,000 to 240,000, a rate of approximately 3,500 per 100,000 population. This rate is much lower than that of the Federal German Republic as a whole.

Kaiser also compared adjacent Swiss and southern German areas and the southern German border area of Südbaden and that of the Basel-Stadt and the Basel-Land cantons of Switzerland. All of these Swiss and German areas collect data on crimes reported to the police and have somewhat similar legal systems and procedures. Crime rates for southern Germany are generally lower than those for the country as a whole or for the central and northern parts. Data from the two Swiss cantons were combined, Basel-Stadt consisting almost entirely of the city of Basel (205,000), whereas Basel-Land is largely the adjoining rural and village areas. The data were then compared with the Südbaden area that consists largely of the city of Freiburg (170,000) and its surrrounding area. The total population of the two Swiss cantons was 990,000 in 1971, and that of Südbaden was 1,868,900. On the basis of a number of assumptions, Kaiser reported that the two adjacent areas had similar crime rates, exclusive of traffic offenses. The combined rate for the Swiss area was 3,463 per 100,000 (Basel-Stadt had 3,503 and Basel-Land had 3,423), which is only slightly higher than the Südbaden rate of 3,339. A more significant comparison was the rate for Basel-Stadt (Basel) and the city of Freiburg, each with nearly the same population: Freiburg's crime rate in 1970 was 7,213, about twice that of Basel. This study, unfortunately, was of total crime rates only and thus does not indicate possible variations in specific offense rates.

Kaiser has also analyzed trends in rates for crimes reported to the police between 1959 and 1968 in fifteen West European countries and has compared them with Switzerland — again assuming crimes known to the police to be three to four times the number of convictions. Although cross-national trend comparisons based on crimes known to the police must be cautiously regarded, Kaiser was able to make some interesting comparisons. During this period reported crime increased 86 percent in France, 62 percent in Denmark, 61 percent in the Netherlands, 55 percent in England and Wales, 34 percent in Scotland, 30 percent in the Federal German Republic, Italy, and Finland, 29 percent in Norway, 24 percent in Sweden, 21 percent in Austria, and 11 percent in Luxemburg. Switzerland was found to have one of the lowest increases in criminality — 3 to 4 percent, based on an increase of 1 percent in convictions.

Even if one were to increase the correction by five times, this still would be less than the increase for the other countries.[2]

Crimes known to the police in selected Swiss cantons and cities

Since the actual rates of crimes known to the police are unavailable at the national level, these data were obtained from three of the largest cantons — Zürich (1,100,000), Bern (990,000), and Basel-Stadt (234,000) — and from four large cities — Zürich (420,000), Bern (160,000), Lausanne (136,000), and in dual fashion for Basel, since the canton of Basel-Stadt is actually a city-canton. Crimes known to the police are not collected in the canton of Geneva, nor in the city of Geneva, and for this reason this important Swiss city had to be omitted. Each canton and city was asked to provide data for the ten-year period 1962–72, and this information was provided by four of them. Two could furnish data for only a five-year period, and not all cantons and cities were able to supply information on all needed crime categories. Crime definitions closely approximated those categories used in the published federal reports on convictions which are based on the Swiss Federal Criminal Code.[3]

Interest was on crime *trends* in the six units. In analyzing trends in each crime, the six units of data will be treated generally as a whole. Trends in the four larger cities will then be analyzed, and comparisons made with the three largest cities in Sweden (Stockholm, 800,000, Göteborg, 400,000, and Malmö, 250,000). Some comparisons will also be made between Switzerland, the United States and other countries. The legal codes of each country may show some differences, but the analysis here is confined to the large crime categories. Moreover, comparisons will emphasize trends in crime, not the differences in the actual rate of crime in different countries.

Three statistical measures were applied to the rates on crimes known to the police, in order to determine trends in selected cantons and cities. A combination of the three measures gave a more adequate measure of the variations in the actual numerical amount of crime, which tended to be particularly small in Switzerland when compared over time with, for example, Sweden. First, *rates* were calculated per 100,000 for the beginning and end of a time period, also percentage increases in rates, with intermediate figures being extrapolated. Second, since rates can be misleading, *correlation coefficients* were run to determine the extent to which a given crime and a time period were associated, despite fluctuations. Third, *regression coefficients* were calculated on each time series to discover the amount of the annual increment of cases that had been added to a given rate and, by so doing, to find out if there had actually been a small or large increase. Correlation and regression coefficients give a more precise meaning than rate increases, for the annual percentage increase may be great, although the number of cases is quite small. Most of the actual figures for each type of crime are in the Appendixes. (See Appendixes A, B, C, and D.)

Murder and nonnegligent manslaughter

Switzerland's rate of murder and nonnegligent manslaughter is extremely low. In the trend analysis of these crimes reported to the police the absolute number of criminal homicides in all six reporting units was very low. Between 1960 and 1972 the largest canton, Zürich (excluding Zürich city) had an average rate of only 0.6 per 100,000, and if Zürich city was included the rate was only 1.4. The canton of Bern had an average rate of 0.3. Of particular significance was the fact that few murders are committed in the larger cities: For example, the average number per year was 3.4 in Zürich, 1.8 in Basel, and 2.7 in Bern.[4] In 1972 the Zürich city rate was 0.5, and Bern had no murders. In the United States the rates for murder and nonnegligent manslaughter were several times higher in 1972: For the country as a whole the rate was 9.2; for cities between 250,000 and 500,000 it was 16.5; and for cities between 100,000 and 250,000 it was 10.7.[5] The rate of 3.8 for cities under 10,000 in the United States was higher than that for the largest of the Swiss cities.

Correlation and regression coefficients for the six sets of data generally showed that murder had either not increased or had decreased. For the largest Swedish cities, on the other hand, the trends show much higher increases in murder rates, correlations, and regression coefficients than the large Swiss cities. (See Appendix A.) United States murder and nonnegligent manslaughter rates nearly doubled between 1962 and 1972 and increased by one-half between 1965 and 1972.[6] Rates for murder and second-degree murder reported to the police in the Federal German Republic increased by two-thirds between 1963 and 1970; in Baden-Württemberg in the south, where crime rates are generally lower, murder and manslaughter increased by one-fourth between 1964 and 1969.

Assault

In two out of three available sets of data, the assault rates in Switzerland have in general decreased or remained constant. Similar to murder, however, assaults reported to the police were numerically small. With one exception, none showed a substantial regression coefficient, the other two being either small or negative. In two out of three larger Swiss cities for which data were available, assault was either negatively correlated with time or showed only a slight correlation or a negative regression; only one city had a strong increasing assault rate trend, but the numbers were small. Swedish cities, on the other hand, showed a far greater general increase in assault, higher correlations, and significantly higher regression coefficients. Assaults reported to the police increased by 148 percent from 1962 to 1972 in the United States.

Robbery

Robbery is a minor problem in Switzerland, as compared with other countries. Total robberies reported to the police in Zürich city between 1962 and 1972 were 359, a yearly average of 32.6 and a rate of 7.7 per 100,000. In comparison, three United States cities of comparable size reported many times the 67 (only 8 against stores) reported in Zürich in 1972, for example. Denver reported 2,014 (thirty times greater), Portland, Oregon 1,715 (twenty-five times greater). In fact, Denver had six times as many in a single year, and Portland five times more, than Zürich in a ten-year period. Stuttgart, a slightly larger city than Zürich, had 379 reported robberies in 1972, approximately six times as many as in Zürich and a rate four times as great. Moreover, these low official robbery figures for Zürich were supported by the crime victimization survey, where only 1.2 percent of the households reported a robbery and only 1.1 percent of the individuals said they had been robbed.[7] (Chapter 5.) Bern had an average robbery rate of only 7.9 from 1963 to 1972; arrests for robbery in Geneva from 1969 to 1972 averaged 7.5 annually, a rate of 2.3 per 100,000. In comparison, the United States robbery rate for 1971 was 180.0 per 100,000 persons, with a range from 45.2 in towns of less than 10,000, 218.7 for cities of 100,000 to 250,000, to 375.8 in cities with populations of 250,000 to 500,000.

The robbery rates for the large Swiss cities were less than the average rate for small United States cities under 10,000 population.

While data from selected cantons and cities indicate a continuous rise in robbery rates, the absolute yearly increase has generally been very small, numerically. Rates for four of the six sets of data, from approximately 1962 to 1972, show a rate increase as well as substantial correlations, but the more significant measure, the regression analysis, confirmed that in both cantons and cities the numerical addition each year to the robbery rate was very small.

Swedish cities showed a much greater increase in robbery rates, no matter how they are measured. In the three major cities the increases ranged from 51.3 percent to 218.2 percent, an average of 132.1 percent. The correlations were much higher, and the regression coefficients for the Swedish cities showed a much more substantial increase, with average regression coefficients two and a half times greater than that of the Swiss cities. Official robbery rates in the United States increased about 200 percent from 1960 to 1972 and 153 percent from 1965 to 1972. Official rates on reported robberies increased by 84 percent between 1963 and 1970 in the Federal German Republic.

Switzerland's low robbery rate is particularly amazing, in view of the extensive opportunities offered for such a crime in this highly affluent country. Swiss people are accustomed to carrying large sums of cash, often bills of large denomination, as they pay in cash or use their well-developed system of paying bills through postal accounts, rather than by checks. A large proportion of them maintain postal account numbers, bills are generally paid by this means, and advertisements often contain forms to be used for order payments at the post office. Often individuals hand over or receive several hundred, even thousands, of Swiss francs at the post offices, many of which are small and located in residential neighborhoods. Large stacks of bills are kept in these post offices, and also in stores and railroad stations, with almost no security and often in open drawers at unprotected windows. This situation sometimes exists even in banks.[8] Tradesmen often handle large sums of cash, carrying it to the post office for deposit or collecting payments there.

Burglary

Burglary is not defined as a separate crime under Swiss law. It is considered a part of *Diebstahl*, or general theft; the law does not distinguish as to how articles are stolen. Thus, whether someone steals some-thing outside a building or enters a building to steal it, the legal cate-gory of the offense is the same. However, separate figures were ob-tained for burglaries reported to the police in the canton of Zürich and in Zürich city. These data indicated an increase in burglary rates from 1960 to 1972 of 36.8 percent in Zürich canton and 127 percent in Zü-rich city: Both the correlations and the regression coefficients were sub-stantial. In Sweden between 1965 and 1972, burglary rates increased 47.3 percent: The range for Swedish cities was from a rate increase of 24.3 percent in some to a high of 92.4 percent (in Stockholm). The rates started from a much larger numerical base: However, both the cor-relations and the regression coefficients were considerably higher than in the Swiss cities. In Göteborg, which is about the size of Zürich, the increase in burglaries, as measured by rates, correlations, and regression coefficients, was much greater. In the United States the increase from 1965 to 1972 was 86.4 percent. As in the case of Sweden, however, the base for measuring the increase was much larger.

The statistical increase in burglary in Zürich canton and the city of Zürich is difficult to interpret, as it does not appear to have resulted in great public apprehension in the Zürich area or in the country as a whole, as was shown, for example, in the attitude survey. Moreover, many residents continue to leave their houses unattended for extended periods of time when they are on vacation. Often, they do not rent their houses or apartments during extended absences, preferring usually to leave their dwellings unoccupied. For this reason it is particularly dif-ficult to find short-term rental accommodations in Swiss cities. Little emphasis is put on special security precautions in houses and apart-ments, and many apartment houses may be left unlocked during the day without fear of unauthorized entries. No advertisements were no-ticed for special security locks and bolts, security measures frequently seen advertised in the United States and in Sweden. This lack of serious concern, and the absence of much security, may well account, however, for this increase in burglaries and in the increased belief that this of-fense is increasing as revealed in the attitude survey in Zürich. In con-trast, Sweden has been experimenting, in Stockholm, with the construc-tion of "security houses which include burglarproof locks and various reinforcements and front doors without glass."[9] It was reported in *Time* magazine, for example, that "Despite Sweden's prosperity, a sharp in-crease in burglaries and robberies has produced a sudden sales boom in police locks and other anti-theft devices."[10]

Burglary and theft (Diebstahl)

Three sets of data for the cantons of Zürich, Bern, and Basel-Stadt revealed no definite trend in *Diebstahl*.[11] The rate of change showed considerable variation, ranging from no change to 48.6 percent. Correlations and regression coefficients with time trends were substantial in Basel-Stadt and in Bern, but not in Zürich canton. As in the case of the cantons, the large cities also exhibited considerable variation in trends. Zürich and Bern showed little increase over a ten-year period (1.9 percent and 16.9 percent), but Basel and Lausanne showed more marked increases (48.5 percent and 43.2 percent). Correlations and regressions were substantial in three cities, but not in Zürich.

It is difficult to reconcile the more general, but not uniform tendency for larceny increases in the police statistics with the observations and the results of the Zürich crime victimization survey. Swiss people seldom seem to show concern about the safety of their personal possessions, including purses, wallets, or suitcases; most Swiss — and foreigners in Switzerland, as well — seem to regard personal items and unattended property as being relatively safe, an impression largely supported in the Zürich victimization survey where larceny was shown to be a minor problem. (Chapter 5.) Displays of all types of articles, clothing, fruits, and the like are often left in the open, even when the stores close for lunch, and one has the feeling that any item dropped or left in a shop or restaurant would either be found there on return or kept in a lost-and-found department. This same respect for private property is noted in shops and restaurants, where chairs, tables, umbrellas, and other items are often left in the open, unattended and unattached, day and night. I once saw a group of new metal tables and chairs on a restaurant veranda, covered with snow and left for several days in a Zürich suburb.

Passengers leave all kinds of items at railway and tram exits and entrances without apparent fear of having them stolen. On one occasion I left a fairly expensive water flask on a train, and when I asked the station master about getting it back, he telephoned to the next station. On the following day I retrieved it at the local station, carefully labeled as to where it had been left, my name, and the station to which it was to be returned. During the skiing season ski racks carried by most automobiles may have as many as four pairs of skis, often new and expensive, left unlocked and unattended on the streets for long periods of time. A Zürich automobile dealer, for example, said that ski racks with locks were available for new cars, but that they were generally for purchase by foreigners accustomed to using them.

The *Diebstahl* form of shoplifting probably accounts for a considerable part of the official increase in theft. As self-service merchandising has spread throughout the Western industrialized societies, shoplifting has become an increasingly serious problem. It is reported to be very common, for example, in the Federal German Republic. Kaiser estimates that such offenses average more than 1 million annually and that the value of the goods stolen from stores and self-service shops total 75 million marks.[12] Swiss authorities have become increasingly alarmed about shoplifting increases. The people themselves feel it is increasing, as indicated by the responses in the attitude survey (Chapter 5). The problem appears to be less serious in Switzerland, where the estimated loss is slightly less than 3 percent of the merchandise, than in the United States where it runs between 4 and 6 percent, including employee theft.[13] Stephani's study of shoplifting of groceries and general merchandise in Migros (Switzerland's largest supermarket chain) stores in the cantons of Bern, Aargau, and Solothurn found that one in every 430 Migros customers was a shoplifter.[14] This study concluded that three times as many foreigners (particularly foreign workers) were apprehended for this offense as were native Swiss, although the Swiss were found to steal more expensive items than the foreign-born.

A significant factor in the rapid increase of shoplifting in Switzerland is that as of 1977 wide use was not made of the increasingly sophisticated and extensive security measures found in the United States. Virtually unknown, for example, are metal tags that stores can attach to garments. These are electrically activated at exits unless removed by the sales staff, thus alerting the management to an attempted shoplifting. Even expensive items such as Scotch whiskeys and brandies are sold on a self-service basis, and in most cases the use of closed-circuit television cameras is confined to some new supermarkets. Uniformed exit security guards are almost nonexistent, and passageways in many discount stores are set at such angles that customers cannot possibly be closely observed — although in some stores customers can be observed from raised booths.

Another factor that contributes to increased shoplifting is the likelihood that an apprehended offender generally will not be prosecuted if the value of the stolen goods is minor. The case will often be considered as petty theft, and prosecution will be only upon the request of the vic-

tim. Although offenders who take items of greater value will be officially prosecuted, authorities in the past have generally advised shops not
to press charges for first offenders. So rapidly have these larcenies increased in the country, however, that criminal charges are now being
urged if the value is in excess of Sw. F. 50 or if the offender has been
caught twice and the amount is in excess of Sw. F. 30. The estimated
chances of apprehension, however, remain low.

Auto theft

Since 1969, data on auto thefts have been collected (for each canton
except Aargau) for the Swiss federal government by the Canton of Zürich. In 1972, 4,156 autos were stolen in Switzerland, a rate of 69.9 per
100,000 population. The Swedish rate of 335 and the United States
rate of 423 are much higher, but the data also include attempted thefts.
This omission from the Swiss statistics, however, is probably far out-
weighed by the fact that the Swiss data include a large number of autos
that do not belong to Swiss citizens. Although all three countries have
high rates of auto ownership, each year an estimated 50 million autos
not registered in Switzerland enter or cross the country in transit to
other countries. The Swiss auto theft rate could thus be considered to
be comparatively low. Most of the theft involves teenagers who take
them for joyrides. Officials estimate that about 90 percent of all auto
thefts in Switzerland fall into this category, and the car is eventually re-
covered. Increasing theft by youth thus explains the increase in auto
theft.

Auto theft rates have definitely increased in Switzerland, although it
is important that the actual numerical increase has not been great. The
Swiss auto theft rate, as a whole, increased by approximately one-third
between 1969 and 1972, with an average annual increase of 10 percent.
However, the increase between 1969 and 1972 in absolute numbers was
only 11 percent.[15] Eight of the larger cantons were chosen for trend
analyses.[16] All cantons showed considerable increase in auto theft; although six showed substantial correlation between auto theft and time,
on the whole the regression coefficients were modest.

As yet, the Swiss citizens and foreigners who live there appear to
show only minimal concern either about the possible theft of their
autos or the possibility of their autos' being broken into. Autos are frequently left on the streets, at the end of tram lines, even for days at a

time while the owners are away from the city. Car owners customarily lock their cars, not primarily to prevent break-ins but largely because insurance companies are reluctant to pay out claims if the owners have not taken these precautions. The Swiss generally feel that they need have no fear about the safety of the auto if the windows have been rolled up and the doors and trunk locked. They do report taking extra precautions, however, when they travel abroad — particularly in Italy, where they not only lock their cars securely but remove valuable contents. While steering-wheel locks have been compulsory in Sweden for a long time, they did not become compulsory for new cars in Zürich canton until 1971.

Illegal drug use

The Swiss have become increasingly concerned about drug use, particularly among the youth in large urban centers. As contrasted to ordinary crime, much interest is now evidenced throughout the country in research on drug-related problems, particularly in the French-speaking area. Drug use appears to be of greater concern than any other problem of a criminal nature, and the federal government now gathers statistics on investigations of drug trafficking and usage throughout the country — the only statistical data on any type of criminal investigation at the national level. The press has given much coverage to this problem since 1970, and this has undoubtedly been significant in terms of the public's view of the increasingly serious nature of drug usage, as was shown in the Zürich attitude survey (Chapter 5). The perceived gravity of the problem is illustrated by a number of discussions in the parliaments at both the national and cantonal levels. A comment by a member of the National Assembly in 1972 is typical: "People in Switzerland are worried about the increase of drug offenses. In spite of the revision of the law of drugs it is urgent to fight drug dealing by means of heavier punishment and to give better protection against drugs to the population."

Parliamentary discussions finally resulted in changes in Swiss drug laws at the federal level in 1975, with more severe penalties for dealing in drugs. The law prohibits possession and use of marijuana and hashish, but punishment is generally only a fine unless it is a case of a repeated offender. Punishment may be severe by Swiss standards if large amounts of drugs are involved or if any illegal drugs are sold.

The increased use of illegal drugs has occurred rather late in Switzerland, largely since 1970, which is much later than in the United States, in Sweden, and in most other affluent countries where it has been a serious problem. In 1968 no more than a hundred cases were investigated in the entire country: In 1969 there were 521, and by 1973 there were 4,836, more than nine times as many cases as in 1969.[17] Although this increase is significant, it has not been as grave as it has been in other Western European countries. The problem is less serious than it might appear to be, because a relatively high proportion of foreigners are arrested for drug use in the country, as compared with other offenses. In 1973, for example, 18.4 percent of those arrested for drug offenses were foreigners; evidence suggests that they are foreign visitors, not workers. That they are primarily foreign visitors and not resident foreign workers is indicated by the fact that the proportion of men to women arrested is almost the same, although in the work force the proportion of women is much smaller. Of the total investigated, the proportion of foreign women was 17.3 percent, slightly less than the percentage of 18.4 for the foreign men: The proportion was higher in the 21–24 age group. Between 1962 and 1971, drug cases in Sweden increased 2,583 percent.[18] Increases were even more marked in the three largest cities: In Stockholm drug rates increased 796 percent per 100,000 population from 1962 to 1970, in Göteborg, 5,617 percent, and in Malmö, 3,333 percent.

As is the case almost everywhere, the drug problem in Switzerland, primarily marijuana and hashish, involves young urban males.[19] According to data for 1973, 82.2 percent of the drug cases involved males – most of them under the age of 25, with far higher rates per 100,000 population. Informed persons have suggested that Swiss youth use drugs increasingly as a protest against the more conservative adult society, much in the same way that they change hair and dress styles. Although they would not generally steal the property of another, as this would harm someone, they believe that the use of drugs is a personal decision. The use of marijuana or hashish is increasing among Swiss youth.[20] Although the figures alarm the Swiss, they show far less drug usage in general than in the United States and many other countries. For example, three-fourths (77 percent) of a group of 4,082 twenty-year-old Swiss Army recruits were reported in 1975 never to have used drugs.[21] Even during their initial period of military training little change was seen.

Trends in criminal convictions

As has been previously pointed out, data are available at the national level in Switzerland for convictions only.[22] These statistics, which have been published since 1948, include all juvenile and adult convictions under the Swiss Criminal Code, as well as convictions under other laws. Exceptions not included in the criminal code are violations of law by adolescents punished by a reprimand, young adult or adult fines of less than Sw. F. 100 (about $33) — changed in 1975 to Sw. F. 200 — and local cantonal law violations. Also not included as criminal code violations are income tax regulations punished by civil and administrative actions. Data on dispositions and sentences of all cases are provided by the court that gives the judgment. The analysis of convictions presented here is limited to violations of the Swiss Criminal Code. Not included are violations of the military criminal code, of the federal traffic code, or of other federal laws except fiscal violations.[23] The national penal code was first established in 1937, put into force in 1942; it has been subsequently amended (in 1943, 1950, 1966, 1968, and 1971). Prior to the establishment of the national penal code, each canton had its own criminal laws. A number of them even had the death penalty, which has been abolished nationally under the Swiss Criminal Code, except in time of war, at which time the death penalty can be imposed under the Swiss Military Code.

Convictions in Switzerland

As measured by convictions, the total Swiss rates for violations of the Swiss Criminal Code have remained almost constant from 1960 to 1971, as have offenses against property rates.[24] (See Appendix C.) Although the conviction rate trend has remained fairly constant since the mid-1960s, it has generally declined since 1960. This is demonstrated by a negative correlation of −0.84 and a decline of one-fourth in the conviction rate per 100,000 population between 1961 and 1971. Conviction trend data in five European countries (Switzerland, Belgium, Denmark, Norway, and England and Wales) have shown that Switzerland was the only country with general stability in the conviction rates, and even some decrease.[25] This relative stability, or even decline, has been due to movements in two directions: the decrease in official criminality among those over 29 and the increase in those younger.[26]

Rates for "offenses against life and body" were quite low, and the correlation with time highly negative. (Appendix C.) Likewise, practically no changes occurred in the trend in convictions for crimes against property. The rates showed little variation, and there was only a slight correlation. There was a decline of one-third and a negative correlation for convictions for "offenses against morality." Crimes against morality, however, have generally declined in many other parts of Europe as well, including England and Wales, France, and the Federal German Republic.[27] This decline has probably been due to the decriminalization of certain crimes, such as homosexual activities, and to the public's increased tolerance of illegal sexual behavior such as prostitution and fornication.

Among specific offense convictions, only two major offenses, larceny and petty larceny, showed a definite increase, both with trend correlations of 0.82. Petty larceny rose quite dramatically, with a total rate increase of 518.2 percent and a steady rise, as measured by the coefficient of regression. This marked rise in petty larceny is difficult to explain, inasmuch as small fines were eliminated in the reporting period. It might have been due to peculiarities of the base year selected. The trend for *Diebstahl* (burglary and larceny) showed a rather steady increase, with minor fluctuations, in the conviction rate; but the yearly variance was low. Convictions in England and Wales showed increase of 237 percent for burglary and 56 percent for larceny between 1960 and 1971.[28] Some offenses, such as robbery, showed a slight increase during the twelve-year period, in terms of percentages, correlations, and regression coefficients. From 1951 to 1972 the robbery conviction rate not only was low but it was remarkably stable, being 1.4 per 100,000 in 1951 and only 1.7 in 1973. (See Table 3.1.) Robbery convictions increased in England and Wales by 94 percent between 1960 and 1971. Other offenses showed declines in convictions, the greatest being in auto theft. Murder convictions declined by 20.4 percent, and the correlation was low. There were also substantial declines in fraud and embezzlement and minor decreases in vandalism, forgery, and falsification.[29]

Crime convictions in predominantly German-speaking cantons

Conviction data reflect a later stage in the criminal process. They are also subject to marked shifts that result from changes in prosecution policies, as well as the effects of bargaining for reduction in charge or

Table 3.1. *Convictions for crimes of robbery in Switzerland, rate per 100,000 for selected years, 1951–73*

Year	Number of convictions	Rate per 100,000	Rate index
1951	65	1.4	100
1955	44	0.9	64
1960	64	1.2	86
1964	65	1.1	79
1967	74	1.2	86
1968	67	1.1	79
1969	99	1.6	114
1970	76	1.2	86
1971	93	1.5	107
1972	159	2.5	179
1973	109	1.7	121

Source: Conviction statistics from *Die Strafurteile in der Schweiz/Les Condamnations Pénales en Suisse* (Bern: Eidgenössisches Statistisches Amt). Population statistics from *Schweiz: Wahnbevölkerung 1951–1972* (Bern: Eidgenössisches Statistisches Amt, 1972).

sentence for guilty pleas that affect the number of convictions as well as sentences.[30] In the German-speaking cantons, however, conviction statistics have much more stability, and they have more reliability for a *trend analysis* than do the statistics for Switzerland as a whole. In the German-speaking cantons, comprising approximately three-fourths of the population, plea bargaining to a guilty plea for a reduced charge is not possible, but it is sometimes used for sentencing. In fact, the prosecutor is required to prosecute all criminal cases where the evidence warrants it. With this procedure, trials are held before a judge only, or a panel of from three to five judges, and conviction rates are high. Convictions are so common that prosecutions and convictions are quite similar, numerically. At least, this is the way it appears and the way in which it was described by various informants. Analyses of convictions by cantons were thus limited to the nineteen predominantly German-speaking cantons. If the French-speaking, the mixed predominantly French-speaking, and the Italian-speaking cantons had been included, the trend line would not have been as reliable, as the public prosecutor may, and frequently does, drop prosecution. In these cantons plea bargaining is frequent; however, plea bargaining for a reduced charge in the American sense is not common.

Analysis of conviction data between 1960 and 1971 from the seventeen German-speaking cantons (plus the two predominantly German-speaking cantons of Bern and Graubünden) did show results similar to the country as a whole, however, revealing a high degree of consistency in a low crime conviction rate trend. Only three cantons showed increases in the rate of total crime convictions between 1960 and 1971, and two of them were in small cantons.[31] (See Appendix D.) Nine of the remaining sixteen cantons had modest rate increases, and two of the most populous cantons, Zürich and Bern, had substantial decreases. Moreover, the correlation analysis showed somewhat similar results: Seventeen cantons had negative correlations, eleven of which were substantial, two of them occurring in the most populous cantons (Zürich and Bern). Regression coefficients, however, indicated considerable variation among the cantons. Conviction rates for offenses against "life and body" generally showed slight increases or decreases, as measured by rates, correlations, and regression coefficients. As a whole, the Swiss rate for property convictions remained constant from 1960 to 1971, but the rates decreased in eleven cantons and increased in only eight. As reflected in rates, correlations, and regression coefficients, "morality" convictions – primarily sexual offenses – were found to be declining or stabilizing in most cantons.

Foreigners entering Switzerland to commit crimes

Most persons knowledgeable in legal matters and in law enforcement believe that for Swiss residents the official crime rate is actually lower than the total rate. In the opinion of these persons, many foreigners, not the foreign workers residing there, come into the country to commit crimes. They claim that this is particularly true in the border areas near Basel and Geneva and in Ticino near Italy; such persons are particularly German, French, and Italian residents, they claim. This opinion appears to be supported by the facts and is not to any degree a product of selective arrests. Many convicted foreigners, for example, are not resident in Switzerland; rather, they are visitors who may have entered the country for purposes of committing a crime.[32] More than one-third (37.1 percent) of the 5,390 foreigners sentenced in Switzerland in 1972 for offenses against the Swiss penal code resided outside the country.[33] The nature and scope of this problem was well illustrated early in 1977, when several serious armed robberies occurred in Geneva and one of its suburbs and also in Zürich.[34] In all of these cases, in which large amounts of money were taken and two police officers wounded, the offenders were definitely identified as having come from Italy. Through the cooperative efforts of Italian and Swiss police authorities one of the armed robbers, an Italian with a long police record, was apprehended with a female accomplice at the Nice airport as they were leaving for Madrid, en route to Brazil.

It is extremely difficult to apprehend persons entering Switzerland for criminal activities, as many crimes cannot be solved, even under optimal circumstances, in a matter of hours or even days. It is quite simple to enter Switzerland at the many border cities: In fact, many foreigners come daily to work in Geneva and Basel, and the tourist traffic is heavy. Other possibly significant factors are Switzerland's greater prosperity, and even the shorter sentences known to be given to convicted offenders and the better prison conditions. If apprehended for an offense, generally, the nonresident alien would probably have to serve less time than he would have to serve for a similar offense in his own country.

Obviously, this belief about the criminality of foreigners coming into the country to commit crimes is almost impossible to verify, as it is often difficult to apprehend such offenders. Analyses of data from Zürich, Basel, and Geneva, however, did indicate that in spite of these limitations, foreigners constituted a large proportion of arrests for robbery. Between 1971 and 1972, for example, over one-third (37.5 percent) of those arrested in Zürich for robbery were foreigners, nearly all of whom were nonresidents. Five cases involved Algerians; two, Italians; two, Austrians; and one each from France, England, Scotland, Jamaica, Hungary, and Yugoslavia. The median value of a robbery committed by a Swiss national was $17; this compares with a median value of $113 for robberies committed by foreigners.

Prosecutors in the Ticino area that borders less affluent Italy attribute much of the burglary, auto theft, and stealing from cars to Italians, rather than to the Italian-Swiss, and their opinions are supported by a study of the proportion of foreigners in the canton prison.[35] A prosecutor in the Lugano area, for example, estimated that 50 percent of all crime, and at least 80 percent of serious crime, is committed by persons who are residents of Italy. Many cases involve theft of cigarettes and other contraband to be sold in Italy. During the summer tourist season, offenses rise considerably.

Prosecutors and police officials may tend to exaggerate these estimates, as it enables them to explain the high percentage of unapprehended offenders. Analysis of insurance claims for various types of theft appears, however, to support the view that foreigners who enter the country from France, Germany, and Italy commit many of these crimes. Data from Mobiliar, a large Swiss insurance company, revealed that claims from insured persons in Zürich and in Bern cantons, both of which are highly urbanized, are about equivalent to the national average. Border cantons, on the other hand, have higher claims; Geneva is 60 percent above the average, Ticino is 35 percent higher, and Basel-Stadt is 10 percent higher. In Geneva and Ticino many of the theft claims result from burglaries of vacation homes; in Geneva, particularly, the police report a low rate of solving such crimes as stolen motorcycles, most of which have probably disappeared across the border. One statement can be made with certainty, and this is that Swiss citizens rarely commit these offenses in other countries. Even questions about this possibility were met with amusement. On the other hand, some persons in the less affluent surrounding countries appear to look upon Switzerland as a suitable place to loot with reasonable impunity.

Summary

Official statistics generally reflect a comparatively small amount of crime in Switzerland, as well as a low upward trend, or even a decrease, in the rates of various crimes. In most cases crimes have shown an increase, as might be expected, but the amount of these increases, as measured by correlations and by regression coefficients, have been comparatively small, particularly when compared with similar Swedish data. While exceptions are found in certain crimes, they are not numerous and do not alter the general trend. This stable, or downward, trend is more marked for convictions than for crimes known to the police in the six cantonal and large city units for which such statistics were collected.

Official data on crimes known to the police and convictions indicated that crimes of violence are extremely low in the country as a whole, for the nineteen predominantly German-speaking cantons, and for the large cities. This situation contrasts sharply with that found in the United States, in Sweden, and in the Federal German Republic. Likewise, assaults reported to the police have shown a general decline or have remained stationary, which was also true of convictions. Robbery remains a minor problem in Switzerland, with very low rates, even though some increase was seen. Annual increases in robbery rates, moreover, are numerically infinitesimal, as compared with increases in Sweden and in the United States, particularly if comparisons are made for large city rates. Surprisingly, the rates for criminal homicide and robbery remain extremely low, in spite of the general availability of firearms in Switzerland. (Chapter 8.)

On a nationwide basis, and for the nineteen predominantly German-speaking cantons, criminal convictions, convictions for crimes against "life and body," property crimes, and offenses against morality re-mained either fairly constant or declined in the period from 1960 to 1971, depending upon the statistical measures used. These trends in convictions contrast sharply with other European countries such as England and Wales, with the exception of crimes against morality.

All official statistics, even those for trends as used in this study, must be viewed with caution in making definite conclusions about the actual amount of crime. This is primarily due to the problems involved in re-porting crimes to the police; this factor, together with arrests, affects the statistics and even the convictions as well. The question of the ac-curacy of the reporting of crimes to the police will be the subject of the following chapter; Chapter 5 will present the results of a crime victimi-zation survey of Zürich.

4. The Swiss police and crime reporting

As in any country, several factors affect the reliability of Swiss police statistics. It is important, therefore, to examine the Swiss police and their relations to the public in order to ascertain the relevance of official crime statistics, particularly statistical trends, provided by the police. If the ratio of police to population were increased in Switzerland, for example, official crime rates would be expected to rise because of the likelihood that the police would be able to detect more crime. Similarly, a marked increase in crime, or greater public concern about it, would lead to an increase in the size of the police forces. Any significant changes in law enforcement policies or changes in methods of recording crimes reported to them by the public, would also affect crime rates, increasing or decreasing them. Likewise, if the citizens lacked respect for the police, or if they were hostile to them and thus did not wish to report crime victimization, a marked effect would result in the crime rate.

It should be kept in mind throughout the discussion of the role of the police in crime, however, that throughout the world the police are generally involved in many activities that are not for the most part related to the commission of crimes. They regulate traffic, enforce various ordinances, help with many problems of the citizens, and so on. United States studies show that about 80 percent, or even more, of police activities are unrelated to crime, and there is no reason to doubt that this is not also true in Switzerland.[1]

The Swiss police

From conversations with police officers and with other knowledgeable persons outside the police, it seems clear that police law enforcement practices remain fairly constant in most of the Swiss cantons and that they have had no major effect on crime statistics. The Swiss police are a professional career group. Changes in political administration are not

53

significant, and it appears that political pressures have also had little or no influence on their policies or practices. Although no studies of police discretion have been conducted in Switzerland, there is no evidence to indicate that such studies would show a significantly different variation over time.

Swiss police crime statistics appear to be reasonably reliable. Crimes reported to them, or coming to their attention, seem to be carefully recorded, according to professors of criminal law and various public officials. Any inaccuracies that do arise are more often due to the rather crude methods of tabulation; computers were not yet being used in 1973, although the police are now planning to use them in several larger cities. Furthermore, the analysis of crimes reported to the police that was done in this study was concentrated on trends, so that minor statistical inaccuracies would probably not be significant.

Contrary to most European countries, nearly all Swiss police forces are under local authority, either city or cantonal. The federal police force is numerically small and is strictly limited to the handling of offenses against the state and illegal drugs. During the 1960s it was recognized that cantonal police forces were inadequate or insufficiently trained either to carry out the numerous duties given them during the frequent international conferences in Switzerland or to deal with problems associated with the protection of embassies, consular residences, and international organizations there — particularly in Geneva, Bern, and Zürich. In the past it was customary for cantons to request additional police forces from neighboring cantons or cities when the need arose, or even to call on the army for help, a procedure often criticized by the press. Largely as a result of these situations certain police directors and members of Parliament sought in 1964 to create a specially trained federal police force to be sent wherever needed. This proposal was rejected by the cantonal police directors, who feared that greater police authority at the federal level would result in a gradual reduction of cantonal authority, and by the press and others who disliked the prospect of a "flying police corps" instructed to defend the security of foreign diplomats and to fight demonstrators. Subsequently, a number of canton police directors worked out a proposed treaty for an intercantonal mobile police force with specified methods of operation.[2] An intercantonal agreement involving collaboration of the police in five eastern cantons (Schaffhausen, Appenzell A. Rh., Appenzell I. Rh., St. Gallen, and Thurgau) was approved, however, by the Federal Council in 1977. Collaboration involves joint police controls in criminal and traffic matters and in such extraordinary events as catastrophes, acts of terrorism, the taking of hostages, and crimes of violence.

The actual size of the cantonal and city police forces cannot be ascertained. No national statistics are available — probably because it might appear that the government is attempting to learn more about, and possibly eventually to control, the cantonal forces. Fortunately, in 1973 the police administrator of the canton of St. Gallen gathered statistics from the cantonal and city police, and they form the basis of the analysis made here of the Swiss police.[3] The total effective cantonal and large city police forces numbered 8,724 at that time; the rate for the country is thus 1.4 per 1,000 population. Excluded in these statistics were the small federal force and the very small local forces. Even if this total were generously increased to 10,000 to include these "extra" forces, the rate would be only 1.6 per 1,000. Either estimate would be lower than that of the United States, where the rate is 2.0 for cities, but it is higher than that of 1.0 for rural United States areas.[4] Eight cantons had less than one policeman per 1,000 population; ten had between 1.0 and 1.5; and seven had more than 1.5 per 1,000. Zürich and Bern cantons, with the respective cities included, were 1.8 and 1.4, respectively. If only the city forces were used, the rate for the city of Zürich was 2.4 per 1,000 and that of Basel 3.4, as compared with 2.8 for United States cities of over 250,000 population. The rate for Bern city was 2.7, compared with United States cities of populations between 100,000 and 250,000, where the rate is 1.8.

These slightly higher ratios of police forces to population in the more urban Swiss cantons does not necessarily mean that there is more suspected crime, nor that they are more active in crime-related work. About two-thirds of all Swiss police are engaged primarily in traffic matters. The number of automobiles in the country has increased, for example, from 89 per 1,000 persons in 1960 to 207 in 1971. One Zürich city police official estimated that only about 300 of the 1,000 member police force dealt primarily with crime.

An attempt was made to find out if there has been an increase or decrease in police forces in terms of population, a situation that might have affected the crime statistics. Data were obtained on the size of the effective police forces between 1962 and 1973 in the cities of Zürich and Bern and in the cantons of Zürich, Bern, Basel-Stadt and St. Gallen. Rates were then calculated on the basis of population estimates. The large city police forces were found to remain fairly constant in size, but those of the cantons had increased considerably. During this ten-year period the Basel police force (canton) increased only 8.6 percent; the city of Zürich, 9.1 percent; and the city of Bern showed a 37 percent increase. The Bern increase largely reflected the changes from a previous small force that was significantly augmented to provide adequate police services for the embassies and for other functions of the nation's capital city. On the other hand, cantonal police forces increased by one-third in Zürich and in St. Gallen and those in Bern increased by 50 percent. A significant factor in these cantonal increases was the greatly increased traffic problems associated with the absorption of rural cantonal areas into the metropolitan areas.

Attitudes toward the police

People's attitudes toward police influence their reporting of crimes. In the survey of heads of representative households in Zürich city (Chapter 5) an attempt was made to ascertain attitudes toward the police and the reporting of crime to them. The survey showed that Zürich respondents had significantly high opinions of police performance: Two-thirds of them were "very satisfied." The police were thought to be doing an "average" job by 31 percent, and less than 3 percent thought that they were doing a "poor job." A Stuttgart survey reported a somewhat similar high regard for the police: One-half considered them to be doing a "good job"; forty-five percent thought that their performance was "average"; and 5 percent thought that they were doing a "poor job."[5] In a 1970 national survey in the United States 64 percent thought the police locally were doing an excellent or "pretty good" job, and 33 percent thought they were doing only a fair or poor job.[6]

In the Zürich survey no significant differences by income or education were found, but there were significant differences by age groups. Younger persons had less high regard for the police, but even among the young adult groups, 46 percent thought that the police were doing a good job, and 42 percent an average job. The foreign-born also expressed high regard for the police. Zürich respondents were not quite as enthusiastic about the courts as they were about the police. About one-half (51 percent) felt that they were doing a good or a very good job, and almost one-fourth of the respondents expressed no opinion. They did approve of the courts more than did respondents in the Stuttgart sample, where 44 percent thought that they were doing a good or a very good job.

When respondents were asked what might be done to improve police performance, few persons (4 percent) referred to discourtesies and discrimination on the part of the police. Two-thirds of the respondents felt that limited manpower was the most serious problem; forty-two percent felt that more police were needed, and 22 percent said that more police should be assigned to patrol and investigative work. Some (14 percent) felt that the police could be better trained and should receive higher pay. In the Stuttgart survey the main suggestions for improving police services were quite similar: need for more police, 50 percent; need for more patrolling, 18 percent; and improved training, 16 percent. Only 2 percent of the respondents referred to discourtesy and discrimination.

While Zürich residents had a general high respect for the police, they did not indicate equally high opinions of their abilities to solve criminal cases. Only 44 percent believed that the police solved more than 50 percent of the robbery cases; corresponding percentages were 41 percent for burglary cases, 32 percent for larcenies, 35 percent for auto theft, and 38 percent for assaults. Actually, in 1972 the Zürich police solved 28 percent of robberies and attempted robberies, and they solved nearly one-half (47 percent) of all the reported burglaries. The Stuttgart respondents estimated an even lower level of police ability to solve cases: robbery, 33 percent; burglary, 29 percent; larcenies, 21 percent; auto theft, 22 percent; and assaults, 33 percent.

Reporting crime victimization to the police

Most crimes are brought to the attention of the police by the citizens involved — in fact, in about 80 percent of the cases. A complex social psychological process often is involved in this act of reporting the crime to the police. First of all, the individual must himself regard the act as a crime.[7] A trivial slap or threat in the form of a minor assault, or the theft of an object of little value, may not be regarded by the victim as being a crime. Should it be regarded as such, however, the consideration still remains as to the merits of reporting it to the police. In the 1973 Zürich victimization survey a large proportion of household heads, as well as individual household members, indicated that they had not reported offenses committed against them. (Chapter 5.) This proportion

Table 4.1. *Percent of victimizations reported to the police, by type of victimization: Zürich, Stuttgart, Denver, and Portland*

Type of incident	Percent reported			
	Zürich	Stuttgart	Denver	Portland
Household	56	42	47	43
Burglary	64	52	57	50
With entry	68	84	77	71
Attempted entry	58	19	37	28
Larceny	51	54	30	29
Completed	57	—	31	30
Attempted	78	—	19	21
Auto Theft	NR[b]	69	78	79
Completed	NR	—	94	91
Attempted	NR	—	39	37
Vandalism	13	37	—	—
Personal	34	50	35	34
Assault[a]	28	55	38	37
Actual	35	55	46	48
			32	30
Attempted	17	—	42	46
			29	26
Theft	39	38	32	31
With contact	33	44	46	39
Without contact	43	35	31	31
Robbery	NR	NR	44	45

[a] Figures for assault in the United States cities reflect differences in categorizing. For *actual* assaults, the first figure (upper) represents aggravated assault, and the second figure (lower) represents simple assault. For assault *attempts,* the first figure represents attempted assault with weapon (aggravated), and the second represents attempted assault without weapon (simple).
[b] NR means that the number of cases was too small for percentages.

is about the same, or higher, than is reported in the cities of most other countries. Figures vary greatly by offense, however. For total crime incidents, 44 percent were reported, whereas slightly more than half of the offenses against the household itself and a third of the personal offenses were reported.[8] (See Table 4.1.) In Stuttgart and in the United States cities of Denver and Portland, Oregon, the percentages of household crime victimizations reported to the police were about the same:[9]

A third of the personal offenses were reported in Zürich, Denver, and Portland, but one-half were reported in Stuttgart.

The low incidence of reporting household victimization in Zürich is somewhat surprising, inasmuch as a large proportion of the households are well covered by burglary and theft insurance. In fact, three-fourths (76 percent) of all individual household respondents, aged 20 and over, reported having insurance to cover burglary and theft, as compared with 62 percent of the Stuttgart respondents, although the respondents in this city did not include foreign workers, who generally do not carry this type of insurance. Only minor differences were found in Zürich in the reporting of crime victimization by nationality and by sex, but considerable differences were found by age, younger persons being less likely to report the incidents.

Two-thirds of burglaries and attempts were reported, which was higher than in Stuttgart and in Portland. About one-half of all household larcenies were reported — about the same as in Stuttgart but much higher than in Denver and Portland. About one-fourth of the actual and attempted assaults were reported, in comparison with 55 percent in Stuttgart, slightly over one-third in Denver and Portland, and 15 percent in Denmark, Norway, and Sweden.[10] No robbery cases were reported to the police, probably because eight of the ten robbery cases were attempts, and none with a gun or involving much violence. In Denver and Portland about half of the robbery cases, and about a third of those attempts that did not result in injury, are reported to the police. Slightly more than a third (39 percent) of all personal thefts were reported in Zürich, which is about the same as in Stuttgart and slightly higher than in Denver and Portland.

The reason given most commonly by the Zürich respondents for not reporting offenses was that they did not consider them to be serious or important enough to be reported to the police. This response constituted a much larger proportion of the responses in Zürich than in Stuttgart, Denver, or Portland. (See Table 4.2.) Personal offenses such as assault, household larceny, and burglary were not reported for the same reason. In general, there was no significant difference by sex, age, or nationality in this response. Three possible explanations might be suggested for this attitude: (1) The offenses actually were trivial (and there is some evidence in the victimization survey for this, in terms of the low value of the objects usually stolen); (2) such losses of a fairly minor nature can be absorbed without undue hardship in a country as

Table 4.2. *Reasons for not reporting crime victimization to the police*

Categories	Zürich	Stuttgart	United States Cities Personal	Household
Not serious, or not important enough	70	49	28	32
Nothing could be done about it; lack of proof	7	26	34	38
Too inconvenient	1		3	2
Wish to avoid trouble, or fear of reprisal	5	2	2	1
Did not know whom to contact	2			
Police would not be bothered			5	7
Other	15	23	28	20

affluent as Switzerland; and (3) the fact that all of the assaults were regarded as trivial. Whatever the reasoning, nonreporting appears not to have been due to any feeling that the police would not wish to be bothered, as the survey revealed a generally high regard for them.

Summary

A survey of the Swiss police indicates that police statistics, and the consequent analysis of crime trends in Switzerland, are reliable. Likewise, there has been no marked increase in police forces for the purpose of crime control. No significant changes have occurred in law enforcement policies or in police policies of recording crimes reported to them by the public. Swiss citizens have marked respect for the police.

Although a large proportion of offenses are not reported to the police in Zürich, similar situations have been found in Stuttgart, in Denver, and in Portland. In some offenses, there was higher reporting of crime in Zürich. The most common reason given for the nonreporting of a crime was that the offense was not of a nature sufficiently serious to warrant going to the police about it. This reason was given more frequently in Zürich than in Stuttgart, Denver, or Portland. The nature of crime and Swiss society lends considerable support to this reason.

5. Crime victimization in Zürich

The foregoing analyses relied mainly on the Swiss national conviction statistics and on a sample study of crimes reported to the police in the larger cantons and cities. Their adequacy was checked against possible changes in police practices, the size of the police forces, and the relation of the public to the police. Criminologists today, however, generally agree that no matter how adequate official police statistics are, they cannot present the actual extent of crime. This failure is due chiefly to the fact that they depend for the most part on the citizen reporting of crimes to them. They themselves discover only a minor percentage of the crimes actually committed. Citizen reports to the police are dependent on many variables, such as their attitudes to the police, the extent to which they feel that the police will do something positive about the crime, and the seriousness of the offense involved. Many of these factors (as well as the extent to which the police themselves discover crimes) are related to the size and efficiency of the police force.[1]

A new technique of crime victimization surveys has been developed over the past decade to meet these objections to, and partially to replace, official statistics, as well as to check on their reliability. The first major pilot surveys of this type were done in Boston, Chicago, and Washington, D. C., by the President's Commission on Law Enforcement and the Administration of Justice in 1966. This commission also arranged for the National Opinion Research Center to interview a national sample of 10,000 households about their experiences as victims of crime.[2] Initial surveys showed three to ten times more crimes than were reported in the official statistics. They also made contributions to methodology, as, for example, the need for proper phrasing of questions to insure more correct responses. As a result of these initial surveys and a limited number of other studies the technique developed rapidly, and many such surveys have been carried out in the United States. Similar victimization surveys have subsequently been conducted in Europe and elsewhere. Although practically all of these surveys have dealt with individuals and households, a few of them have studied the extent of crimes committed against business concerns.

Victimization surveys have been carried out by the United States Bureau of the Census since 1972, under authorization by the Law Enforcement Administration (LEAA) of the Department of Justice. Some criminologists hope that periodic surveys will become a permanent procedure to determine the extent of crime and crime trends, reflecting the actual situation more adequately than official statistics generally do. As it is now being carried out, the survey involves periodic interviewing of a national probability sample of 75,000 households and 15,000 business establishments. Termed the National Crime Panel, it provides data for the United States as a whole and also a subnational grouping of metropolitan areas by size. In addition, surveys of representative samples are being made in sixteen major cities, and it is hoped that eventually data will be made available for thirty-five cities. In each of the five largest cities about 10,000 households have been covered in interviews, and approximately 2,500 commercial establishments have been included in the sample. The first published reports of the survey, dealing with crime victimization in the five largest United States cities, appeared in the spring of 1974.[3] In each of the eight other largest cities, an average of 9,700 households (consisting of about 21,000 persons aged 12 and over) were covered during 1972.

Crime victimization surveys may make it possible to compare rates of crimes in various countries, comparisons that have been difficult or impossible with official crime statistics. By 1976 this means of measuring crime was being increasingly accepted. It was, in fact, widely discussed at the Fifth United Nations Congress on the Prevention of Crime and the Treatment of Offenders, which was held in Geneva in 1975. Several crime victimization studies had been carried out jointly in the Scandinavian countries from 1970 through 1974.[4] A pilot victimization survey had been done in London in 1973 by the Institute of Criminology of Cambridge University.[5] Surveys of crime victimization had also been conducted in Stuttgart[6] and Göttingen[7] in the Federal German Republic, in the Netherlands,[8] in Abidjan, capital of the Ivory Coast, [9] and in Japan. Similar surveys were being planned in Australia and in Canada.

In connection with the Swiss crime research project a victimization survey was carried out in Zürich, and simultaneously a similar survey was done in Stuttgart under the auspices of the Criminological Institute of the University of Freiburg. Many problems and limitations remain unsolved, however, and until solutions to them can be found it will remain difficult to make completely valid comparisons on an international level. These problems include closer similarities in sampling techniques, in the questions asked, in the training of the interviewers, in the choice of respondents, in the age of the victims and in the methods of analyzing data.[10]

The Zürich victimization study covered a representative sample of 482 households, covering approximately 940 individuals aged 14 and over. An attitude survey was also included. (See Appendix F for sampling procedures used.) It was designed along the lines of the United States surveys, but the interviewing was conducted by Publitest, one of Switzerland's largest and best-known opinion survey organizations, which has carried out several surveys for the Sociological Institute of the University of Zürich. This crime victimization survey was one of the first to be done outside the United States.

In this survey only household *heads* were used: husband, wife, or the equivalent "head," but with approximately equal numbers of males and females. It was assumed that this type of respondent would be better informed about all household members than an indiscriminately chosen adult household member. Some of the studies in the United States have shown that household respondents tend to underreport victimization of other household members, but these surveys have generally used any respondent above a certain age, not necessarily the head of the household.[11] Interviewers were instructed to ask questions in as much detail, and with the same time allotment, for each member of the household as for the household respondent. The results of the survey would, of course, have been more accurate if each household member had been interviewed, but the additional expense involved precluded the more extensive interviewing.[12]

Despite this limitation, the household "head" survey gave far more complete data on crime victimization than was available through official police statistics. It was also thought, for a number of reasons, that a higher degree of reliability could be assumed in the Swiss family milieu than in the household milieu in large United States cities. First of all, it is generally felt that the Swiss household, even in a large city like Zürich, is a much more closely knit unit than households in most large United States cities, particularly those in slum areas. It would be expected, for example, that the female household head would be more knowledgeable about the activities of household members, particularly since the majority of married Swiss women do not work outside the home.[13] Second, the fact that crime is not as common in Switzerland, as shown by official statistics, as in the United States or in Swedish cities, would tend to make any criminal incidents more memorable in a family.[14] Third, the large proportion of one-person households, as well as those consisting of husband and wife only, made it reasonable to expect that information from these respondents would be highly reliable. Although Swiss household respondents were thought to provide reasonably adequate victimization information about other household members, reliability was increased by applying certain corrective factors to increase the total number of assaults and small thefts reported in the sample.[15]

The interview schedule

The interview schedule consisted largely of questions selected from the United States Census Crime Victimization surveys, which were then translated into colloquial German.[16] In addition to crime victimization information it dealt with attitudes reflecting concern about crime and the reporting of crimes to the police. Victimization questions were designed to obtain information about assault, robbery, burglary, theft, auto theft, and vandalism; experience has demonstrated that questions about offenses such as fraud fail to produce reliable responses. Also included were questions about attempts, if the incidents had been reported to the police, and if not, why not. Some adaptations of the United States interview schedules were made; for example, more emphasis was put on possible thefts of motorcycles or parts.

Interview schedules must be formulated in such a way as to insure that they will reflect the interviewee's perception of a crime. In other words, the terminology should elicit answers as similar as possible from all respondents. Some persons, for example, regard minor law infractions as crimes, but others do not; some do not consider the taking of an object of little value, or of a small sum of money, as a "theft," and others do. Similarly, one may recall a minor assault involving a slight hit or threat with an object, but another may not define such an act as having been a "crime" serious enough to be reported as such.[17] The object of a victimization survey is, of course, to find out about all such acts, and it is for this reason that the results obtained cannot actually be compared with official statistics that involve a person's taking the time to report the incident to the police. Consequently, careful study and several years of experience have been devoted to terminology in the Census — LEAA surveys. It was found, for example, that such legal terms as "assault" mean little. The wording of the question must be so descriptive that the respondent understands exactly what the interviewer wants to know: "Did anyone beat you up, attack you, or hit you with something, say, a rock or a bottle?" Because of careful attention paid to the wording of the questions on the interview schedule it appears that the Swiss respondents reported fully on such incidents, even minor assaults and small thefts as well as attempts.

After the interview schedule had been carefully structured thirty of them were pretested, and certain questions were then modified or dropped. Interviewing was then done after a letter of introduction and explanation had been sent to each household head. (As explained in Appendix F.) Questionnaires were checked for completeness and accuracy, and later a sample of 10 percent was rechecked for accuracy by telephone. Individual case sheets were prepared on each reported crime, including detailed information about the nature of the offense, the value of the loss sustained, and whether or not it had been reported to the police.

Data were collected on whether the respondents had been the victims of a crime during the preceding twelve months. The interviewing took place immediately after the annual summer vacation period because it covered the period from the previous vacation, a time span thought to be most appropriate to aid in memory recall. In studies similar to this, a twelve-month period has been found to be quite reliable for questions dealing chiefly with crime incidents. A six-month period is preferable for more detailed questions, due to recall problems — a factor that is of greater significance if the respondent is also answering for other household members. In some United States studies considerable fading of memory has been found between the first and second six months of the year in recalling offenses against individuals, particularly in personal crimes. This problem was not felt to be a serious one in Zürich, where crime is not common and thus represents a more unique event subject to more accurate recall by the head of the household.

Cross-cultural comparisons

The Zürich survey data were compared with similar data from the United States, Stuttgart, and, in a more limited fashion, with Scandinavian and

London data. Such comparisons must be viewed in quite general terms, however, due to some differences in sampling methods, choice of respondents, age of victims, and questionnaire construction.[18] Moreover, there may be cultural variations in an individual's perception of behavior that would lead him to believe he had been the victim of a crime. Some attempted assaults, for example, may be regarded with less concern in the United States than elsewhere. In spite of all these qualifications, crime victimization surveys offer more adequate cross-cultural comparisons of the extent and nature of crime today than do official statistics.

With the use of data from surveys conducted by LEAA and the Bureau of the Census in 1973, comparisons were made with two United States cities, Denver (515,000) and Portland (383,000), two cities comparable in size to Zürich (420,000).[19] A replication of the Zürich survey, with a sample of 440 fairly representative households, was made at about the same time in Stuttgart, a German city of 630,000, slightly larger than Zürich.[20] Stuttgart is the largest city in Baden-Württemberg, in the southern part of Germany, where the rates are generally lower for all serious crimes than for the northern part of the Federal German Republic.[21] For this reason it was believed that a comparison between Zürich and Stuttgart would be particularly useful. Comparisons were also made with a survey of the victims of violence conducted in Copenhagen, Oslo, Stockholm, and Helsinki in 1970–72 on representative national samples of persons aged 18 to 80. Unfortunately for comparative purposes, this study covered victimization over a two-year period, rather than a one-year period as in Zürich.[22] A 1971–72 victimization survey of property offenses in Denmark and in the city of Copenhagen also provided some comparisons,[23] as did a pilot London victimization survey of three city areas carried out in 1972.[24]

Because the major comparisons of crime victimization in Zürich are with Stuttgart and the two United States cities of Denver and Portland, it should be pointed out that only the head of the household was interviewed in the Zürich survey, whereas in the United States surveys the head of the household was interviewed only in connection with offenses against the household of burglary, household larceny, and auto theft. Individuals were interviewed in the case of assault, robbery, and personal larceny, thus making the number of these offenses more complete. In Stuttgart both the heads of households (440) and individuals over 14 (633) were interviewed in connection with offenses against the household and against the individual. The differences between Zürich, on the one hand, and Stuttgart, Denver, and Portland, on the other, are generally so great, however, that this difference in interviewing procedures had little effect on the general conclusions that can be drawn from the comparisons. It is also important to recognize that whereas professional interviewers were used in the Zürich survey of household heads, students were used in Stuttgart, so that gains in accuracy from the interviewing of individuals may have been counterbalanced by the competence of the interviewers.

Extent of victimization in Zürich

On the basis of the survey findings, neither household nor personal crime victimization is extensive in Zürich.[25] Of the total criminal incidents reported, 47.2 percent involved crimes against the household itself (63 percent if vandalism and unspecified miscellaneous offenses are included). Thirty-seven percent of the incidents were offenses against individuals: Crimes of violence accounted for 14.5 percent and 22.4 percent were personal thefts. Crimes of violence, including robbery, totaled only 14.6 percent (robbery accounted for only 4.2 percent of all reported offenses).

Approximately one-third (34 percent) of the households reported at least one crime against them during the preceding twelve-month period.[26] Slightly less, 32 percent, in Stuttgart reported having been victims of some crime. The average Zürich household victimization was 0.5: almost 10 percent reported more than one victimization of any type, 5.8 percent reported two, and 2.6 percent, three. For the household as a unit, one-fifth (20.9 percent) were victims of a crime against it, and 16.0 percent were victims of an offense against individual household members. Of the Zürich households, 5.6 percent were victims of violent offenses (assault, rape, robbery), as compared to 3.9 percent in Stuttgart. Property victimization was 31.3 percent, as compared with 25.2 percent in Stuttgart. Overall in Zürich, 4.0 percent were victims of an assault, 1.2 percent, of a robbery, and 5.4 percent, of a burglary. Slightly more than one-fifth (22 percent) were victims of either household or personal larceny, whereas in Stuttgart total larceny of households and household members was 17 percent. An act of vandalism was committed against 6 percent of the Zürich households.

Table 5.1. *Crime victimization rates per 1,000 households and 1,000 persons: Zürich, Stuttgart, Denver, and Portland*

	Zürich	Stuttgart	Denver	Portland
Household victimization				
Burglary	83	96	158	151
With entry	54	71	120	120
Attempt	29	25	38	31
Household larceny	116	138	158	149
Actual	108		145	136
Attempt	8		13	13
Auto theft	10	23	44	34
Actual	6		31	27
Attempt	4		13	7
Vandalism	60	84	—	—
Victimization of persons				
Assault	25	15	47	40
Actual	15	15	13	13
Attempted	10	—	34	27
Robbery	10	22	18	17
Actual	2		12	11
Attempt	8		6	6
Personal larceny	58	92	134	123
With contact	21	25	6	5
Without contact	37	67	128	118

Household victimization

The most accurate victimization statistics appear to involve offenses directly involving the household itself, burglary, larceny, auto theft, and vandalism, acts with which the household respondent is obviously well-informed.

Burglary. Burglaries or attempted burglaries per 1,000 households in Zürich were 83, whereas Stuttgart had a considerably higher rate of 96. (See Table 5.1.) Rates for both cities were only one-half that of Denver or Portland. The actual burglary rate of Zürich households was slightly lower than that of Stuttgart but approximately 45 percent of the rates for Denver and Portland. The Zürich survey indicated that the households most subject to burglary were the Swiss, rather than the foreign-born, those headed by a person in the 35–49 age bracket, larger households, those in high-income groups, and those who lived either in the Old Town or in predominantly working-class areas.[27] (See Appendix I for victimization rates by household characteristics.) In Denver, households most subject to burglary were more often headed by a person under the age of 35 and in the low-income group, but in Portland burglaries occurred more often in the middle- and high-income groups.

Household larcency. Larcenies and attempted larcenies in Zürich, outside and around the household and including vehicle parts, were fewer than in Stuttgart and much lower than in Denver and Portland. The rate for reported attempted larcenies was very low and lower than that for Denver and Portland. While the differences were small, the households with the highest larceny rates were Swiss, headed by a person between 35 and 49, larger households, those belonging to higher income groups, and located in areas populated predominantly by salaried persons. Households most frequently victimized in Denver were headed by a younger person, between 20 and 34, but in Portland household heads were in the same age group as the Swiss. The victims were most often from middle-income groups in Denver and Portland.

Auto theft. Auto thefts or attempts were of such a limited number that it was difficult to analyze them. Only two autos were stolen from the total sample of 482 households, and attempts were made to steal only four others, a total rate of only 10 per 1,000 households. This rate was less than one-half of Stuttgart's, one-half of Portland's, and one-fourth of Denver's. One-half of the households in the Zürich sample owned an auto.

Vandalism. The vandalism, or property damage, rate for Zürich was 60 per 1,000 households, much lower than that of Stuttgart (84). In the Copenhagen survey respondents reported an even higher rate of 110 per 1,000 households. Zürich rates were highest in those households headed by a person between 35 and 49 in high or moderately high-income households.

Crime victimization of persons

The total household sample consisted of 940 persons aged 14 and over[28] who were considered potential victims of crimes of assault, rape, sexual threats,[29] robbery, or personal larceny.[30] In general, the rates of individual crime victimization were low, either in absolute figures or in comparison with rates in Stuttgart and United States cities, Sweden, or London.

Assault. Assaults occur infrequently in Zürich. The combined rate for both actual and attempted assaults, aggravated and simple, was only 25 per 1,000. Denver had a rate almost twice as great, and Portland, a rate of 40 per 1,000. In Stuttgart, however, it was much less than in Zürich. The actual assault rate of Zürich was the same as that of Denver and Portland. The Zürich assault rate was several times lower than that of Copenhagen (90), Oslo (70), Helsinki (310), and the rate of 160 for the three largest Swedish cities of Stockholm, Göteborg, and Malmö. The age groups most likely to be assaulted in Zürich were the Swiss, males, those aged 20–24, and those residing in the predominantly salaried urban districts. (See Appendix J for victimization rates by characteristics of victims.) Assault victims in Denver and in Portland tend to be much younger, being highest in the under-20 age group.

Robbery. Official statistics show that Switzerland has little robbery: The victimization survey confirmed this fact. For combined actual and attempted robberies, the rate was only 10 per 1,000 population. The rate of 22 in Stuttgart was slightly over twice as high as that of Zürich, and the rates in Denver and in Portland were nearly twice as great. The rate for actual robberies in Zürich was 2, while that for attempts was 8. Numerically, robberies were too few to analyze by personal characteristics.

Personal larceny. Larceny generally constitutes the largest proportion of total crimes. By definition, personal larceny is the theft of personal property or cash from any place other than the home of the victim or its immediate vicinity. As in the U.S. Census – LEAA surveys and in the Stuttgart survey, no distinction was made in the analysis of the Zürich larceny victimization as to the value of the items involved.[31] Two-thirds of all thefts reported in the Zürich survey were of small value, probably under $15.

The rate for personal larceny in Zürich was 58 per 1,000 persons: This rate was more than one-third less than that of Stuttgart and one-half as great as that of Denver and Portland. The Copenhagen survey reported a theft (regardless of value) victimization rate of 150 per 1,000, or three times that of Zürich. The Swiss and the foreign-born (foreign workers) were about equally vulnerable to larceny, males slightly more so than females, and persons living in predominantly salaried and higher-income districts. Both in Zürich and in Denver and Portland, victims were more common among the younger age groups.

There are two types of larceny: with or without contact. That with contact includes purse-snatching and pickpocketing. The rate for larceny without contact was 37 per 1,000 persons — about one-half the Stuttgart rate and about one-third that of Denver and Portland. For larceny with contact the rate was 21, slightly lower than Stuttgart's but much higher than that of Denver or Portland. It is difficult to explain this rather high Zürich rate, in view of the much lower rate for larceny without contact. Unattended personal possessions appear generally to be safe in Zürich, and it may be that personal objects have little resale value in a highly affluent country, whereas money obtained through purse-snatching or pickpocketing is of immediate use.[32] Much of the latter may be due to victimization by foreign visitors — particularly during the summer — and to increased drug usage in Switzerland, as addicts require increasing supplies of cash to support their drug habits. In any event, it is generally this low rate of larceny without contact that probably accounts, more than any other factor, for the relatively low total crime rate in Zürich (and probably for the country as a whole). Even if it were assumed that an even larger proportion of theft cases were unreported by household respondents, the rate would still be quite low.

Crime victimization outside of Zürich

About 13 percent of reported victimization occurred within Switzerland but outside of Zürich: A similar percentage was found in Stuttgart. No differences were found by sex, age, or nationality. In addition to victimization within Switzerland, about one in twenty-five respondents (four percent) reported having been victimized outside the country while traveling abroad. This question had been included because Swiss citizens have a reputation in Europe for traveling a great deal outside their own country. Eighteen of the twenty offenses reported involved "something stolen," and only one assault was reported. Nearly one-half of the offenses had occurred in Italy, followed by France and the Federal German Republic, with the remainder in a wide variety of countries.

Any valid interpretation of the distribution would have required the knowledge of the percentage of Zürich householders who had traveled abroad, and to which countries during the year. In the Stuttgart sample slightly fewer (3 percent) had been victims of crimes while they were outside the country. Nearly all had been victims of property offenses, although 9.1 percent reported robbery or assault committed against them. Those in Stuttgart reported that they were most likely to be victimized in Italy, followed by Spain and Austria.

Summary

One can conclude from the victimization survey that total (household and personal) crime is not high, comparatively, in Zürich. The rates for crimes against the household were generally low. Rates for burglary were considerably lower than they were in Stuttgart and also lower than those of comparable United States cities. Thefts from about the household area were lower than in Stuttgart and much lower than in the two United States cities. The vandalism rate was lower than that of Stuttgart. Rates for individual victimization in Zürich were low for assault, robbery, and personal larceny other than from the person. While total larceny is low, larceny from one's own person is fairly high, but this may be due in part to victimization by foreign visitors during the summer. Auto theft appears to be much lower than in Stuttgart or in the two American cities.

It is generally difficult to compare adequately the official police statistics and crime victimization surveys, and no effort was made to make such comparisons in Zürich. The time periods did not coincide, and this might have affected any comparisons. Also, police often reclassify a victim's report of a crime, and thus their categories might differ from that used in the survey. In addition, the victimization survey covered only Zürich residents, while police data include crimes against nonresidents as well. For example, while the Zürich population is 420,000, about 150,000 others commute daily to the city, and many tourists and other visitors pass through constantly. Along with the city residents themselves, these individuals are also potential crime victims.

6. Measuring crimes by theft insurance

Burglary and theft insurance, rates charged and claims paid out, can provide valuable information on the extent and trends for this type of crime. Because they are seldom used for this purpose, however, their use in 1974 by the Council on Municipal Performance (COMP) to estimate the extent of crime in thirty-one United States cities (as part of an economic survey) was quite unique. In this survey the Council used 5 million home insurance theft policies: They concluded that the data they obtained were more accurate than were official police statistics, and even more accurate generally than the city rankings from the 1974 crime victimization surveys of the United States Census Bureau – LEAA. It was conceded that this survey covered only insured theft victims and that householders in crime-ridden city neighborhoods found it often virtually impossible to obtain insurance, but the report asserted that "claims filed by policy holders, and investigated by the insurance companies, were more likely to be accurate than FBI data compiled entirely from police reports or Census Bureau surveys that relied exclusively on interviews of victims."[1] In surveying the results of the COMP survey one scientific journal stated:

Insurance theft records are a neglected source of crime information. Statistical needs mandate the collection of the data. They have never before been systematically compared with FBI crime reports. Yet they represent an inexpensive, potentially important new crime measure to supplement FBI reports and the victimization surveys. . . . Unlike the two existing crime information sources, insurance data are based on a bilateral agreement on the nature of the crime. A policyholder has a financial incentive to report very significant theft and the insurance company has a corresponding incentive to investigate it. Neither side can arbitrarily reclassify thefts.[2]

Some insurance companies are rather reluctant to make public data on their operations, primarily to protect their rate structures from becoming known. Moreover, as these structures involve administrative overhead and other factors, as well as claims, some feel that certain misconceptions might arise if uninformed persons should be given access to the data. In Switzerland, fortunately, considerable basic information was obtained from two of the large insurance companies, the Schweizerische Rückversicherungsgesellschaft (The Swiss Reinsurance Company) in Zürich and the Schweizerische Mobiliar of Bern. The data provided by them made it possible to study insurance theft claims and thus determine levels of crime and trends. Household theft and burglary insurance rates were then compared with those in the United States and in selected European countries. A comparison of auto theft rates with those in the United States and in several European countries was also made possible by these data. Comparisons were made of business theft and burglary claims as a percentage of premiums paid in Switzerland and in other European countries, as well as in Australia and in Japan. Obviously, the conclusions drawn from all such comparisons must be somewhat more general than precise.

Household theft insurance rates

Swiss citizens commonly carry household theft insurance. In fact, one insurance company estimated that about 90 percent of Swiss households are covered by this type of insurance. In contrast, a company in the state of Wisconsin estimated that about 60 percent of Wisconsin households have this type of coverage and that the average for the United States as a whole is about the same.[3] The Swiss coverage is high for several reasons: It is not necessarily due only to the crime rates, as is generally thought to be the reason in the United States. Approximately thirty companies sell insurance in Switzerland, and throughout the country fire insurance is compulsory. Along with this compulsory insurance, most people pay a quite modest additional premium to cover insurance on household theft. In five Swiss cantons it is also compulsory to carry theft insurance.

Swiss household theft policies are very comprehensive, including burglary and theft of furniture, appliances, paintings, and rugs, among other things. They also cover "simple theft," an insurance term meaning the inclusion of thefts of any kind of personal goods, inside or outside the dwelling (money, jewelry, cameras, camping equipment, and the like).[4] Such broad coverages contrast markedly with coverage in the United States and in most other European countries. In the United States, generally, for example, there are various deductibles, and the extent of these exclusions determines premium rates. In addition to the limitation of payment for losses only in excess of $50 to $100, such items as jewelry and furs are specifically limited. Special policies must be written if such expensive items as cameras, valuable jewelry, or expensive paintings are to be covered at their specified values. Normal household insurance policies in the Federal German Republic exclude most simple theft; special insurance must be obtained to cover money and many other objects. Household insurance in Italy covers only furniture and household effects. In view of the far more comprehensive theft insurance coverage in Switzerland, the actual premium rates are much lower than in most other countries mentioned here.

United States theft insurance rates vary greatly by state – even by cities within states – and in large cities like New York and Chicago the rates differ within the city itself. In Switzerland, however, rates are the same throughout the country, and this uniformity in rates is an indication that less marked variation is found in crime throughout the country, regardless of canton or city size. It is of significance, furthermore, that the "simple insurance" policy is applicable only in Switzerland. Should a Swiss citizen wish to travel abroad or to reside in another country, insurance on baggage and other possessions is limited.

Despite the unusually high cost of living in Switzerland, household theft insurance rates are lower, and the coverage greater, than they are in Sweden or in many other European countries and the United States. In 1973 the rate for normal (comprehensive) household theft insurance in Switzerland was Sw. F. 1.30 per Sw. F. 1,000 – or a rate of approximately $1.30 per $1,000 insurance, calculated at the rate of exchange at the time. At that time similar insurance rates in the Federal German Republic were the equivalent of Sw. F. 0.80 per Sw. F. 1,000 (about $.86 per $1,000) on such limited coverage that if it existed in Switzerland the rate would be much less. In Italy limited coverage is between $1.20 and $2.40 per $1,000 of insurance coverage, which costs about the same or considerably more than that of the comprehensive Swiss insurance.[5] Rates for additional coverage in Italy range from $12.00 to $24.00 per $1,000 for jewelry and $6.40 for paintings. French rates could not be obtained, as the companies charge not by objects but rather by each room, and the rates vary by region.

Since both Switzerland and the United States are highly affluent countries, with many similar economic indexes, a comparison of the 1973 rates of the two countries is significant, in spite of the many variations in the United States. For purposes of comparison, two states with fairly low crime rates — Wisconsin and Minnesota — were selected, along with Ohio, which has a medium crime rate. Cities chosen for comparison were Denver, Colorado, Chicago, Illinois, and New York. [6] It was necessary to compute average rates in order to make comparisons; for example, whereas Swiss rates vary little by amount of insurance, in the United States they decline by each $1,000 increment to a final rate for "over $5,000." As relatively few persons carry more than $5,000 in burglary and theft insurance, and the rates decline sharply after this amount, the averages were computed on the first five units of $1,000.

In the comparisons, calculations were based on the Swiss rate in 1973 of $1.30 per $1,000 of insurance throughout the country. The Wisconsin statewide rate for household theft insurance was more than six times that of Switzerland. Moreover, it excluded coverage on furs and jewelry. The Minnesota rate, also statewide, was twelve times greater. A more marked comparison is seen from Ohio figures, where the four insurance district rates were from twenty-two to forty-two times greater than the Swiss.

Coverage is far more costly in large United States cities than the average rates in the states in which the cities are located; variations of this type do not exist in Switzerland. The rate for Denver, as well as the county in which Denver is located, was eleven times larger than the $1.30 per $1,000 insurance paid by, for example, Zürich and Geneva residents. The average rate for Chicago, and for Cook County, is also eleven times larger. The differences are even more marked when one considers that the Chicago and Cook County rates are for policies in which the first $50 loss is deductible, while Swiss rates are on an all-inclusive basis. New York City rates vary considerably by area, and they average twenty-two times greater in Manhattan, eighteen times greater in Queens, and fifteen times greater in Brooklyn.

Auto theft insurance rates

Auto theft insurance coverage is optional in Switzerland, but more than 50 percent of auto owners carry it. Rates are considerably lower than they are in the surrounding countries. Moreover, they do not increase proportionately with the insured value of the auto; instead, they decrease. The rate in 1973 for an auto worth $2,000 was approximately $5.00, and the premium for an auto valued at Sw. F. 10,000 ($3,000) was $6.50. Rates for automobile theft insurance are uniform throughout Switzerland. In the United States they vary greatly by state, within states, and by cities. In addition, there is no provision in the United States for a decrease in rates according to the increased value of 'an insured auto, as is the case in Switzerland. While some United States auto rates are lower than those of Switzerland, in general, they are higher. The Swiss rate of approximately $2.17 per $1,000 (based on a $3,000 auto but proportionately lower for a higher priced car) was higher than the average of $1.27 in Minnesota or $1.80 in Wisconsin. Ohio rates varied from $.93 to $6.92, an average of $3.01, about one-third higher than the Swiss rate. New York City auto theft rates are extremely high, ranging from $5.35 to $26.62 per $1,000 of insurance, depending upon the area. The lowest rate would be two and a half times, and the highest, twelve times as great as that of Switzerland. Rates for the four different Chicago areas ranged from five to sixteen times as great.

Theft insurance claims

Increases in property crimes cannot easily be measured by analyzing increases in insurance rates or in claims paid out. Both indexes reflect the general contemporary inflation that has also occurred in Switzerland, although it was generally much less there than in other countries. Some inflation is also reflected in the increased value of objects stolen and in automobile values. During the 1962–72 period the consumer price index rose by 21.2 percent, and wholesale prices by 15.4 percent, in Switzerland. Theft insurance rates, however, have risen somewhat more in Switzerland than can correctly be attributed to these economic inflationary trends. Between 1962 and 1972, figures for all insurance companies combined showed an increase of from 50 to 60 percent in household theft insurance rates, with approximately the same increase in rates for business establishments.

An officer of Schweizerische Mobiliar, one of Switzerland's largest insurance companies, which sells about 40 percent of all insurance, stated that the experiences of the company indicated a real increase in thefts of motor vehicles and personal effects, as well as in burglaries. Mobiliar submitted considerable evidence, but the actual amount of the increase cannot be entirely determined because of the many other variables — for example, changes in the population, the number of insured persons, and the nature of their insured possessions and inflation. In 1943, for example, they had dealt with 1,454 theft cases; in 1972 there were 80,000 cases. Of the latter, 59,000 were personal-effects thefts, cases of some rarity in 1943. Mobiliar reported steadily increasing theft claims: There were 38 claims per 1,000 insured persons in 1965 and 85 per 1,000 in 1972, with the greatest increases occurring between 1969 and 1970, when the figures rose from 72 to 82 per 1,000. The average claim per case has also steadily increased, from Sw. F. 160 ($52) in 1963 to Sw. F. 280 ($93) in 1972, a 75 percent increase. For the ten-year period 1962–72, the average claim for a theft case increased from Sw. F. 201 ($67) to Sw. F. 287 ($95), or an increase of 43 percent.

Claims paid for burglaries (household and business) by all Swiss insurance companies increased from Sw. F. 20 million in 1970 to Sw. F. 32 million in 1972, a 60-percent increase.[7] Simple larceny payments increased 67 percent, and claims on bicycles and motorcycles increased by 63 percent. During this same period, however, consumer prices increased about 19 percent, and production worker wages and salaries, 35 percent. A partial explanation for these increases in theft claims may well be the increased amount of traveling by the Swiss abroad, where they have become victims of crimes.

Home insurance coverage is particularly high in Sweden; from a 1962 coverage of 80 percent it had risen in 1973 to 90 percent of all households being covered.[8] It is a comprehensive insurance coverage that includes not only burglary and theft but also fire, damage, and personal liability. Although coverage has increased, conditions for insurance have become much more strict. When claims are made for insurance payments, or even to obtain the insurance, the applicant must show that certain precautions against theft have been taken and that specific risks are avoided.

Due to the differences in the nature of the coverage in Sweden and in Switzerland, it is not possible to compare either the rates or the increases in theft and burglary insurance premiums. Data are available for Sweden, fortunately, on claims for theft and burglary and also for auto theft. According to figures provided by Folksam, one of Sweden's largest insurance companies (and one which is probably representative of the others) both the amount of the theft and burglary claims and percentage of total household premiums have increased enormously from 1963–72. In absolute amounts, claims increased fivefold in this time span, the most marked increase occurring since 1969. As a percent of total household insurance premiums, the increase in claims was from 6.3 percent in 1963 to 17.5 percent in 1972. In 1972 the most common items stolen in home burglaries were furs, television sets, radios, more expensive furniture, and liquor, which is very costly in Sweden. Automobile theft insurance claims have shown a similar pattern of steady increases, claims at the end of this period being 1.4 times those at the beginning. As a percent of claims on total insurance premiums, auto theft increased from 21.6 percent to 35.4 percent.

Percentage of claims to total premium revenues

The relative incidence of crime, as well as trends, can also be measured in terms of the percentage of claims to the total premium revenues from theft and burglary insurance policies. This particular ratio is generally said to become critical when total damage claims constitute more than 60 percent of the total premium revenues, although in the United States this ratio is said to have gone up currently to about 75 percent, due to increased overhead. At 60 percent, total damage claims, added to administrative costs and such expenses as sales and appraisals, begin to exceed total premium revenues, and the company is then said to be operating at a loss — at least in this type of insurance. If the situation in Switzerland is examined in these terms, the country had, from 1954 to 1971, one of the most favorable insurance situations of nine countries, with the exception of the Federal German Republic and Japan. (See Table 6.1.) For example, the average percentages were as follows: Switzerland, 41; France, 48; Italy, 70; and the United States, 54.

The Swiss figures also showed less change in theft and burglary as a percentage of premiums between 1960 and 1971: The increase was from 44 percent in 1960 to 59 percent in 1971, an average of 58 percent and a range from 41 to 59 percent. In contrast, other European countries showed a much more rapid increase and a generally greater range. The percentage of claims in the Federal German Republic increased from 21 to 78, averaging 45; in Italy, from 51 to 163, averaging 94; in Denmark, from 27 to 128, averaging 74; and in France (1960–9), from 51 to 76, averaging 59. The United States, with a high rate already, had a decrease from 56 to 47, with an average of 61 and a range of 47 to 66.

Of the eleven countries for which theft and burglary insurance claims data were available in 1971, Switzerland ranked fifth, ahead of Spain,

Table 6.1. *Theft and burglary claims as a percent of theft and burglary premiums for selected countries, 1954–71*

Year	Switzer-land	Federal German Republic	France	Italy	Denmark	Norway	Finland	Spain	Australia	Japan	United States
1954	23	20	25	37	26	15			28	11	47
1955	24	18	21	43	27	16			29	19	44
1956	26	18	26	42	26	21			33	27	46
1957	30	18	37	54	25	34			44	31	50
1958	33	19	37	47	26	40			42	82	54
1959	36	19	38	47	27	36			45	79	51
1960	44	21	51	51	27	38			55	42	56
1961	45	24	52	54	29	50			62	45	54
1962	48	27	68	64	33	69			61	45	52
1963	43	31	65	73	40	56			64	32	55
1964	47	33	47	75	46	57	46		70	23	59
1965	44	40	45	62	49	56	40	18	73	37	58
1966	41	48	51	62	56	69	46	21	79	27	59
1967	45	55	60	62	79	71	70	28	78	28	65
1968	49	55	71	77	102	75	98	35	62	32	66
1969	49	57	76	104	126	80	84	45	55	37	60
1970	58	72		140	128	90	75	42	54	40	55
1971	59	78		163	128	85	83	43	54	46	47

Source: Material from Schweizerische Rückversicherungsgesellschaft in Zürich (Swiss reinsurance company).

Japan, the United States, and Australia, but considerably lower than the high rates of 78 for the Federal German Republic, 83 for Finland, 85 in Norway, 128 in Denmark, and 163 in Italy. Although data were not available for Sweden, one might assume that it would be higher than either Denmark or Norway, and therefore considerably higher than Switzerland.

Summary

It might be concluded from an analysis of Swiss crime insurance rates that, on the whole, the country ranked lower in crime than the United States or many other European countries. Household burglary and theft insurance rates were unusually low, and the coverage was much greater than that in the United States, Sweden, the Federal German Republic, and Italy. Rates for auto theft insurance were higher in some cases but generally lower than those in the United States if considered in terms of the value of the auto. Household theft policies in Switzerland were far more comprehensive than policies in the United States and most European countries, covering personal goods both inside and outside buildings, including jewelry, money, paintings, cameras, and the like. Claims are also paid without the deductibles and other limits on claims paid, as in the United States, for example. Burglary, theft, and auto insurance rates are uniform for the entire country, while rates in the United States vary greatly by state, within states, and even within cities. Rates and claims on burglary, theft, and auto insurance policies increased in Switzerland over the 1960–71 period, and these increases could not be accounted for entirely on the basis of population increases and inflation. Available data have shown, however, that both the rates and the claims have increased far more in Sweden.

The trend in the ratio between theft and burglary claims to total premium revenues is perhaps the most significant measure of crime with respect to insurance. In this regard, Switzerland had one of the most favorable situations of nine countries examined from 1954 to 1971: It ranked fifth among the nine countries for which burglary and theft insurance data were available, ahead of the Federal German Republic but behind Japan. Between 1960 and 1969 the Swiss claim figures showed little change, in contrast to other countries where increases had been more rapid. A marked increase did occur in 1971, however, in the percentage of insurance claims. If the Swiss insurance rates and the percentage of claims increase in the future their significance must be measured against the low rates and percentages of claims from which they start, as well as the extent to which rates and percentage of claims also increase in other countries.

7. White-collar crime and tax violations

Any analysis of crime in Switzerland would be incomplete, as well as biased, if it failed to present a discussion of white-collar crime. It would also serve to perpetuate the stereotyped picture of crime and the criminal as a lower- or working-class phenomenon, thus generally omitting — or at least defining as not being criminal — most illegal activities of persons in upper-status occupational positions.[1] A double standard of justice exists when illegal behavior among the lower or working classes is viewed with strong disapproval and is prosecuted readily, while illegal behavior among business and banking interests, for example, is defined as nothing more malevolent than shrewd business and financial practices.

White-collar crimes are committed by persons of relatively high social and occupational status, members of the middle and upper socioeconomic classes, in connection with their occupations.[2] These violations of law are found among businessmen, as well as among doctors, lawyers, politicians, and government employees. Particularly extensive are violations in the business and financial world. Financial losses to society in a single case of white-collar business crime may well equal the total amount involved in thousands of larcenies and burglaries. The discussion of white-collar crime in Switzerland will be limited to business and finance, particularly banking, but it will also include a general discussion of income tax violations.

The white-collar criminal is set apart from other offenders by his distinctive conception of himself. In fact, in his use of the term "avocational crime" as a substitute for white-collar, as well as other related crimes, Gilbert Geis makes this the key to his definition: "The crime is committed by a person who does not think of himself as a criminal."[3] This offender tends to reserve the concepts of "crime" and "criminal" for the lower socioeconomic groups who engage in the more overt larceny, burglary, and robbery.[4] He even gains support for this image of himself from the general public and from those in his own occupation.

83

While this public does not necessarily condone, and may even condemn, him and his activities, it still finds it hard to identify him as really being a criminal. Both in their work and throughout their social activities, businessmen associate chiefly with other businessmen: Thus, the nature of the illegal activities or the attitudes of others toward them are generally shielded from outside scrutiny. Moreover, the mass media generally continue to present the stereotyped picture that "real" crime is almost entirely committed by people of low socioeconomic status. Even when flagrant white-collar crime is discovered there has been a tendency to treat these cases in a different manner, often with far less censure. A study of convicted British white-collar offenders shows how they found it difficult to accept the label of criminal. One social scientist maintains, "They were, in general, popular members of social groups. Their clubs included two prominent London clubs, Masonic lodges, Rotary, and a host of minor political, social, and sports clubs of various kinds. . . . Club membership was considered important mainly for the social prestige which it carried and for the opportunity of mixing with people of superior status."[5]

Swiss white-collar offenders in the area of business and finance operate in a general situation where the overall affluence of the country, and its generally conservative nature, have led to strong desires for profits in investment dealings and in expanding economic enterprises. Economic success is highly esteemed, and this may well account for the public's somewhat tolerant attitude toward the moral and ethical standards in business and finance. People expect a certain amount of deception and exploitation without demanding criminal sanctions. One criminal prosecutor in Zürich canton has written that to many persons white-collar crime does not require social outlawing, as it is looked upon as a sort of national sport.[6] These practices might even be expected in Swiss society, as there is a strong ethic directed toward making money but great disapproval of its being stolen directly, as in the case of larceny, burglary, or robbery.

Extent of white-collar crime in Switzerland

In Switzerland, as in other countries, relatively little basic criminological research has been done in the area of business and financial crime. Consequently, considerable reliance has had to be put on the work of qualified journalists, rather than criminologists. The journalistic references and case materials referred to here, however, have all been well documented.

White-collar crime in Switzerland in business and finance appears to be extensive: In contrast to much ordinary crime, it also appears to be increasing.[7] Particularly serious are the banking violations, fraudulent insolvency and bankruptcy, the illegal mismanagement of funds, false bookkeeping, and tax and customs violations.[8] A Zürich police official has written that the number of felonious bankruptcies is very high, yet criminal charges are rare.[9]

This generally extensive nature of white-collar crime is significant, particularly as it has been widely claimed that the high rates of ordinary crime, in the United States especially, are partly due to widespread law disobedience in business and financial circles. The report of the President's Commission on Law Enforcement and Administration of Justice in 1968 emphasized the serious erosion of morals as a result of these flagrant law violations.

It is reasonable to assume that prestigious companies that flout the law set an example for other businesses and influence individuals, particularly young people, to commit other kinds of crime on the ground that everyone is taking what he can get. If businessmen who are respected as leaders of the community can do such things as break the antitrust laws or rent dilapidated houses to the poor at high rents, it is hard to convince the young that they should be honest.[10]

The situation in Switzerland appears to contradict this assumption, as the extensive white-collar crime seems not to have affected substantially the law compliance of other groups. So far, the behavior of the country's youth has not been markedly — or, at least, overtly — affected by the illegalities practiced, for example, by the exceedingly complex banking institutions. In all probability, as will be shown later, many other factors, such as the assumption of responsibility by Swiss citizens and the lack of pronounced intergenerational conflict, tend to mitigate the effect that white-collar crime has had on the general crime picture.

Economic power and the Swiss definition of crime

One senses in the Swiss situation a birfurcation in law somewhat similar to that which exists in most Western countries. Certain antisocial acts committed by lower- and working-class persons are rigorously defined as crimes, while antisocial acts of business and commercial groups generally are not so defined or prosecuted. As Richard Quinney points out, "criminal definitions are applied by the segments of society that have the power to shape the enforcement and administration of criminal law."[11]

The Swiss Federal Criminal Code deals largely with conventional crime. There is no special criminal code for economic and commercial offenses; monetary speculation is not a criminal offense; there is virtually no federal control over investment companies; and business firms are more or less free to issue stocks and bonds with little supervision. Most of the legal regulations controlling both business matters and tax payments are the cantons' responsibility, usually handled by civil or administrative bodies. Assessments are made, and taxes are collected, in 3,000 communes. In most cantons, and even at the federal level, income tax violations have not, in the past, been criminal offenses. However, a new law went into effect in 1974 providing criminal penalties for federal tax frauds. Most prosecutions of white-collar crime cases fall within the section of the criminal code under the broad general categories of fraud, embezzlement, or falsification of goods, all of which are subject to local enforcement.

The general lack of comprehensive control of white-collar criminal activities is quite a different situation from ordinary crime, and this tends to encourage these activities. As will be shown later, the decentralized Swiss political system helps to prevent and to control ordinary crime, but it works in an opposite manner with much business and criminal activity that cannot be dealt with successfully at the local commune, city, or cantonal level. For example, many businesses operate throughout the country. In order to improve prosecution, changes have been suggested in the Swiss criminal procedure laws that would result in greater centralization of the prosecution of large-scale business crimes.[12]

In prosecuting cases — particularly for fraud — it must be proven by the prosecution not only that there has been fraud but also that the offender had intended at the time to commit the fraud.[13] In a country like Switzerland, where many business firms operate internationally and where legal prosecutions require the cooperation of varied authorities and a great amount of case preparation, many serious problems are encountered. These problems become even more difficult, in view of the limited prosecution staffs trained in white-collar cases — with the possible exception of the staffs in the cantons of Zürich and Basel-Stadt. Prolonged delays are met in the disposition of these cases. In 1970, for example, several Zürich canton cases had been pending five to six years. The situation is aggravated by the tendency of the Swiss to have more complete confidence in securities and bonds than is warranted, without their ever fully realizing how little scrutiny has been given to their issuance. When an individual is defrauded he often is insufficiently motivated to prosecute, as long as he hopes he can get his money back or he does not incur heavy losses. It is chiefly for this reason that those white-collar offenses that do come to the attention of the authorities are largely those that have failed to produce the profits expected. Bernhard Rimann points out that the general public is more interested in profits than in security in boom years, and that this attitude results in much unreported white-collar crime.[14] During periods of economic depression, on the other hand, many fraudulent activities cannot be concealed.

Diffusion of white-collar crime

Whether it occurs in Switzerland or in any other country, white-collar crime cannot be fully understood without comprehending the value conflicts presented to persons in higher-status positions, conflicts that vary according to the social structure and the value systems of a society.[15] In Swiss society, as elsewhere, the acquisition of greater profits and increased economic power often stand in sharp contrast to the restrictions of law, the ethical ideals of the society, and the reputation of the business or financial concern. The values involved in the state regulation of commercial enterprise conflict with the values of a free-enterprise system. When these conflicts occur, attitudes involved in the selective obedience to a "good" or a "bad" law become keys to compliance.

Switzerland's position as an international center of business and banking, particularly for Europe, creates increased pressures as well as temptations, for its business and banking concerns to violate legal or ethical norms. The unique Swiss Bank Secrecy Law, to be discussed later, has greatly facilitated illegal and unethical activities. A United States District Attorney in New York has explained how this operates:

Swiss banks are able to buy stocks for their customers on the New York Stock Exchange without using the name of the customer (although a recent Treasury regulation obligates them to identify any known United States residents on whose behalf they may be acting). Omnibus accounts opened by Swiss banks at New York brokerage houses allow the banks to keep the identity of their customers secret if they wish to disregard the Treasury regulations. Thus white collar criminals find it convenient to use Swiss banks to conceal stock manipulations and insider trading since Swiss bank secrecy makes it difficult for the SEC [Securities and Exchange Commission] and other government agencies to find out who is the real owner of a stock in question. In the past, Swiss banks have played a more active role in white collar crimes by advancing margin to customers on stock purchases below the level set by the SEC. A number of Swiss banks have been indicted for this offense.[16]

From research done in the United States, one can assume that the illegal behavior found among certain Swiss businessmen and bankers is learned from associates. They learn the values and the rationalizations that enable them to violate the law and to feel justified in doing so, as well as the techniques of fraudulent practices.[17] As the illegal and unethical practices are diffused from one business or banking establishment to another, they often become the accepted mode of doing business. Sometimes the diffusion results from efforts to meet illegal competition from another business or banking concern. For example, in an effort to get lucrative international banking business, a large number of banking institutions have been established in Lugano, a city of only 25,000 population. The number far exceeds that needed to handle the local financial transactions of the area.

Information about unethical and illegal practices is circulated in the business group as part of the definition of the situation, and rationalizations to support these violations of law are transmitted by this differential association.[18] Many rationalizations to support illegal activities are in common circulation: "Business is business"; "one cannot conduct a profitable business in any other way"; "others are doing it"; and "it is necessary if one is to be successful in business."

A great deal of organization is involved in white-collar crime. This organization ranges from the comparatively simple reciprocal relationships involved in business transactions to the more complex procedures typical of the illegal activities of several large corporations and banks. Violations in the latter may extend to other companies and may also involve subsidiaries. Edwin H. Sutherland pointed out that corporate crime is not only deliberate but highly organized. "Organization for crime may be either formal or informal. Formal organization for crimes of corporations is found most generally in restraint of trade, as illustrated by gentlemen's agreements, pools, many of the practices of the trade associations, patent agreements, and cartels."[19]

Types of white-collar crime

Wide variation is found in the types of violations of laws regulating business in Switzerland. Fraudulent loans often result from attempts to secure high-interest rates or profits without requiring the usual securities or without checking the transaction carefully. Similarly, bonds involved in commercial transactions are not always adequately studied to determine if interests and dividends have been checked. Frequently businessmen are caught with fraudulent bills of exchange. One police official reported that in the last few years bad bills of exchange worth millions of Swiss francs have been issued in Zürich.[20] Accounting practices are not infrequently so loose and improperly supervised by governmental agencies that it is extremely difficult to prosecute the guilty parties. In fact, such cases of white-collar crime reveal the apparent lack of supervision over security issuance that is reminiscent of the situation that existed in the United States prior to the enactment of the Securities and Exchange Act. When loose security supervision is combined with secret accounts and when most tax frauds are not considered to be criminal acts, one can readily understand why the volume of these cases is great. Two examples here will illustrate the exceedingly intricate manipulations involved.[21]

The AG für Plastik-, Immobilien- und Finanzgeschäfte (PIF). In 1962, the Centraf AG was founded in Neuchâtel with a share capital of Sw. F. 50,000. From a firm in Vaduz (capital of Liechtenstein) they took over a license for the fabrication and sale of a plastic product. Instead of going into production of this product, the owner of the firm established other firms (Poly Plast AG in Zürich and Dista AG in Bassersdorf) and did not disclose this arrangement. The director of the AZAD Bank in Zürich cooperated by granting the founder credits in an almost unlimited amount. Together with the AZAD Bank, a larger plastic firm (PIF) was founded, with a share capital of Sw. F. 2 million. However, these shares were not backed with securities. As the debts of the different firms rose, bonds were issued that, naturally, again were not backed with any kind of securities. Shortly afterward, the firm went into bankruptcy, with great losses. In turn, the inactive firm of Poly Plast AG in Zürich was used to found another firm, and machines were taken over from another firm that had gone bankrupt. These machines, however, already belonged to a bank that had taken over the material after the bankruptcy. In order to produce a balanced statement, the value of these machines was reevaluated to the amount of Sw. F. 200,000. As the overhead and expenses could not be covered with the profit of this new firm, bonds were issued. At the time of bankruptcy, the value of the bonds in circulation amounted to about Sw. F. 2 million.

The Chiasso Branch of Crédit Suisse Bank. The largest bank scandal in Swiss history occurred in 1977. It involved extensive illegal banking transactions amounting to Sw. F. 2.2 billion ($880 million) and an estimated loss of Sw. F. 1 billion ($400 million) or more. The Chiasso branch of Crédit Suisse (located in Italian Switzerland, near the Italian border) is one of the three largest Swiss banks, with assets of $17 billion. Contrary to certain emergency rules of the Swiss central government, this branch bank had received large illegal deposits of Italian lire. Because of political and financial instability in Italy, large sums of Italian lire had been flowing into Switzerland. The Swiss federal government issued an order of a 10-percent "negative interest rate" for large foreign non-Swiss deposits to protect the value of the rapidly falling lire and to prevent the Swiss franc from moving to such unrealistic levels that exports might be affected. It was charged that instead of putting the funds in the bank as deposits or in readily saleable stocks, the top manager of the Chiasso branch channelled large amounts of Swiss francs into a Liechtenstein-based holding company, Texon Finanzanstalt. This company then reinvested the converted lire in Italian companies dealing mainly in wine, plastics, and in resort management. In January, 1977, the capital of Texon was only Sw. F. 50,000; later it rose to Sw. F. 500,000, and the debts to the Crédit Suisse Chiasso branch were more than Sw. F. 2 billion. The Chiasso branch bank also apparently offered the Italian clients high returns and gave company guarantees never registered on the bank's books. The money was routed in such a way as to avoid Swiss withholding taxes and the negative interest rate imposed by the Swiss authorities to halt the inflow of foreign funds.

Investigations of the Chiasso branch by the Crédit Suisse home office in Zürich in late 1976 had revealed the illegal transactions; about the same time a blanket amnesty from the Italian government resulted in large withdrawals from the Chiasso branch. The branch manager of the bank and two of his top assistants were arrested and charged with criminal mismanagement. As a result of the scandal the chief executive of Crédit Suisse and his deputy, as well as the bank's honorary chairman, resigned.

So large was the financial loss in these illegal activities that the Swiss National Bank and two other large banks offered to give a credit of Sw. F. 2 billion to Crédit Suisse in case of need. The President of the Swiss National Bank and various members of Parliament called for stricter banking controls and for changes in certain aspects of Swiss bank secrecy laws in order to reduce the threat of misuse. A proposal was also made to enlarge the very small staff of the federal banking commission, whose function it is to act as the watchdog body for more than five hundred banks in Switzerland. This staff increase, however, would not free commercial banks from the obligation to tighten their own internal controls to prevent illegal behavior. Eventually, the case resulted in substantial changes in the operation of the bank secrecy law. Crédit Suisse (Swiss Credit Bank) was penalized $28 million in negative interest penalties in November 1977.

Switzerland, and the city of Zürich particularly, constitute one of the largest centers of international banking in the world. In 1972, for example, the collapse of Investors Overseas Services, an enterprise operating out of Switzerland and involving Robert Vesco and Bernard Cornfeld, resulted in losses of more than $200 million. Cornfeld was arrested by Geneva cantonal police officials and was imprisoned on charges of fraud and abetting speculation and mismanagement, but he was later released on bond of $1.5 million, the largest in Swiss history. Due to situations of this type, in 1970, the Zürich Canton Parliament asked for an increase in the number of district attorneys, due to the increases in the time-consuming white-collar offenses that had been developing as a result of Zürich's position as an international financial and trade center.

Numerous other forms of white-collar crime are prevalent in Switzerland – many on an international level and often involving mass swindles. Very common are those involving international trading in stocks, bonds, and real estate; others involve the establishment of supplies or deliveries of stock against high security deposits. Firms usually do not maintain their headquarters in the country in which their manipulations are aimed; rather, they operate from legally independent trading companies. They often appear to be respectable companies, and neither their methods of doing business nor their acquisition of new customers differs from those of respectable firms.

A common method of international white-collar crime involves the misuse of bills of exchange, rather than fraudulent bills. Today, there is a form of international black market stock exchange for bills of exchange not only in Switzerland but in other European countries as well. Individuals learn from various sources about firms whose credit has been exhausted and are thus in financial need. Often, they are offered cash, but acceptances are kept anonymous and are made marketable by using the name of some limited-liability company that maintains headquarters abroad, barely more than a cover. The agent receives about a 20-percent commission from the discount gain.

Illegal banking activities and the Swiss bank secrecy law

Banking has high prestige in Switzerland, and it has an incomparable reputation internationally. In fact, Zürich is one of the largest monetary centers in the world, particularly in gold transactions. The development of banking has a long history in Switzerland. Two aspects of this development are of particular importance. Swiss banking followed the pattern of Crédit Mobilier, founded in Paris in 1853, namely that a bank was not only to collect capital but was also meant to participate in the development of new industries like railroads and manufacturing. In the 1850s the Swiss Credit Bank (Crédit Suisse) and others that later were set up, *banques d'affaires,* no longer were mere depositories and trading houses in gold and silver or the discounting of notes. They also granted loans, formed industrial or other companies that they conducted as if they were their own accounts, participated in new and old enterprises, issued securities and their own bonds, bought gold and silver as well as stocks and merchandise, discounted bills, and accepted deposits.[22] The second aspect of Swiss banking development was the stability of Switzerland as a neutral, the only country that did not impose restrictions on foreign exchange and where capital, gold, and currency were free to move. Swiss banks actively encouraged deposits of foreign capital, and this was further aided by the bank secrecy law that will be discussed later.

For a country the size of Switzerland, the number of banks is extremely large — more than 4,000 including branch offices — although five principal banks actually control most of the banking empire. A large Swiss bank encompasses the activities of a savings bank, brokerage house, money exchange, investment bank, credit union, commercial services, investment counseling, and a storage company. Checking account activity is lower than elsewhere; many transactions of this nature are handled through the postal service. T. R. Fehrenbach explains how this system works:

Inside Switzerland the personal cheque account is almost unknown. The Swiss developed a similar clearing system, but administer it through the federal post office. This is called the *giro* account. Most Swiss people and businesses maintain one; Swiss stores send money orders with their bills. The post office then transfers money from one giro account to another, acting exactly like a bank. If a payee or payor has no account, the post office accepts or delivers banknotes. Money can be sent anywhere in one day or less; the system works. Oddly, in the most overbanked nation on earth, the post office is also in what most foreigners would consider the banking business.[23]

Banks are of three types — the large, publicly owned commercial banks, the famous Swiss private banks, and those banks owned by foreigners and referred to by the Swiss as "other banks." Many of these banks are accustomed to dealing in international business on a large scale, and a Swiss bank gains foreign exchange profits through a number of types of transactions, as well as profiting from normal international banking charges. Between 1956 and 1965 at least $500 million a year, mostly in gold, was deposited in Swiss banks.[24] This gives to Swiss banks large funds for investment abroad, sums that would never have been possible by Swiss deposits alone. The extensive foreign activities of Swiss banks have been criticized as actually beneficial only to a banking establishment and contributing little to the growth of investment capital in the country itself.[25] Large amounts of funds are termed *capital en fuite* ("capital in flight") funds whose transfer is not connected with the settlement of a debt or a merchandising transaction. No official figures are available on the amount of money "in flight" in Switzerland, but it is used in innumerable complicated financial manoeuvers.

Switzerland has long attracted foreign funds as a result of its history of political and financial stability, its conservative nature affecting many aspects of Swiss life, the so-called Calvinistic moral values of the Swiss that emphasize work and profits, and the country's bank secrecy law. Fehrenbach has elaborated on the attitude of the Swiss toward the importance of money:

Sociologists generally agree that banking and high finance are Protestant fine arts. Zwinglianism did not reconcile Christ and Mammon. Zwingli and his national spiritual descendants never saw any conflict. The Swiss did not learn to love money. That is a misconception. The Swiss *respects* money, a very different thing. Respecting it, a Swiss pursues, handles and husbands money as an end in itself, which is utterly different from German materialism with its emphasis upon *things,* or American status-seeking with its drive for power or prestige. A Zürich millionaire of today lives hardly any differently from his grandfather — at work before eight, in sober dress, fretting over every franc as if it were personally vital. In Basel or Bern it is impossible to distinguish between first-generation and sixth-generation banking rich. There are thousands of playboys in Switzerland, but they usually have Arab or Hispanic names.[26]

At the same time, the Swiss banking system has been charged by the world press, as well as by many governments and bureaus, as offering a hiding place for stolen or looted money, providing a screen for stock manipulations and shady promoters, and helping tax evaders to conceal both income and assets.[27] There is no question but that, due largely to the concentration of the large-scale international banking interests, the bank secrecy law, and the more tolerant attitude toward the type of depositor, Switzerland — particularly Zürich — has become a center for "dirty money" transactions.[28] In these transactions international deposits are "washed" or "laundered" to obscure their illegal origins; through new commercial transactions the money is made legal and is also concealed from tax authorities. Those banks which engage in international transactions often violate many Swiss laws, as well as the laws of other countries. Deposits consist of large sums of money removed from the fiscal control of foreign countries (which their laws forbid), money often acquired by illegal operations or simply money put in Swiss banks for "security" reasons. Thus, these large financial operations every day violate many laws of Switzerland and other countries.

The Swiss Bankers Association claims that Swiss banks "cannot be held responsible if criminal elements take advantage of Swiss bank secrecy. It is claimed that the large reputable Swiss banks would never knowingly take 'hot money,' and that every precaution is taken to prevent criminals from opening accounts in Swiss banks."[29] Cases like the Clifford Irving—Howard Hughes affair would seem to stand in direct rebuttal to such claims; they show, in fact, that the banks fail to take "real precautions" to find out if large and suspicious deposits have been criminally obtained, that some bank managers will accept obviously "dirty" money, and that such actions "cannot be attributed just to the smaller private banks and to the 'other banks.' "[30] In his book Irving has described the fraud in which a purported Howard Hughes biography was sold to the McGraw-Hill Company for $750,000, this money then being deposited by his wife in a Swiss bank.[31] In making the deposit his wife used a forged passport, as well as a forged endorsement that differed from the passport. Later, $350,000 was withdrawn from this bank and deposited in another.

For a century or more, Swiss bankers have been accustomed to accepting large deposits from foreigners escaping confiscatory taxes, individual businessmen trying to avoid foreign exchange difficulties in their own countries, and from political refugees and heads of states who fear their tenures might not last indefinitely. United States banks have no such freedom, and the "kind of government regulations that would require the Miami banker to report his new mysterious cash customer are unheard of in Switzerland."[32] A recent study of the problem of these "dirty money transactions" concludes that:

Few Swiss banks have been guilty of seeking out and encouraging the dirty-money business. However, as a matter of course, a Swiss banker leaves himself wide open to this business by dealing with a number of foreign clients whom he may never have met, accepting cash deposits that are often sizable, and scrupulously protecting the confidentiality of his clients' transactions. These are the banking customs that, in addition to the legally enforced tradition of bank secrecy, have made Switzerland a favorite financial center for the dirty-money men.

Swiss bankers have reacted to their popularity among international manipulators by simply denying that it exists, an unrealistic position in light of overwhelming evidence to the contrary, or by placing all of the blame for dirty money on the "other banks." The "other banks" foreign ownership makes them convenient scapegoats for Swiss bankers who charge that they are the setting for most, if not all, of the criminal activities that have tarnished the image of Swiss banking. The fact that some of the more notorious Swiss banking scandals in recent years have involved the "other banks" has not served to dampen these prejudices. However, the Swiss themselves must shoulder some of the blame. Swiss laws regulating the opening of new banks have been so lax that almost anyone, scalawag and legitimate banker alike, has been able to open a Swiss "other bank."[33]

Following a major scandal, in 1969 the Swiss enacted a new law regulating foreign-controlled Swiss banks. Clarke and Tigue explain:

Before an "other bank" can even open its doors, it now has to fulfill a number of conditions to the satisfaction of the Swiss Banking Commission. The countries in which the shareholders of the "other banks" are nationals must agree to allow Swiss banks to open reciprocal branch offices. The name of the "other bank" must reflect its national character, so that depositors are not misled into believing that they are dealing with a bank operated by Swiss nationals. The "other bank" must send a written undertaking to the Swiss National Bank that it will not contravene Swiss monetary and economic policy. The bank must agree not to engage in exaggerated publicity in Switzerland and abroad about the advantages of Swiss secrecy, numbered accounts, and other such aspects of Swiss banking. It must guarantee that its management is "beyond reproach." (It is difficult to imagine a bank opening any-where and refusing to make this guarantee.) These regulations are in effect a cata-logue of the sins of which the "other banks" have been guilty — in fact, and in the eyes of the Swiss banking community.[34]

The Swiss Federal government exercises weak controls over commer-cial and banking transactions, and the cantons are for all practical pur-poses generally too small to control large-scale financial manipulations. Financial circles exercise great influence on legislation, thus preventing the enactment of strong and effective control measures. It is, further-more, relatively easy to avoid detection of infractions of monetary con-trol measures, because bank accounts are largely secret. Switzerland is one of the few countries in which bank secrecy is prescribed by law, thus making infringements punishable. Bank employees are expected to keep secret any observations made in the execution of their profession-al duties. This secrecy is derived, by common accord, from the contrac-tual relations that exist between the banks and their customers, rela-tions subject to mandatory law.[35] For many years before bank secrecy was codified into statutes it was recognized as an essential feature of the banker–customer relationship. Although this relationship is recog-nized in most European countries and in the United States, the great difference is that in Switzerland bank secrecy "was written into *penal law* and it was specifically and *deliberately applied* to all government."[36] Hans Schultz points out how far-reaching has been the protection of banking secrecy under penal law, covering not only the deliberate and intentional violation of confidence but negligent violation as well.[37] The Banking Law of 1934, officially protecting bank secrecy, was put into effect during the period between the two World Wars, largely to protect exiles from Nazi Germany, where severe restrictions were in effect to prevent refugees from taking money out of the country. The revision of the Swiss Banking Law (Article 47) of March 11, 1971, provided that:[38]

1. Whoever divulges a secret entrusted to him in his capacity as officer, em-ployee, authorized agent, liquidator or commissioner of a bank, as a repre-sentative of the Banking Commission, officer or employee of a recognized auditing company, or who has become aware of such a secret in this capac-ity, and whoever tries to induce others to violate professional secrecy, shall be punished by a prison term not to exceed six months or by a fine not exceeding Sw. F. 50,000.
2. If the act has been committed by negligence, the penalty shall be a fine not exceeding Sw. F. 30,000.

Several limitations in the bank secrecy laws have been pointed out by Schultz.[39] The obligation to maintain secrecy can be lifted by the individual for those persons stipulated by him; a bank cannot involve the claims of banking secrecy toward the heirs of a client; banks are required to inform authorities in criminal cases if they are requested to furnish evidence or to produce documents; the claims of bank secrecy cannot be invoked when criminal proceedings are in process; in the prosecution of a tax fraud banks must provide information, as well as in prosecutions for illegal bankruptcy. This obligation to supply information applies as well to the governments of other countries with which Switzerland cooperates in legal matters, provided that the offense precipitating the request for legal help is also punishable in Switzerland — as in the case of the Swiss treaty with the United States.[40] Thus, the laws of the two countries must agree on the question involved. The help requested also cannot be in contradiction with Swiss constitutional principles. In accordance with this ruling, recognized by international law, Switzerland traditionally provides no legal assistance in respect to political offenses or those not punishable under Swiss law, such as those involving currency. When the cases fall within the Swiss category of criminal offenses, assistance is generally given by Switzerland. In the case of Clifford Irving, the fraud was discovered and bank secrecy was suspended in order to permit the arrest of the offender. Bank secrecy thus can constitute no basic obstacle to the efforts to combat international crimes if such efforts are made, but this is not always done.

Banking secrecy is a recognized element not only of constitutional law but through practice and legal pronouncements. This has developed as a natural process from the sociopolitical principles upheld in Switzerland in respect to the right of the individual to a private sphere completely free from state intervention. In fact, this individual right is what bank secrecy has been developed to protect, and a Swiss public opinion poll in 1976 found that approximately two-thirds of those questioned supported the bank secrecy laws.[41] Bank secrecy is also well established by an important humanitarian consideration, as Switzerland has served as a political sanctuary for centuries. During World War II, for example, bank secrecy was a useful means of protecting the deposited fortunes of individuals endangered under totalitarian regimes. It is claimed that the banks do not, however, accept deposits from persons whose names and origins are not known to them. Hans J. Mast writes:

They accept no anonymous moneys, and a numbered account offers no anonymity within the bank. Its only effect is to restrict knowledge of the account holder to a limited circle of bank officials. In this way it offers clients, particularly those in the public eye, better protection against the risk of infringement of bank secrecy. In the eyes of the law, however, such an account differs in no respect from a normal account. The point where the legal validity of bank secrecy ends is the same for the numbered as for the ordinary account.[42]

The numbered accounts system has a particular effect in protecting white-collar crimes. Since only a limited number of bank officials know the identity of the customer, both the depositor and the banks are protected, to a certain extent, from sanctions of the civil or penal law. These laws do not require the banks to inform any governmental agencies about certain possibly illegal transactions on the part of their customers, a situation quite different from that in most other countries. Banks are not allowed, furthermore, to release information to the revenue service regarding the business of persons subject to taxation.

Changes were made, however, in the operations of the bank secrecy laws in 1977, as a result of the difficulties of Crédit Suisse and its Chiasso branch. The Swiss Bankers Association, representing about 85 percent of Swiss banks, entered into a voluntary five-year agreement with the Swiss National Bank, in which a bank is not obligated to inform on a client but is required to sever relations with any client whom the bank suspects of violating the law. It provides that the identity of the banks' clients be reliably ascertained and that the bank be responsible for seeing that it does not aid and abet illegal capital transfer, that it abstains from helping clients to seek to evade taxes either in Switzerland or abroad, and that it accepts no funds that are recognized as having been acquired by punishable acts. Moreover, the agreement establishes sanctions for banks violating the pact, with fines for violations up to Sw. F. 10 million. To ascertain and punish offenses, an arbitration committee is to be established, comprised of two representatives of the central bank and two of the Bankers' Association, the chairman to be a federal judge unanimously designated by the committee members.

Income tax and property tax violations

Switzerland has an unusual income tax situation, both in terms of the basis on which the tax is levied and in the prosecution of tax cases.[43] Tax resources are largely raised from property assessments and through indirect taxation: Income taxes are quite low. In Zürich canton, for example, the total income and property tax assessment at local, cantonal, and federal levels does not exceed 30 percent. Each of the 3,000 communes levies and collects nearly all taxes on salaries and property. There are additional taxes, such as the indirect tax on imports and other items, that are levied by the federal government. Each commune retains a certain amount of the taxes collected, a certain percentage is transmitted to the canton, and some goes to the federal government. Factory taxes are levied according to the plant's location. Tax rates thus vary according to communal needs; because of this variation, persons often decide where to live on the basis of tax rates. Throughout Switzerland communal tax collectors are elected officials. In 1977 a national referendum rejected an amendment to the constitution that would have given some national uniformity on commune income tax rates.

Swiss citizens must declare to the tax authorities the exact amount of income and assets, but the authorities cannot, except in two cantons, check this information with the bank. This type of tax system results in considerable variation, with more compliance being assured in some communes, less in others. While a tax commissioner in a small commune may have more intimate knowledge of a person's real income and property — which might be conducive to greater compliance — he might also be subject to influence or corruption from certain individuals, particularly the more wealthy. Where the system provides no methods of cross-checking and is not computerized, individual returns contain only receipts for salary payments and deductions. Taxpayers are simply asked to pay additional sums if errors have been found. Because most tax violations are handled as civil or administrative actions, and not under criminal law, taxpayers have less substantial fears of any actions resulting from false reporting.[44]

In Switzerland, a "tax amnesty" involves no additional taxes, penalties, or prosecutions of persons for misrepresentation to the government of taxes due, providing they declare them. In the first tax amnesty in 1969, a total of capital assets declared for the first time in all of Switzerland was Sw. F. 11.5 billion, about $3.5 billion.[45] (See Table 7.1 for the cantonal amounts and the per capita distributions.) The average for the country was Sw. F. 1,837 ($450) per capita (not per tax individual) and ranged from a high of Sw. F. 4,026 in Geneva to a low of Sw. F. 919 in Luzern. One cannot compare the cantons, however, because there have been sixteen cantonal tax amnesties since the initial one in 1945, and

Table 7.1. *Results of Swiss tax amnesty, 1969*

Cantons	Population	Amount of amnesty	
		Millions of francs	Sw. F. per capita
Zürich	1,107,708	1,965.1	1,774
Bern	983,296	2,200.0	2,237
Luzern	289,641	265.0	915
Uri	34,091	34.3	1,006
Schwyz	92,072	155.7	1,691
Obwalden	24,509	46.8	1,910
Nidwalden	25,634	32.0	1,248
Glarus	38,155	75.0	1,966
Zug	67,996	135.8	1,997
Fribourg	180,309	333.9	1,852
Solothurn	224,133	312.0	1,392
Basel-Stadt	234,945	405.7	1,727
Basel-Land	204,889	256.7	1,253
Schaffhausen	72,854	85.0	1,167
Appenzell A.Rh.	49,023	100.3	2,046
Appenzell I.Rh.	13,124	39.7	3,025
St. Gallen	384,475	850.0	2,211
Graubünden	162,086	250.0	1,542
Aargau	433,284	676.2	1,561
Thurgau	182,835	378.8	2,072
Ticino	245,458	430.2	1,753
Vaud	511,851	470.6	919
Valais	206,563	335.1	1,622
Neuchâtel	169,173	347.6	2,055
Genève	331,599	1,335.0	4,026
Total	6,269,783	11,516.5	1,837

Source: Report of the Federal Government to the Members of the Federal Parliament Concerning the Success of the Tax-Amnesty of 1969 (June 1, 1972) (mimeo). At that time the rate of exchange was four Swiss francs to the dollar.

federal taxes were not included in these amnesties. For this reason the "success" of the amnesty was low in those cantons having recently declared tax amnesties.

As a minimal analysis, the amount of undeclared capital assets was computed for different property classes. Although the results refer only to sixteen cantons, they are considered to be reasonably representative

Table 7.2. *Distribution of persons who made use of the 1969 tax amnesty and the ratio of formerly undeclared capital assets, according to property classes*[a]

Amount of property owned (in Sw. F. 1,000)	Users of the amnesty (percent)	Property declared for the first time (percent)
0–49	8.3	9.1
50–99	19.1	7.7
100–199	22.2	7.4
200–499	22.1	6.8
500–999	20.7	6.9
1,000 or more	19.4	7.0

[a]In percentage of all persons subject to taxation and in percentage of the total capital assets.
Source: Report of the Federal Government to the Members of the Federal Parliament Concerning the Success of the Tax-Amnesty of 1969 (June 1, 1972) (mimeo). At that time the exchange rate was four Swiss francs to the dollar.

for the country as a whole. Table 7.2 gives the percentage distribution of persons who made use of the amnesty and the distribution of the formerly undeclared parts of capital assets, according to property class. Persons taking advantage of the tax amnesty were chiefly in the upper property groups, and the percentage increased with the lower income levels. As a result, 8.3 percent of those with up to Sw. F. 50,000 used the amnesty, as compared with 19.4 percent of those with property assets of Sw. F. 1,000,000. The proportion of those who declared property for the first time — that is, previously undisclosed property — was almost the same for all groups: There were 9.1 percent in the lowest income group up to Sw. F. 50,000, as compared with about 7 percent for those with incomes of Sw. F. 200,000 or over.

Summary

As in the United States and in many other Western European countries, Swiss persons with economic and social power have largely been able to avoid having criminal sanctions imposed on them in areas of business and banking. White-collar crime in these areas appears to be extensive, however, and it is increasing, in contrast to much ordinary crime. An interesting situation is thus presented, as it refutes the claim that a country with extensive crime in business and finance will, as a result, have much ordinary crime as well.

White-collar crime at the international level appears to be extensive. It includes such forms as swindles in stocks, bonds, and real estate, the misuse of bills of exchange, and the "laundering of dirty money" from abroad through Swiss banking facilities. Although Swiss banking enjoys high prestige, the federal government has only weak controls over commercial and banking transactions, and the cantons are far too numerous — and many of them are also too small — for any practical control over large-scale financial dealings.

The extensive nature of white-collar crime in Switzerland is due to the fact that the country is an international center for business and finance. It is also the result of the economic power differentials in what is defined as real crime, the tolerance of the Swiss public of these illegal activities (as contrasted with other kinds of crime), the bank secrecy laws, and the inability of the cantons to deal with the national and international complexities of white-collar crime. Tax violations are also extensive, but they generally do not come under the criminal law.

8. Political decentralization and the criminal justice system

According to the evidence presented, crime other than white-collar offenses appears not to be a major problem in Switzerland or in major Swiss cities. This conclusion constitutes an important exceptional instance in respect to the crime picture found among the most highly developed, urbanized countries of the world. In the search for the processes and scientific explanations underlying any phenomenon – in this case the phenomenon of criminality – such an exceptional situation warrants a careful analysis.

Many factors are significant, but certain processes and phenomena appear to be of more importance than others in this analysis. Certainly, the slower rate of urbanization and urban growth and the absence of slums play an important part. The governmental responsibilities assumed by the citizenry have been unique in the Western world and provide a certain counterforce to the development of criminality. The ready access to firearms has not resulted in much violent crime, including robbery, because the Swiss society does not have a cultural pattern of using violence to settle disputes or to achieve monetary objectives. The criminal justice system itself has not contributed greatly to further increases in crime as it frequently has in other countries. Among Swiss youth, who constitute the bulk of the property offenses cases, a pronounced subculture has not been widely developed, partly because communication with adults has been maintained in the society. Finally, crime has not been found to be a serious problem among the large foreign worker population. These various issues will be analyzed successively.

Slow growth of urbanization and absence of slums

Everywhere throughout the world – in the developing, as well as in the developed countries – urban areas have high rates of crime, and it is here that most crime is concentrated. Studies in the United States,

France, and Japan, for example, show this relationship between crime and urban areas.[1] Almost without exception, developing countries report rapidly increasing crime, due almost entirely to the accelerated urbanization accompanying industrialization and the migration of rural youth to the cities.[2] Most crime in the less developed countries, in fact, is concentrated in cities, particularly the large ones. Almost universally, studies show that crimes reported to the police increase as the size of the city increases. For example, in the United States rates generally rise as the size of a city increases from under 10,000 to 1,000,000 or more for murder, robbery, burglary, auto theft, and, with minor exceptions, aggravated assault.[3] Larceny increases steadily in cities up to 1,000,000 or over. Crime victimization surveys, however, do not show as clear a relationship. The victimization rates increase progressively from cities of 50,000 to those 1,000,000 or over for robbery and auto theft and, with some fluctuations, for burglary.[4] Household theft, assault, and theft, however, do not show a consistent pattern by city size.

The urbanization has been slower in Switzerland. Partly as a result of the unique governmental and political structure of the country, as well as its historical development, the Swiss urbanization processes have also been quite different from those in many other European countries. These factors plus the slower rate of urbanization have produced greater stability in economic and social conditions.[5] In fact, the urban growth rate was generally slow until about 1960, so its rapid acceleration has occurred only within the last decade or so. In 1850, when the population was about 2.4 million — almost one-third of what it is today — only eight cities had more than 10,000 inhabitants. The total urban population, in places with 10,000 or more, was only 154,000 — or about 6.2 percent.[6] In 1920, Switzerland had twenty-eight places with more than 10,000 persons — or 27.6 percent of the population. While the country is highly industrialized, the growth of urbanization has been only moderate, due to the decentralization of industry into the rural and semirural areas. For some time the country's lack of coal, around which both industrialization and population centers have developed in most countries, has forced the dispersion of industry along the rivers, where water power — and later electricity-producing water power from the mountains — was available. E. A. Gutkind points out that in Switzerland "industry was less effective as a social 'dislocator' and 'catalyst' than in many other countries."[7] Even though cities grew much faster than the rural areas, the same appalling physical conditions that characterized English cities, for example, were never created in Switzerland. This difference was graphically pointed out in 1860 by C. B. Arwed Emminghaus:

Switzerland has whole industrial villages, industrial valleys, industrial cantons. She is herself an industrial country *par excellence* – but she has no industrial cities, no Manchester, no Leeds, no Dundee, or Belfast, no Sheffield or Birmingham, even quite apart from the size of these cities. But the Swiss cities are by no means large working-class conglomerations; they have nothing in common with those dismal centers of the English industry; they are seats of small trades and industries and of commerce; and they are also centers of the intellectual and political life of the country.[8]

The linguistic and cultural differences in the country have had a pronounced effect on internal migration, particularly urban migration. Where migration has occurred, it has largely been restricted to the same language area, those inhabiting the German-speaking area (65 percent of the country) seldom leaving this area to move to the smaller French-speaking (18 percent) or Italian-speaking (12 percent) areas. In a conversation I had with a leading forensic psychiatrist, he stated that "in interviewing persons in prison in Geneva one is likely to find that their families had lived several generations in the same area." There is even little mobility of faculty or students between universities in the various language areas, and universities are generally regarded as German-speaking or French-speaking.

All of these factors inhibited the growth of very large heterogeneous cities, with their distinct sets of norms, values, and slum cultures, and there was only a limited development of an urban proletarian class. The gulf between city and country was far less marked than it was rapidly becoming elsewhere. Centralization of rapid urban growth has only developed within comparatively recent years as the larger cities have expanded into the surrounding metropolitan areas. Even with this expansion, however, no city has exceeded 500,000 inhabitants, as has certainly been the case in other small countries like Sweden, Denmark, Belgium, and the Netherlands. Zürich's population is less than 500,000, and Basel and Geneva have fewer than 250,000, but Stockholm proper has almost a million, and Copenhagen, more than a million. Even if the larger metropolitan area is included, Zürich's is still only 700,000 – much smaller than, for example, the city population of Stockholm or Copenhagen.

Even with the more rapid urbanization of the last decade, however, no typical slum areas have grown up in the large Swiss cities, as compared, for example, to such cities as Hamburg, Munich, Paris, Marseilles, London, or comparable cities in the United States. A combination of political, economic, and historical factors have effectively inhibited the development of such slum or "criminal" areas, where certain criminal norms have evolved along with opposition to the police and poor sanitation and health practices.[9] Citizen responsibility has also been an important factor in preventing the growth of these areas, as well as in the development of socially positive norms. As a result, norms favorable to the growth of criminal patterns have not been established in specific areas of the cities. It appears, for example, that youth crime is not concentrated in specific areas of Swiss cities. A study made in Geneva reported that only 8 percent of a group of 100 youth offenders, most of whom had committed theft and had appeared before the penal court, came from what might be considered a slum type of environment.[10] Another study, also made in Geneva, compared youth offenders from the central city with those living elsewhere in greater Geneva and found little difference in the nature of youth crime in the two areas.[11] Similarly, a Basel study presented no conclusive relation between the area of the city and youth crime: It was considered to be an important factor for about half of the delinquents (52.5 percent) but not important in any of the other cases.[12] A Basel study of 498 criminal cases appearing before the high court in 1960 found that the educational level had no significant influence on either the amount or the type of the crime.[13]

Modern Switzerland is generally considered to be, and actually is, a very urbanized country, but there is much less urbanism – or an urban way of life – in its large cities. Even after years of residence in large cities, most persons still think of "home" as their traditional cantons or communes, even though they may be some distance away. A large proportion of urban inhabitants have never broken in spirit with the soil or the rugged mountain lands of their ancestors. In fact, in order to be a Swiss citizen a person must first have cantonal citizenship, which, in turn, depends upon citizenship in one of the 3095 communes. Many Swiss prefer to live in their traditional areas even when they work in the cities. Each day, for example, approximately 180,000 persons commute from their homes to their work in Zürich, and Bern has an even larger proportion of commuters. Due to these factors, some 60 percent of the Swiss still live in the cantons where they were born, a situation that is quite unusual in an affluent, industrialized nation.[14]

Remaining as they often do in the local areas, the people tend to know their neighbors better than they would have, had they moved into the cities. They are perhaps also more aware of what is going on in their own communities. With less mobility and urban migration, furthermore, the Swiss youth have had more stability in their schooling and in their various social contacts, and they more likely have developed greater family and regional ties. This, in turn, has probably been associated with greater personal responsibility for compliance with norms. A prosecutor in Ticino canton, or the Italian area of Switzerland, stated that "in Bellinzona the people feel they belong, while in Italy there is more impersonality in cities of this size." In his opinion, this feeling of "community belonging" prevents them from committing thefts. As the cities continue to grow, however, more large impersonal suburban areas develop with large apartment complexes, and the natural consequences of these developments will be an increasing deterioration of community ties. Informed officials in both Geneva and Zürich state that suburban areas are increasingly becoming problem areas for youth crime.

Political decentralization of government

The comparatively slow urbanization process and its effect upon citizen responsibility for compliance with normative standards have been enhanced by the great political decentralization in the country. The extremely decentralized system has resulted in the restriction of federal governmental structure and power to certain limited aspects of Swiss life. In comparison to Sweden, for example, the Swiss government's central power, particularly at the federal level, is much weaker. Even the highest level of government, at the federal level, consists of a seven-member council, rather than a single official such as a prime minister. Although one member serves as council president, the presidency changes annually, on a simple rotating basis. Fehrenbach summarizes the system in this manner:

Switzerland has the loosest form of national organization of any modern nation, and the weakest central government in the West. Its tiny area is divided into twenty-five sovereign cantons, each of which retains real powers. The federal capital at Bern manages foreign affairs, controls arms and alcohol, regulates the currency, and runs the mails and railroads. Almost everything else is left to the several states. The President of the Confederation is a figurehead, selected annually from a federal cabinet of seven, whose overall powers are small. There are two legislative houses, the Nationalrat and Ständerat, modelled on the American House and Senate. Both houses must issue bills to make them law — but any law can be repealed by popular initiative and national referendum, and some have been. The federal judiciary has no powers of legislative review.[15]

Swiss citizens dislike the delegation of too much responsibility to the federal government, a situation quite different from the strong governmental power and responsibility found in most European countries. Most of these countries, including Sweden, for example, have centralized police forces, while Switzerland continues to resist proposals for a centralized system. The Swiss police system is completely decentralized, and the units are locally based. With political decentralization has come a more active local concern in the operation of agencies such as the police, the courts, and the schools. As a result, problems related to law violation and to crime prevention have become a built-in part of the decentralized Swiss political system. This situation is in sharp contrast to the larger and more centralized governmental structures found in almost all other countries. This appears to work in the prevention and control of ordinary crime in Switzerland. White-collar crime, on the other hand, seems to flourish in the absence of strong federal measures. This type of offense is not amenable to local governmental controls because it is generally broadly based — throughout the country as a whole, or even on an international level.

Of great significance in Swiss political life is the importance of cantonal and communal citizenship. In fact, the cantonal flag is generally flown above the national flag — just the reverse of the situation, for example, in the United States. This country of approximately 6 million persons is divided into twenty-five cantons (actually twenty-two, with three divided into so-called half-cantons), and the responsibilities of each canton are as great as or even greater than those of the individual American states, even though six cantons have less than 50,000 persons, and one, only 14,000. Each canton has its own legislative body, its own criminal justice system, and its own educational system, which may vary from canton to canton. Sorrell states:

It may seem bewildering that such a small state has twenty-five different school systems, but, just as everything else is decentralized and decided upon on a local level by a population that differs from its neighbors in culture, religion, and language, so is education. Switzerland has no national ministry of education, but great efforts are being made by the Federal Government towards a rather unified school system to find more common denominators in most areas without depriving the populace of its right of self-determination on whatever issue.[16]

The cantons are subdivided into a variety of communes (generally four types). The detailed organization and extent of local self-government in these various communes is left to the canton, so great diversity is found in the specific cantonal commune system. All cantons, however, have residential or political communes (Einwohnergemeinde) — over 3,000 of them — some of which have fewer than a hundred inhabitants. They consist of all persons who live in the commune or local area, whether or not they are citizens. Whether or not he is a citizen of the commune, each Swiss who lives in the commune is allowed to vote. The political communes are responsible for the registration of all inhabitants and all public acts relating to them (for example, civil marriage is also compulsory in Switzerland) — taxes, local police, building regulations, and so on. In addition, there are other types of communes. The commune of citizens (Bürgergemeinde), consisting of the citizens of the commune, deals with communal possessions such as land, administers relief funds, and handles the naturalization of foreigners, who must first obtain communal citizenship before cantonal or federal citizenship is granted. The school commune (Schulgemeinde) is made up of citizens in a given school district: They handle all school problems, including school buildings, election of teachers, teacher pay scales, and other school affairs. Finally, the religious commune (Kirchgemeinde) is open to all Swiss (as well as foreigners in some cantons) who belong to a specific faith. They deal with the church buildings, election of ministers, and they have tax authority. In an effort to improve cantonal administration, a trend is developing to combine the commune of citizens and the school commune with the political commune, as in the Zürich canton, where large communes are united. In fact, cantonal and federal government units have had to assume more responsibilities through social security, compensation or equalization funds, and the like. The fairly autonomous communes near urban centers are also faced with expansion into their areas, and although villages farther removed from urban centers are not faced with immediate problems of containing urban expansion, their situation is equally critical and essentially the same. If they are not to become integral parts of the big cities and survive as separate entities, they must at least become much like the city, bigger, more complex, more diversified, more industrialized, more centralized, and more efficient. Barber believes that "autonomy, full participation in public affairs, consensus on significant issues and communal collectivism are simply not compatible with modernization of this kind."[17] The political communes eventually will be forced to decide if they will retain their communal identity, thereby risking economic stagnation and political obsolescence, or if they will trade their communal goals for what Barber calls a "mindless prosperity."[18] In spite of this present trend, the Swiss communal system, along with the cantons, remains one in which the average citizen is able to exercise a strong role of democratic responsibility.

Citizen assumption of responsibility for social and crime control

As a republic, Switzerland has the oldest continuous form of government in the world, from its origin as a confederation of its three cantons, formed in 1291, to its final cantonal structure in 1815 and the Constitution of 1848. This is not to say that it has been entirely a continuous democracy, as throughout the centuries great power and control were vested in many of the cantons by an aristocracy of birth and wealth. It is only beginning in the period between 1831 and 1848 that Switzerland can be called a real democracy. Historically, Switzerland has had a lengthy process of integration of a large number of socially and legally distinct cantons, small feudal manors and states, ecclesiastical possessions, and city-municipalities into a federal state. These integrative processes have occurred at two levels — at the cantonal level of small feudal entities[19] and at the federal level, in more numerous and closer alliances between the cantons.[20] The process of integration developed in such a way that the many smaller units survived (as communes, districts, and cantons) in the new union. This process came to an end at the cantonal level in 1815, from which date no changes have occurred either in the cantonal boundaries or in the number of cantons.[21]

Throughout many centuries the small country of Switzerland was bordered by the two powerful countries of Austria and France, and, for the last hundred years, by a modern Germany and Italy as well. Communication has been hampered by the geographical conditions of mountain barriers and limited passes that have also affected communication within the country; the many feudal states and other units within the country have frequently been isolated from each other. As a result of these factors, the Swiss people have had to be self-reliant, developing a broad interest in politics and in political decisions at all levels. Today, Swiss citizens feel that they are their own masters, and they tend to dislike authority in the form of an impersonal government. Although they dislike authority, they do like order. The individual citizen's self-reliance was enhanced by the possibility that he could influence political developments, over long periods of time, in relatively small geographic entities such as the cantons, districts, and communes. Swiss citizens continue to have strong feelings about these political units, feelings that are manifested in the importance generally attributed to their cantonal and communal citizenship, a loyalty that at times seems even to supersede Swiss citizenship. This sense of citizen responsibility has, to a large extent, been carried over from the rural areas into the large urban centers, although there are current signs that this is beginning to decline — as can be seen in the increasing apathy toward voting.

The famous open-air people's assembly (Landsgemeinde) which meets to discuss and vote upon issues in the cantons and communes was originally traditional in eight cantons: It exists today in five (Obwalden, Nidwalden, Glarus, Appenzell-Ausser Rhoden, Appenzell-Inner Rhoden) and in the districts of Graubünden.[22] In these assemblies any member has the right as an individual to submit proposals, to nominate and elect public officials, and to debate the issues to be decided by majority vote. In the past the Landsgemeinde was not fully democratic in character, as it was largely a gathering of the ruling families, who were usually aristocratic, and they tended to vote by clan, rather than as an assembly of free individuals.

The Swiss today have an ingrained faith in mutual help and solidarity, and the direct democracy of their political system enables each citizen to share the responsibility for running the country.[23] This high degree of democratic participation is illustrated by the widespread use of the initiative and the referendum at all levels to bring about changes and to challenge a law. Only 50,000 signatures are required for an initiative to try to change the constitution by an election at the federal level, and only 30,000 signatures — less than 2 percent of the electorate — or eight cantons are needed to demand a referendum to change a law adopted by Parliament. At the local level, most of the cantons provide a "finance referendum" whereby certain decisions of the legislature to use public funds beyond a certain amount must be ratified by the public. For example, a few years ago, the citizens of Basel voted on the purchase of the famous Picasso painting *Harlequin,* the price of approximately Sw. F. 1,500,000 ($500,000) having been approved. In Zürich in 1973 the citizens rejected a proposal to construct a subway, and in

1974 a referendum to expel foreign workers over a three-year period was rejected by the Swiss people, 66 percent to 34 percent.

The Swiss attitude of self-reliance is clearly revealed in such social-welfare measures as old-age pensions. Older retired persons have always been expected to support themselves from three primary sources: personal earnings or savings, contributions from former employers (where applicable), and the remainder — which usually is only about one-third of the total — from state pensions. The Swiss are a thrifty people who still rely heavily on a spirit of economic self-reliance that involves accumulating savings and extensive voluntary pension and life insurance plans. For example, in 1976 the International Savings Bank Institute reported that Swiss citizens had the highest per capita average savings in the world. This is in marked contrast to the basic philosophy of the extremely comprehensive Swedish welfare state, a system designed to care for the individual throughout his life. Although Switzerland has had a national social security plan since 1948, their system, in contrast to that of Sweden, entitles persons to modest old-age pensions and disability claims. Over the years, attempts have been made through an initiative to introduce a full-scale old-age pension, but these attempts have failed consistently. The Swiss still believe that except for state and vocational group insurance, each person should try to save, with the incentive to build up some capital or to have voluntary insurance.[24] Such an approach, which emphasizes a strong work ethic and the need for future goals, is still being instilled in the Swiss youth.

The pressure of citizen responsibility is enhanced by the more even distribution of income and the generally middle-class position of most Swiss citizens. The lower class is represented primarily by the foreign workers and a small proportion of the rural Swiss. The school system emphasizes democratic traditions and citizen responsibility. Private schools for Swiss children are much less numerous in Switzerland than in England, for example, but there are a number of private schools in the country that are attended both by Swiss and foreign children. Generally, one is not struck with obvious wealth, and most Swiss seem to believe that the wealthy purposely try to avoid much display of their wealth. Most of them believe that theirs is both a political and economic democracy, one in which pretensions of social class and ostentation play an insignificant role, although many bankers and large-scale entrepreneurs are known to have large fortunes.

The Swiss citizen's sense of responsibility and his active participation in community affairs affect his own behavior and that of others, including compliance not only with the generally accepted social norms but also with the law. It is commonly said, for example, that in Switzerland everyone is his own policeman.[25] The people are conscious of the judgment that others make of behavior that violates laws and regulations and risks public censure. The possibility of public censure restrains many from getting into trouble, and they seem to abide by rules and regulations – perhaps more so than in most countries. This desire to avoid public censure is probably more conducive to conformity than is the fear of a police reprimand. It is well illustrated by the negligible amount of jaywalking, even when traffic is very light and there are no policemen. One American newspaper correspondent commented upon the remarkable degree to which the Swiss pedestrian waits to cross the street with the traffic light.[26]

The best example of citizen responsibility and personal honesty is perhaps the self-service ticket-issuing system, the honor system in effect for *all* city trams and buses throughout the country.[27] This particular transportation system relies heavily upon citizen honor to reduce costs and maintain efficiency, for it makes possible the operation of trams and buses of two to three cars by only the one motorman. Passengers are advised by numerous signs to obtain their own tickets before boarding and to retain them, as no tickets are available within the trams or buses. Zürich instituted this honor system in 1970, and since then it has been adopted throughout Switzerland. At each stop there are automatic ticket-dispensing machines (1,000 in Zürich), and one ascertains the correct fare from the adjoining city map, colored according to fare zones. When the correct fare is deposited the ticket that is dispensed indicates the time and the location. If one uses tickets from prepurchased coupon books, they must be inserted into the machine for stamping. The tickets can be used for certain transfers, but all must be retained, in case of possible checks by inspectors, who might board to verify tickets. Should an inspector find a passenger without a proper ticket the person is fined on the spot, Sw. F. 10 (about $4 in 1977). The Swiss maintain that the public embarrassment of being found to be cheating on the system represents a far greater punishment than the fine itself. An estimated 210,000,000 passengers a year use the Zürich trams and buses, but in 1974 only 40,992 persons were found riding without tickets.[28] Many of these persons were undoubtedly foreign tourists, who are often unfamiliar with the system.

General availability of firearms in Switzerland but low rate of violent crimes

It has been shown that both rates and trends for murder, nonnegligent manslaughter, and robbery are low in Switzerland. Yet, firearms are readily accessible all over the country. Members of the citizen army (unless exempted for physical reasons, all male Swiss must serve and remain in the army from age twenty to age 50, and age 55 in the case of officers) keep their weapons in their homes, so they are available to them and also to the other members of the household. The weapons include rifles and − in the case of officers − revolvers, as well as certain automatic weapons and specified amounts of ammunition. Rifles and revolvers can also be purchased from stores, provided the purchaser has been permitted by the cantonal authorities to acquire them.[29] Each year, approximately seven hundred gun licenses are issued in Zürich − mainly for hunting purposes. If anyone sells his gun to another, no registration formalities are necessary. Swiss law does restrict, however, the carrying of certain weapons, including firearms and spring knives.

Firearms are rarely used in crimes of violence in Switzerland: They are seldom used to settle personal disputes or for robberies. During the years 1971 and 1972, for example, firearms were used in only three of the total ten murders in Zürich. According to police officials, during the approximate period 1970−1972 in Zürich, only one homicide − a wife killing her husband − occurred with a gun, and even in the case of robberies, guns are not often used. These facts contrast strikingly with the belief that a low criminal homicide rate is due to strict firearms regulations. It also shows that, contrary to views held by criminologists and others, homicide is due to the tendency to use extreme violence to settle disputes, and not always because firearms are readily available. It appears that the Swiss do not have this tendency to use violence, in terms of a full "subculture of violence," which often involves using weapons to settle serious disputes.[30] A quite different situation exists in the United States in relation to firearms, however, due to the far greater possibilities of using extreme violence in disputes. In the United States more than 100 million virtually unregistered firearms are in the hands of citizens, including 40 million handguns.[31] The United States had a rate of 13,500 firearms per 100,000 population in 1968, compared with 3,000 in Canada and 500 in Great Britain. Firearms, usually handguns, are involved in two out of three homicides, one out of five aggravated assaults, and one out of three robberies.[32] A 1975 Harris public opinion poll found that 73 percent of Americans favor registration of all gun purchases — up from 66 percent in 1967. The Swiss experience indicates the importance of factors other than gun control in violent crimes.

In contrast to the very minor use of firearms in robberies in Switzerland, approximately one out of three robberies in the United States is committed with a gun. In a study made of the weapons used in Zürich city robberies in 1972 and 1973, where the weapon used had been reported, only 15 percent involved the use of a firearm (only 19 of a total 127 cases). In Basel, from 1970 to 1972, only two of nine robberies involved a revolver, three a rifle, the others either knives or other weapons — a beer bottle in one case. This is in marked contrast to Sweden, where firearms are becoming increasingly common in the commission of robberies. In Sweden's largest bank robbery ($340,000), four men armed with machine guns held up an armored car in Göteborg in 1976.

The nature of the criminal justice system

The Swiss criminal justice system commonly provides means of diversion from the use of imprisonment. It begins at the police level in the German-speaking area, where the offender generally is not arrested but released on his own recognizance for a later court appearance, except in the case of certain serious offenses or unusual circumstances.[33] Suspects are usually well screened on the basis of police reports and other information before they are prosecuted. In German-speaking Switzerland the prosecutor makes no plea bargaining deals by accepting guilty pleas for lesser charges — a common practice in the United States, France, and, to a certain extent, in the French-speaking area of Switzerland. Should the evidence sufficiently indicate that a certain crime has been committed, the prosecutor must proceed with the charge.

Following conviction, alternatives to imprisonment are widely used — particularly, the suspended sentence for adults and probation for those aged 15 to 18. In a suspended sentence persons are sentenced to imprisonment, but the sentence is suspended conditional upon no subsequent criminal behavior by the convicted offender. The person does not report to anyone. Suspended sentences are possible only if the penalty involved imprisonment. Except for offenders between 15 and 18 years of age, fines cannot be given in suspended sentences. Under Swiss criminal law there is no provision for adult probation, which is a supervised suspended sentence. The suspended execution of the penalty has apparently met with considerable success. The primary goal is to prevent offenders from slipping into chronic criminality, but it is also believed to be important to provide a rapid penalty, particularly for first offenders.

The suspended prison sentence is being used increasingly; between 1968 and 1972 the number rose from 11,701 to 14,690, an increase of 26 percent.[34] During the same time span, the number sentenced and committed to prison and those whose sentences were not suspended declined from 7,055 to 6,993, or 0.9 percent.[35] According to Schultz, five out of six offenders successfully complete their suspended sentences, with no further infractions of the law.[36] Hardly any changes have occurred in the number of sentences revoked (and the person thus imprisoned), as there was an increase between 1968 and 1972 of only 1,892 to 1,990 in the revocations. Future increases in the use of the suspended sentence will be even greater, due to the fact that in 1971 changes were made in the Swiss Criminal Code to allow a suspension of sentence up to eighteen months instead of one year, the time period customarily used prior to these changes. Moreover, the law was changed to provide for suspension of more severe imprisonment, that is, to penitentiaries (*Zuchthäuser*), in addition to ordinary prisons.[37]

Switzerland appears to use the suspended sentence and probation far more frequently than do almost all other European countries.[38] Approximately two-thirds (60 to 65 percent) of all persons sentenced to detention or to prison, according to Jerzy Jasiński, were given either a suspended sentence or put on probation. The only European country with a higher rate of such usage was the Netherlands. In Sweden about 10,500 persons are generally sentenced each year to prison, and 9,000 are put on probation, or 46.2 percent.[39]

Prisons are less frequently used in Switzerland, in terms of population, than in most other European countries.[40] The Swiss rate of imprisonment in 1972 was 43.5 per 100,000, as compared with Sweden's rate of 61.4, 83.6 for the Federal German Republic, 74.2 for England and Wales, 69.8 for Denmark, 60.2 for Belgium, and 59.2 for France.[41] Only Norway and the Netherlands had lower rates, 37.1 and 22.4, respectively. On the other hand, the *proportionate* use of imprisonment was lower in Switzerland than in most countries, but higher than in some others.[42] One must remember that small fines are not included in

Swiss criminal statistics, thus increasing the percentage of imprison-ment. The percentage of convicted Swiss offenders sentenced to prison without suspended sentences or probation was 17.8 (20 percent in 1974), whereas the percentage for Denmark was 37.5, for Norway, 35.6, for the Netherlands, 33.9, for the Federal German Republic, 22.7, and for Austria, 22.7. In other countries the proportions sentenced to pris-on were lower − 11.5 percent in Poland, 4.1 in Finland, 3.1 in Sweden, and 2.5 in England and Wales.

It is widely known that the United States has the longest prison sen-tences of any country in the world. This contributes to the high United States crime rate, as the rate of recidivism is extremely high, there is general bitterness toward society and the prison staff because of this harsh, lengthy imprisonment, and prison inmates learn increasingly more sophisticated crimes. In Switzerland, on the other hand, offenders receive relatively short sentences and a large proportion of these are sus-pended. On the whole, about 75 percent of the Swiss offenders receive sentences of three months or less, as compared with 38.7 percent in Norway, 21.7 in England and Wales, and 10.1 in Poland.[43] A high per-centage of Swiss offenders (84.7 percent) also receive sentences of six months or less, but this does not differ greatly from what is common in other European countries: 84.1 percent in Austria; 83.7, in Norway; and 82.9, in the Federal German Republic. The percentages are some-what higher than that of England and Wales (70.8) or of Denmark (67.1), and much higher than the percentage of 24.7 in Poland. Similar short sentences are given in Sweden; in 1972 about 69 percent of those sen-tenced to prison received a sentence of less than four months, about 22 percent were sentenced to between four and twelve months, and about 9 percent for a year or more.

Most important, however, is the fact that the persons actually com-mitted to prison, rather than those merely sentenced, generally receive exceptionally short terms of imprisonment. Swiss inmates thus are not incarcerated over long periods of time that enable inmates to acquire additional criminal sophistication. As indicated by the general crime situation, few offenders appear to develop secondary criminal careers that involve a criminal self-identity, the acquisition of advanced crimi-nal techniques, and rationalizations for crime, all of which are likely to lead them into careers in armed robbery or burglary or other crimes of a serious nature.[44] As it appears that few sophisticated criminals are de-veloped in the system, few other persons in the society become "infected" with such criminal norms. All of this tends to reduce both the volume and the seriousness of conventional crime.

In 1971, 11,290 persons convicted under the criminal code were sentenced to prison, but 68.9 percent of those sentenced received suspended sentences.[45] One-half of those committed to prison (51.9 percent) were sentenced for a period of less than a month, 20.9 percent from one to three months, 12.5 percent from three to six months. Only 14.7 percent (1,654 persons) were actually committed to prison for six months or more. These short sentences for those confined to prison are even more surprising when one considers that this group has been highly selected. Generally, those who receive an actual prison sentence are those who have previously had one or two suspended sentences, or have committed very serious crimes.

Even these short prison sentences are not always served to completion. Swiss criminal law permits the conditional discharge of those sentenced to more than three months after they have served two-thirds of the sentence, release being left to the judgment of the cantonal officials. It has been estimated that more than one-half of the 2,000 offenders committed annually to more than three months' imprisonment are discharged conditionally after having served two-thirds to three-fourths of the original sentence.[46] Sentence reductions total about 20–25 percent of the original sentences imposed. The average time served, for example, at Regensdorf — the maximum-security prison for the Eastern region, which includes Zürich — is less than a year.

In addition to these short sentences and the shorter time actually served, the nature and general conditions of the Swiss prisons serve as factors that inhibit the growth of crime. The Swiss federal government collects no statistics on prisons and their populations.[47] Consequently, a special study was made of the number, type, capacity, and the average population of Swiss prisons. The data presented here were obtained through correspondence with the various cantons, and although every effort was made to assure both completeness and accuracy of the data, at best they can be only approximations, in view of the diversity of the data. Prison populations are not clearly defined, as there is no official definition of long- and short-term prisons. A few contain some persons awaiting trial and administrative detainees, along with sentenced prisoners. It is the author's opinion, however, that the margin of error is probably small.

Prisons are of small size: The four largest of the prisons for those serving six months or more ("long-term") have capacities of three hundred to four hundred inmates; six others hold between one hundred and three hundred; others, between fifty and one hundred; and one, less than fifty inmates.[48] Size is somewhat misleading, however, inasmuch as the prisons operate considerably below capacity. As a total, an average of only 60.1 percent of the long-term prisons' capacities were used during the year. Five prisons operated at an average 75 percent of capacity; seven, between 50 and 75 percent, and two at under 50 percent of capacity. There are three young-adult institutions (ages 18 to 25), with an average population of 103. Only two prisons are for women — one in the Geneva area and the other in the German-speaking part of the country — with an average total daily population of 71. There are four prisons for recidivist and habitual offenders.[49] There are also prisons for persons serving short sentences, usually less than six months. Four of these short-term prisons have capacities of 100 to 150, three hold 50 to 100, and 50 have capacities of fewer than 50 inmates.

One of the several factors related to the small size of Swiss prisons has been their developmental history. Originally, they were small and under individual cantonal control, but as this became too expensive they were increasingly developed and administered under joint canton compacts (Concordats) involving three regions: Eastern (eight cantons); Northwestern (eleven); and Central (six). There are no federal prisons for the country as a whole, whereas all Swedish prisons are under federal control. Most juveniles who require some type of custodial care are placed in private institutions — which also serve as residences for "difficult" juveniles — or private homes, so they can continue their schooling.

The smallness of these institutions is probably conducive to a prison regime that appears not to be extremely harsh, and this may well be an important factor underlying criminal careers in burglary, theft, or robbery. One study has indicated that prison regimes in most of the institutions are liberal, few inmates presenting a real security risk. Günther Stratenwerth concludes that Swiss prison inmate subculture seems not to be highly developed.[50] An informal atmosphere generally prevails in these small prisons, particularly if they are compared with those in most countries. First-offender institutions are usually open, although there are closed institutions for recidivists. Even the maximum-security prison for the Eastern District was found to be relaxed, with much less emphasis on security than one might expect. Long hairstyles are permitted, and furloughs home are granted after one-half of the sentence is served. Inmates at the prison for first offenders are permitted one weekend's leave or furlough every two months after having served six months. Mail is censored only on a spot-check basis, and an inmate council deals with disciplinary and other matters.

In spite of these positive aspects of the Swiss prisons, the system does not emphasize "therapy" programs for inmates. One might argue that an overemphasis on such professional "treatment" in other countries, particularly in the United States and in Sweden, may contribute indirectly to the development of a criminal self-concept and to a criminal career by making an offender more aware of his being a "criminal." Programs for Swiss inmates emphasize work, either in agriculture or in shops. Long-term inmates can choose an apprenticeship, and the others receive training in several occupations. Long-term prisoners have the possibility of being allowed work release outside of prison, the so-called *semi-liberté,* after eighteen months — or after six months in special cases. Inmates are also permitted to take correspondence courses to improve their educational levels.

In spite of these differences in prison size, the short sentences, and the work programs, the recidivism rate — at least as based on a limited number of studies — appears not to differ greatly from that of other countries. The rate runs between 50 and 70 percent.[51] It must be remembered, however, that Switzerland uses imprisonment primarily for offenders who have been previously committed to prison or for those who have had one or two failures on suspended sentences. Still, one might question how effective a system can be when this high rate of recidivism exists. It does appear, however, that the use of imprisonment has not led to a marked increase in more sophisticated offenses like armed robbery. It has been reported that this has not been the case in Sweden, where the recidivists have been more likely to commit more serious offenses than before. The recidivism rate in Swedish prisons is very high. According to 1972 data, 81 percent of those sentenced to youth prisons committed a new registered offense within three years.[52] It should also be recalled that despite the similarity between Switzerland and Sweden in the use of short sentences and small institutions, a far smaller number of persons (relative to their respective populations) are sentenced to prison in Switzerland, because of the more extensive use of the suspended sentence. Even a short exposure to prison can result in the development of a criminal self-conception and the acquisition of criminal norms. The Swedish government has recognized this problem and has moved recently to reduce further the length of sentences, to diminish the use of imprisonment, and to increase the non-institutional methods of dealing with crime.[53]

Nearly every country in the world has a uniform criminal code, but the United States has a separate criminal code for federal offenses and fifty separate state codes. The establishment of a uniform criminal code nationally was a unique step in Switzerland, a country where the cantons exercise a high degree of autonomy and where federal governmental powers are limited. Through this federal code many cantonal inequities were eliminated in criminal definitions and penalties. However, the administration of the federal criminal law was left to each canton, and there are considerable variations in procedures. This historical development leads one to ask why, if such a uniform criminal code could be established in Switzerland, where government at the national level is far weaker than in the United States, a similar uniform criminal code could not be established in the United States as well — as at present many gross inequities exist in penalties, as well as in the legal definitions of offenses. Such a uniform code could provide greater fairness to United States citizens, as one out of five persons moves annually and hundreds of thousands — if not millions — daily cross state boundaries. At least, disparities in sentences would be minimized by the establishment of a maximum penalty. In many states, sentences of up to thirty or more years are given, and in Illinois, Texas, and some other states they may be for fifty years or longer. As in Switzerland, the administration of the law would be left to the authorities of the individual states. Such a uniform code could be drafted by a commission appointed by the President or by Congress, which might well enact such a code under a broad interpretation of the interstate or general welfare clause of the Constitution.

9. Youth and Swiss society

Property crimes, which constitute the bulk of all serious offenses, reflect primarily a problem of youth. This is the case in all countries today, regardless of the political and social systems involved or how highly developed they may be. The majority of property offenses are committed by a youth under the age of 18 years, or at most 20. Even older persons engaged in more serious criminal activities such as burglary and robbery generally have histories of having begun these activities at an early age. Several important factors underlie this fact, which has been well established in many studies. The modern urban world has become separated primarily by age or peer groups and a decline in intergenerational communication. The greater impersonality of the urban setting has increasingly produced a weakening of the social controls over youth that are ordinarily exercised through the family, the neighborhood, or the community. As a result, an increasingly distinct youth subculture has developed, with its own styles of dress, music, and forms of recreation and excitement. Youth groups often look upon crime as an exciting adventure, particularly because it involves the risks of danger and the challenge of breaking the law. Attitudes favorable to crime are acquired primarily through companions and through participation in small, intimate groups such as youth gangs. Many studies of youth, as well as older offenders, have established the view that most ordinary crime arises through the adoption of deviant norms, and particularly from the tutelage of others.[1] Groups and gangs serve to define criminal activities as excitement and to furnish informal training in techniques and rationalizations for this behavior to the new members.

One of the major explanations of Switzerland's lower crime rate is that it has a considerably lower percentage of offenders among its youth. This generalization was ascertained through a comparison of Swiss youth crime rates with those of other countries, all of which have approximately the same proportion of youth in the age group 14–20. The percentage of youthful offenders is lower in Switzerland than in the

United States, the Federal German Republic, or England and Wales, but not as low as in Austria.[2] Swiss youth offenders are also somewhat older (in the age group of 18—20) than are offenders in other highly developed countries. As yet, crime has not seriously involved the younger groups, as it has in Sweden and Scotland, where the typical offender is aged 14; in the United States, Denmark, and Japan, where the modal age is 15; or in Canada, where the age is 16.[3] Furthermore, Switzerland has almost no real organized youth gang behavior, and there is far greater conformity in the younger age groups than is found in most Western European countries. This is probably due primarily to the fact that there has been less alienation and unrest among the Swiss youth, as well as greater communication between the young and the adult population. Each of these issues will be examined separately.

Less youth crime

Although everywhere the proportion of youth involved in property crime is large, the crime rates for Swiss youth aged 14 to 18 are generally not high. A study of convictions between 1950 and 1961 showed that offenders in Switzerland, the Federal German Republic, and Austria were more likely to be older (17 to 20), while those in Sweden and in England and Wales tended to be younger (14 to 17).[4] A study of 498 criminal cases handled by the Basel High Court in 1960 found most offenders to be in the 20—30 age group.[5] Youth crime, not including traffic offenses, increased by one-half (50.5 percent) between 1964 and 1968 in the Federal German Republic, and in Baden-Württemberg, 53.2 percent.[6] A more recent study reported that one-fourth of all crimes in the Federal German Republic, excluding traffic offenses, were committed by persons in the 14—20 age group, and 14.1 percent were committed by persons in the 14—17 group.[7] The same study showed that above-average increases in robbery have occurred in the 14—17 age group.[8] A study in Sweden showed that the number of offenders per 100,000 persons registered by the police in the age group 15—17 had quadrupled between 1935 and 1967, going from a rate of 316 to 1,216 per 100,000.[9]

Although in the United States the typical offender in conventional crime is under the age of 18 and in Sweden under the age of 16, the typical offender in Switzerland is likely to be over 18, and even 20. The fact that the younger age groups in Switzerland do not engage in crime

Table 9.1. *Percentages of selected self-reported committed criminal acts by Zürich sample of 707 males, aged 15—19, 1973[a]*

Delinquency	Never	Once or twice	Three or four times	Five or more times	No answer
Burglary or attempted burglary	86	10	2	1	0.3
Theft of items worth Sw. F. 5—50 ($2—17)	56	28	8	8	0.5
Theft of money from someone or someplace	56	27	7	9	0.4
Use of car without owner's permission	87	9	1	3	—
Vandalism of public or private property	26	36	16	23	—

[a] Decimals are rounded to the nearest number, which results in some instances of totals not always being 100 percent.
Source: John Casparis and Edmund W. Vaz, *Swiss Society and Youth Culture* (Leiden: E. J. Brill), 1978, Chapter 5.

to the extent that they do in other countries considerably reduces the total amount of crime in the country. If one compares data on certain crimes, the implications become more evident. In the United States, for example, a third (32 percent) of all arrests for robbery in 1972 were of youths under 18, as were one-half of all burglary arrests (51 percent), serious larceny (50 percent), and auto theft (54 percent).[10] Marked comparisons exist between the United States, for example, and Switzerland for serious crimes of murder and nonnegligent manslaughter by youth. In 1971 there were no convictions for these offenses in the age group under 18 in Switzerland, but in the United States in 1972, 11 percent of those arrested for crimes in this category were under 18.[11]

In a self-report study (in which the persons answered questions about themselves anonymously) made in 1973 by John Casparis and Edmund W. Vaz of 707 males aged 15 to 19 in Zürich — respondents widely distributed by social class — a large proportion, ranging from 26 to 86 percent, reported never having engaged in any crimes.[12] (See Table 9.1.) Half of them had never even stolen small articles valued at between Sw. F. 5 to Sw. F. 50 ($2 to $17) or money. Almost 90 percent had never committed a burglary or used an auto without permission, and three-fourths had never carried a weapon or smoked marijuana. In another study of youth in Zürich canton in 1973 an even lower percentage of marijuana smokers was found.[13]

Everywhere most autos are primarily stolen by youth. In the United States, for example, generally about one-half are stolen by a person under the age of 18, and three-fourths by someone under 21, as is shown in the reports issued annually by the Federal Bureau of Investigation of the U.S. Department of Justice. In Switzerland the police in Basel estimated the percentage of autos stolen by youth under the age of 20 to be about 80, whereas the Zürich police estimated the percentage at about 90. Still, the country has a low auto theft rate. Rates are increasing and will continue to increase as more youths steal autos for joyrides. It is difficult to make comparisons of youth involvement in this particular offense, however, because of the differences in the ages legally established for licenses to drive autos. Swiss youth are legally forbidden to operate a motor vehicle until age 18; the age for licensing is generally 16 in the United States. Any 18-year-old in Switzerland who has ever been convicted of a crime is required to wait until he is 20 to obtain a license. It is illegal for anyone to teach another to drive until the person has had his own license to drive for a year. These strict licensing regulations, and the lack of driving experience for many Swiss youth, may serve as inhibiting factors in auto theft and in crime generally, particularly in view of the importance attached to the permission to drive a motor vehicle in all modern industrial societies. It is possible, on the other hand, that the restriction on driving before the age of 18 may make the stealing of an auto more novel to an underage youth.

Vandalism is perhaps the most typical of all youth offenses in Western countries. This offense, however, appears not to constitute a major problem in Switzerland. In the canton and city of Bern, for example, only 4 percent of the approximate 4,000 cases coming before the juvenile prosecutor in 1971 involved vandalism. In Basel-Stadt, only 5.4 percent of the 1,643 juvenile and youth cases handled by youth officials were vandalism cases. An analysis of vandalism cases in the canton of Bern from 1963 to 1972 indicated an increase in the rates, but the annual increases, as measured by correlation and regression coefficients, were unusually small.[14] Only one-fourth of the Zürich youth sample studied by Casparis and Vaz, however, reported that they had never committed an act of vandalism — although the definition of public and private vandalism was very broad and was likely to include minor, as well as major vandalism of private property, such as "broken windows or street lights, destroyed gardens or flower beds, cutting up of automobile tires, etc."

A particularly striking difference in Swiss vandalism is its relative absence in relation to public property. One rarely sees damaged seats, windows, or signs on street cars, trains, or buses; seldom are traffic and road signs defaced or destroyed. With the exception of occasional political slogans on billboards or walls, one also seldom sees graffiti in the form of writing or drawings on walls. A significant indication of the low level of vandalism in the country is the limited amount of either defacement or theft from the numerous automatic vending machines of all types located throughout the large Swiss cities. All tram and bus tickets in these cities must either be purchased from (or coupon tickets validated by) automatic ticket dispensing machines; Zürich alone has more than 1,000 such machines. In addition, telephone booths in large numbers are located throughout the cities — many in isolated areas — and innumerable "automats" dispense items such as food and notions. Although they contain many products and often large sums of money, rarely are they damaged or broken into.

In the United States, on the other hand, the malicious destruction of public property by juveniles and youth groups constitutes a major problem. In 1972 vandalism constituted 2 percent of all arrests in the country: Forty-four percent were committed by persons under 15, and 71 percent by those under 18. In the Federal German Republic, vandals known to the police increased from 39,985 in 1965 to 54,083 in 1971, and the percentage of juvenile offenders involved increased from 44 to 55 percent. According to informed persons consulted in Sweden in 1973, vandalism has become increasingly common. Particularly serious has been the damage or destruction of road signs, street lights, bus and tram seats, and telephone booths. The police have estimated that the annual damage reported from vandalism in Stockholm alone is between Kr. 7 million and Kr. 8 million, about $1.5 million. Destruction of the Stockholm bus stop signs, bus equipment, and damage to the underground train system totaled more than Kr. 1 million (about $250,000) in 1970. Our study of Swedish statistics covering the period 1965—72 showed a 50.3 percent increase in vandalism rates, a high correlation with the time trend, and a substantial annual increase, as measured by the regression coefficient. The situation is almost identical in Stockholm, Göteborg, and Malmö.

Little organized youth or adult gang behavior

Although group activity does play an important role in Swiss youth crime, highly organized youth gang activity like that in many large American and European cities is insignificant in Switzerland. A detailed study of seventy youth offenders in Geneva revealed that a third (34 percent) of all offenses involved groups; but these were rarely organized gangs, and there was considerable variation in the role of the groups by type of offense.[15] Almost always, burglary was committed in pairs or a group, autos and bicycles were rarely stolen alone, and 40 percent of the cases of thefts of money involved groups. On the other hand, three-fourths (74 percent) of simple thefts of objects were committed alone. A study of adjudicated youth offenders in Zürich revealed that athough offenses were often committed with others, only infrequently did the groups constitute a gang in the Swiss legal sense.[16] Under the Swiss Criminal Code (Article 137.2) a *Bande* ("gang") is legally defined as two or more offenders who work together, and offenders can be handled under this category as a more serious form of theft or robbery.[17]

An important characteristic of organized gang behavior is a certain degree of permanence in the association of the group members who engage in criminal activities. They usually give themselves a name, make decisions about the division of work, and choose a leader. Such subcultural delinquency in the form of gang activity is extensive in the United States and somewhat extensive in Sweden.[18] Group behavior of this type, however, appears to be minimal in Switzerland. So small is their number that most youth gangs in the large cities are generally known by name to the police and their activities are reported in the newspapers. In fact, Sylvia Staub, in studying the formation and typology of juvenile gangs, used a technique of examining all newspaper reports containing references to youth gangs in the country during the period 1958–63.[19] She found that a total of only thirty-one such gangs had had police contacts throughout the entire country, distributed as follows: seventeen in Zürich; eleven in other large cities, and three in rural areas. She also studied all juvenile offenders who had been subject to an investigation by the Zürich youth prosecutor between 1956 and 1960. Only eight identifiable groups were found; only four of them were organized criminal gangs, the remainder being more or less loosely formed groups.[20] Most of their offenses involved stealing and damaging property, such as auto theft, motorcycle and spare parts thefts, shoplifting, and thefts from parking meters and locker rooms. Their offenses had not involved much planned crime and were chiefly characterized by efforts to have fun together during their spare time. In 1974 the Zürich police commission reported that seventeen juvenile gangs were known to the police, all of them under the age of 18.[21] This would indicate no marked change in the situation during the last decade. Most of these known gangs were generally not highly organized, with the exception of a gang movement of older youths, the "Rockers," who will be discussed shortly.

Even less gang activity appears to exist in other Swiss cities. A study was made in Geneva of one hundred boys, aged 14 to 17, who appeared before the youth penal court between 1965 and 1966, primarily on theft charges (85 percent). This report stated that "absolutely no organized gang behavior as such" was found. Although three-fourths (77 percent) of their illegal acts were committed in groups of twos or threes, the groups were never structured, permanent, or hierarchical; rather, they were simply small, temporary groups of friends who were not primarily or permanently organized for the purpose of committing illegal acts such as theft.[22] The youth prosecutor in Bern stated that youth gangs there have little continuity, most of them remaining as a group for no more than a year. The head of the youth police in Basel stated that no more than five or six organized youth gangs existed in the entire city. The Basel youth prosecutor said that during 1972 he had dealt with only two youth gangs, neither of which consisted of more than five or six persons and which largely engaged in theft, auto theft, and occasionally a minor assault. Youth prosecutors in Lugano and in Locarno, in Italian Switzerland, reported no organized juvenile gangs.

Inquiries about organized youth crime in Switzerland inevitably elicit references to the Rockers, a general term used to encompass more specific groups called Hell's Angels, Black Panthers, Silverbirds, and the like. Their activities began in about 1969, having spread to Switzerland from the Federal German Republic, where they had first appeared in Hamburg from around 1964 — mostly molesting pedestrians and damaging property.[23] Their activities attracted much attention in the press and in public discussions throughout Switzerland. Their activities were associated, in part, with the antiestablishment youth revolt that was taking place then in that country, as well as elsewhere throughout the world. For the most part, they were members of motorcycle gangs who wore special black leather clothing and carried weapons such as chains and flick knives. They liked to act tough, engage in fights, and threaten to assault strangers, and sometimes they used extortion to demand money from restaurants and bars. They generally did not commit burglary.[24] Members of the Swiss gangs, who were primarily aged 16–25, came from no particular social class and, in Zürich, from no special part of the city. Their total membership probably did not exceed a hundred in the entire country, but much police activity was directed against them, and they were heavily prosecuted. Although little remains today of this gang phenomenon, it is to this group that most Swiss refer when asked about organized gang activities. The tremendous publicity and concern about them, however, is indicative of the relative lack of organized gangs of the more conventional type.

Although research on the subject has been extremely limited, a wide variety of respondents were in agreement that Switzerland has almost no adult criminal gangs or organized crime comparable in any way to that found in cities like London, Paris, Hamburg, Bremen, and Marseilles. Where adult gangs are found in Swiss cities, they are quite likely to have come from outside the country and generally remain only long enough to engage in criminal activities. Without much adult organized gang behavior — except, perhaps, in the area of white-collar crime — it may be assumed that both the extent of crime and the sophisticated nature of offenses such as robbery would be much less than in countries where the reverse situation exists.

Youth conformity and communication between youth and adults

The urbanization process in industrialized societies is usually associated with, and, in fact, aids in bringing about, a breakdown of social controls over youth. As the process develops and peer groups are formed, communication between the groups diminishes and the youth become increasingly alienated from the adult generation and from their families. This process appears to have been limited in Switzerland, although it is developing, and this has had an important bearing on the lower crime rate found among the youth. For example, a study in a large Swiss city found that a decline in the bonds of conventional reference groups such as the family and the school has had an effect on the extent of delinquency.[25]

There appear to have been more opportunities to bridge the generation gap, and, as a result, the youth are less separated from their elders. This does not mean that there is not some youth unrest or that they do not seek a degree of independence: They are just not as often alienated as they are in many Western European societies. Of great significance is the fact that some studies indicate that young Swiss persons, unlike many adolescents elsewhere, do not necessarily prefer their peers to adults as significant others.

One recent study of Swiss youth and society concluded that greater conformity was found, and less unrest, among the youth than in many other European countries.[26] The authors, all of whom were sociologists, stated that in spite of some active agitation in some cities, youth in Switzerland "present a rather calm and peaceful image when one compares them with the more explosive actions of youth in other countries."[27] A 1970 study of urban youth who attended a large youth center in Zürich showed that youth revolt had not progressed far and that those who had participated in such revolt were among the more "far out" and independent urban youth.[28] Various measures used in this study revealed no great youth solidarity, little alienation, and few noticeably unconventional ideas.

Two explanations might be offered for this comparative conformity and the lack of serious alienation among the youth.[29] First of all, there appears to be relative harmony in Swiss institutions, backed by a strong desire to compromise conflicting views. Switzerland has the type of democracy that seems to encourage a more continuous discourse between the young and the adults. Young people do not generally contend with problems of employment, or of access to a reasonable level of education.[30] Secondly, and quite a contradictory premise, is the Swiss insistence on youth conformity. A certain formalism exists in the Swiss democracy, local constraints remain strong, traditional models of behavior are powerful, and serious political conflicts are relatively absent. An extensive study on the status of women by Thomas Held and René Levy reveals an underlying conformity in Swiss family structure, a patriarchal system that would be threatened were women to seek more active lives outside the home.[31] Most Swiss marry young, and few women work after marriage, particularly after the birth of the first child. Working women belong largely to lower economic groups. For the most part, the Swiss woman is a homemaker who supervises the children and the household yet remains subservient to her husband in questions of educational and disciplinary matters. Switzerland probably has the smallest proportion of married working women of all the affluent industrial societies in the Western world. As compared with about 50 percent in the United States and Sweden, only 29 percent of Swiss married women aged 15—64 were working, according to the 1970 census. The percentage of foreign married women working was 60. The survey by Held and Levy found a total of 39 percent of Swiss and foreign (Italian) married women were working, but 32.5 percent of them were working for fewer than twenty hours a week. Swiss women were the last women to gain the vote in national elections (1971) in the developed countries (with the exception of the small adjoining country of Liechtenstein, where women still cannot vote). They still do not have the right to vote in cantonal elections in two cantons and some communes. In addition to the conformity stressed in the family situation, the school system also tends to promote youth conformity. As Vaz and Casparis contend:

Compared with Canadian schools Swiss institutions have undergone less change and are hardly "permissive" by our standards. A heavy emphasis is placed on scholarship and discipline is widely institutionalized. . . . The school teacher continues to hold high status, and student-teacher contacts are conducted according to well-established role obligations. Since social distance prevails, a comparatively formal etiquette governs these contacts, and unlike the Canadian high school where teachers perform a variety of roles, the role of "good guy" is not yet available to the Swiss teacher. Swiss schools are concerned mainly with impersonal matters and relatively little organized opportunity exists for extra-curricular activities. Unlike Canadian boys . . . Swiss boys, with their heavy academic load, must often forego many leisure activities and experiences in order to achieve future goals. Swiss boys who do find plenty of time for extra-curricular activities are often those who have left school early and become apprenticed to a trade.[32]

The model stressing youth conformity is probably an overemphasis, however. Within recent years several cantons have rejected lowering the voting age from 20, and some 40 percent of a sample of Zürich canton youths aged 15—25 (studied by Robert Blancpain and Erich Häuselmann in 1973) indicated a belief that they did not have enough rights.[33] A separate youth culture has been emerging, however, and a wider use of marijuana and hashish has been evidenced. In their 1973 study of Zürich city youth Casparis and Vaz reported that they found a youth culture forming similar to that found in Europe and North America, although not as yet as well developed as in many other countries.[34] This youth culture, they believe, is an inevitable natural product of an urban industrial society and of a metropolitan center such as Zürich. Their research indicates that this emerging youth culture is not necessarily a product of the frustrations of adolescents, quasi-adults who are alienated against society and family. It is of significance, however, that although they found the degree of involvement in the growing youth culture to be indicative of a somewhat strong and constant relation to such deviance as gambling, illicit sexual intercourse, drinking, and smoking marijuana, it has not, as yet, led to marked involvement in property crime.

Support for the hypothesis that Swiss youth continue to be more integrated into the general society than they are in most similar societies is perhaps better shown in a study made in 1973 of a representative sample of Zürich canton young persons between 15 and 25.[35] *About three-fourths (77 percent) of the youth preferred to participate in a group that is heterogeneous with respect to age.* In another study only 1 percent of a stratified nonrepresentative sample drawn from the larger study indicated popularity among the peer group to be the most important of five given items.[36]

Although Swiss youth may be on the verge of becoming more emancipated and more peer-oriented, it is also possible that a "hyperconformism" may be developing. One cannot be certain, nor can one determine precisely, about the trend for Swiss youth without further studies of adult society and the effect it has upon the youth society — including the extent to which it encourages a rupture with youth. The 1973 study in Zürich canton found that although Swiss youth are showing increasing political unrest, they regard manifest agitation as of little importance.[37] Still, the data do not indicate a strong consensus on conformity, as only 46 percent of the sample highly regarded conformity and no more than 30 percent supported the *status quo* in Switzerland. In a society in the process of social change it is extremely important to know to what degree, when, and how, the youth will align itself more to confrontation or more to rigid conformity.[38] In this connection Blancpain and Häuselmann have suggested three processes that will be decisive in an increase of political unrest among youth in Switzerland. These factors will undoubtedly also affect the crime situation and other deviant behavior:

1. The expansion of the educational system, i.e., a certain increase and equalization of educational opportunity. With this expansion. the older generation attempts to maintain the legitimacy of the institution and the legitimacy of social stratification based on education. At the same time, the expansion politicizes high school and university students.
2. The increasing saturation of traditional values, institutionalized as a high individual standard of living. This contributes to a growing illegitimacy of the status-giving institutions, including educational institutions, which are oriented toward the needs of the economy, and this in turn promotes the search for new values.

3. The decreasing legitimacy of age stratification, accompanied by escalating generational conflict.[39]

In addition to the general social structure that tends to strengthen the status quo, other factors are important in maintaining more family solidarity and contacts between age groups and more conformity in the family. Although care must be exercised in overemphasizing one aspect of Swiss life, certain traditions act to bridge the gaps between age groups. The long and important tradition of out-of-doors activities that is continued throughout the year and into the older years has resulted in joint activities of all kinds throughout life. Teenaged, and even older youth often travel with their parents and other adults to hike and ski in the mountains, and they participate in non-sports-related endeavors as well. Traditionally, in rural Switzerland annual *Alpenfestes* of sports and singing that involve all age groups are still held. Regardless of age, the Swiss often participate in gymnastics, hiking, skiing, various individual competitions like wrestling, and group singing. A 1964 study in the entire country of a representative sample of 1,808 Swiss youth (army recruits) aged 20 showed that 86.8 percent of young men interviewed were sports-minded.[40] The German-Swiss youth appear to be more sports-minded than either the French- or the Italian-Swiss. Of all activities in which they regularly engaged, the five leading ones were swimming (48.2 percent), skiing (42.3 percent), skating (20.8 percent), soccer (19.1 percent), and target shooting (18.7 percent). (See Table 9.2.) Regular participation in team sports was reported in gymnastics (19.9 percent) and soccer (14.2 percent).

Another factor of significance in the maintenance of more open lines of communication between generations is the greater tendency for youth in their early twenties to continue to live with their parents in the cities while they are going to school or working. They are accustomed to associating with older persons, and Swiss youth are frequently seen drinking beer and wine in association with older men in cafes, taverns, and in other public gatherings. Of even greater significance is Switzerland's long tradition of a largely citizen army. All males between the ages of 20 and 50 (previously, it was 55; this age remains only for officers) are supposed to serve as members of the army unless they are exempted.[41] This produces a great deal of interaction between the youth and the adult men.

Switzerland has no professional army, as such, although there is a small cadre of professional military personnel consisting primarily of 1,600 training and noncommissioned officers, a small contingent of pi-

Table 9.2. *Rank order of the ten principal sports engaged in regularly[a]*
among Swiss youth, taking into account seasonal conditions

Sports	%
1. Swimming	48.2
2. Skiing	42.3
3. Skating	20.8
4. Football (soccer)	19.1
5. Target shooting (300 m)	18.7
6. Athletics (gymnastics)	17.9
7. Cycling	14.8
8. Mountain climbing	14.6
9. Tennis	10.6
10. Boating (sailing, etc.)	10.0

[a] Several times a month
Source: Pierre Arnold, Michel Bassand, Bernard Crettaz, and Jean Kellerhals,
Jeunesse et Société: Premiers Jalons pour une Politique de la Jeunesse (Lausanne:
Payot, 1971), p. 177.

lots (most are civilians), frontier and military installation guards, plus
the administrative and technical employees of the ministry of defense.
The citizen army is divided into three age groups — those aged 20 to 32
(Auszug), 33 to 42 (Landwehr), and 43 to 50 (Landsturm). All groups
serve a certain number of days in the army, a total of approximately
330 days in a lifetime. At the age of 20 (depending upon circumstances,
the recruiting age can range from age 19 to 22) each physically able
Swiss male must serve in the "school of recruits" (Rekrutenschule) a
total of seventeen weeks, and until he is age 33 he must receive military
training — eight courses of twenty days each, often on summer or winter maneuvers. During the next ten years he serves three courses of thirteen days each, but then from age 43 to 50 he is required to serve only
one period of thirteen days. The requirements of time served for officer
candidates are much longer, the periods served increasing considerably
for the higher officer ranks. The Swiss have no military academy; each
officer serves first as an enlisted man and noncommissioned officer, a
procedure that tends to reduce social distance in the armed forces. Due
to their better education, however, officers usually are drawn from the
upper-middle and upper classes.[42]

Throughout Switzerland, both in summer and in winter, one constantly sees thousands of citizen soldiers of varying ages on the move together on the trains, in truck convoys, or on foot maneuvers on the roads. In addition, persons of military age, and particularly the older age groups who do go on military duty, participate in regular army drills and routine target practice in local areas. Target installations are located in settled communities of all sizes, and they are used regularly each week, particularly on the weekend. Premilitary age groups — those aged 16 to 19 — often participate in target practice under the direction of older persons. Restaurants and drinking places display community awards and team trophies for target shooting and other activities, particularly sports events. Each Swiss citizen keeps his personal military equipment in his own home, and he is responsible for its proper maintenance. This equipment consists of an automatic rifle and twenty-four rounds of ammunition — or a revolver, in the case of an officer. As a result, much activity associated with the proper care of weapons, target practice, or conversations about military activities become common in the family. All of this, together with the other varied activities carried out in Switzerland across age lines, has served to inhibit the age separation, alienation, and growth of a separate youth culture that has increasingly become characteristic of the United States, Sweden, and many other highly developed countries. Although these factors represent only one aspect of a total Swiss way of life, they play no small part in the low crime rate and crime trend.

10. Crime and the foreign worker

Swiss citizens are generally convinced that the foreign worker is far more inclined to commit crimes than is a native-born Swiss. Studies have shown this belief.[1] It is also reflected in conversations with the Swiss people and in the letters written to the newspapers. This opinion is understandable, as foreign workers might well be expected to be affected by several factors closely associated with the commission of crimes. They come from the lower classes in their own countries, and they largely make up the lower class in Switzerland. They find themselves surrounded by affluence, and they know that penalties for criminal offenses are usually much less severe than in their native countries. They also belong, for the most part, to the age group between 17 and 30 that constitutes a large part of the offenders. In addition, as will be pointed out, they are economically, politically, and socially discriminated against, and they are more subject to arrest and prosecution.

The foreign worker

Switzerland has the largest percentage of foreign residents of any European country.[2] In 1972 approximately 1 million persons – almost 17 percent of the population, or one of every six persons – were non-Swiss. Although some are simply foreigners residing in the country, most of them are workers, largely semiskilled or unskilled laborers. A small percentage of the foreign workers are highly skilled, and there are also managers and employees of foreign firms, as well as foreign doctors, professors, and students. The laborers come largely from the southern European countries – many Spaniards and some Greeks, Turks, and Yugoslavs – but the majority (55 percent) are Italians.[3] The total foreign worker group constitutes over 95 percent of the non-Swiss in the country, and the remarks made here about the foreign worker and crime refer to this group. Due to a decline in the economic situation, Switzerland's foreign worker population, as well as that of other European countries, began to decrease in 1974.

136

As measured by occupation and income, these foreign workers constitute 30 percent of the work force and the bulk of the lower class. Others who belong to the lower class are primarily some "pockets" of Swiss who live in poor rural areas and some of the older citizens. The foreign workers are associated with innumerable areas of the economy: Large numbers work in housing, highway and bridge construction, in all types of industrial plants, and in the maintenance and service areas in hotels and garages.[4] A decade or two ago, they were predominantly female — domestics, household maids, or cooks — but since 1970 the ratio has become predominantly male. A recent treaty with Italy and other countries provides that foreign workers may be joined by their families after eighteen months, and when the wife comes she is usually also employed. Since housing is at a premium in those cities where most of the foreigners work, groups of male workers often live together in an apartment, room, or barracks widely scattered throughout the city. It is difficult for them to become citizens in most European countries, but this is even more difficult in Switzerland. Federal laws require a residence of ten years before a permit of domicile can be obtained: A residence of twelve years enables a foreigner to apply for citizenship. Federal, cantonal, and communal authorities have also established other requirements, such as character references. Special provisions are made for the children born in Switzerland or if a foreigner is married to a Swiss citizen.

A significant difference can be seen in the role of the foreign worker in Sweden and Switzerland. These groups remain much less isolated in Sweden, where they constitute about 7 percent of the total population, than they do in Switzerland, where they made up 17 percent of the population. In fact, in Sweden they are encouraged to become citizens, a status rarely conferred upon the Swiss foreign worker. Sweden's 1976 partial political enfranchisement of long-term foreign alien residents, without citizenship, was without precedent in the world. In 1977 nearly 59 percent of the 218,000 eligible aliens resident in Sweden voted in the local elections.

In Switzerland even those foreign workers who have lived in the country for prolonged periods of time remain largely an outgroup, socially, economically, and politically discriminated against by the Swiss people. They live chiefly in the German-speaking area, where the cultural milieu is entirely different from their own, and only rarely do they become fluent in the local language. Many have had only a limited education: One study showed that 47.2 percent of the Italian workers in Switzerland had received no more than five years of education.[5] The Greek workers tend to have about the same educational level as the Italians; the Yugoslavs, more; the Turks, less. They work in the lowest-paid jobs, generally the hard, dirty, menial tasks that the Swiss are not willing to do. However, they are usually paid regular Swiss wage rates for the same type of work, rates that are much higher than those paid in their own countries. In 1973, for example, they earned between Sw. F. 900 and Sw. F. 1200 a month (and even more in some cases) and, in addition, they receive workmen's compensation and social security benefits. They find living costs high, but by economizing, the typical single foreign worker can send large amounts of his earnings back home to his family. If he remains long enough in the country he can improve his financial situation but generally not his occupational mobility, a state of affairs that cannot be explained on the basis of any governmental restrictions. Hans Joachim Hoffmann-Nowotny's comparative study of the Swiss and the foreign workers showed that about two-thirds of the native Swiss feel that the Swiss prefer to fill supervisory positions with Swiss. This view was also reflected by the Italian workers, 75 percent of whom felt this to be the case even after a worker had lived there for more than ten years.

Hoffman-Nowotny's study, in which five hundred Italian workers were compared with a similar number of native-born Swiss, showed that the foreign workers entered the Swiss occupational and social structure at the lowest level. As a result, a new social stratum has been developed, one generally lower than the lowest stratification structure of native-born Swiss, thus automatically elevating large segments of the native Swiss population in the social structure. Although this transition and elevation occur in an uneven manner, an upsurge of the familiar tensions that characterize stratified societies has developed, tensions that are then projected upon the foreign workers as a powerless minority. In this process many Swiss frequently perceive the immigrants either as a submerged, or even as a manifest threat, and their fears give rise to the various strategies directed against the foreign worker. In attempts made to deny him occupational integration and mobility, for example, rules may be made to specify certain special skills as prerequisites for various occupational positions. Other discriminatory attempts can be seen in various social and political spheres, and some measures are sufficiently extreme to force a foreign worker to return to his native county. A further type of discrimination can only be described, from a sociological point of view, as "neofeudal" in nature. Often, the native Swiss sets himself so apart, psychologically, from the foreign worker that even though he is allowed to remain in the country, the neofeudal distance that has developed between him and the Swiss denies him any possibility of integration and eventual assimilation into the society.[6]

Interviews with the Italian workers showed not only that they were generally employed in the lowest positions, in terms of occupation and income, but also that the majority of them belonged to the lower socioeconomic stratum in the country from which they had emigrated. Most of them also came from the least developed areas in Italy. Hoffmann-Nowotny has stated:

In other words, a group of people who were marginal in their country of origin remain marginal in the country of immigration. While the situation of the immigrants has improved from an individual point of view, it has remained unchanged in structural terms. With regard to other factors, their marginal situation is worse in the immigration than in the emigration context. These factors are, for instance, the incompleteness of families, the impossibility to choose occupations freely, the lack of political rights, and the insecurity implied by limited residence permits.[7]

Low crime rate of the foreign worker

Research studies show that the total crime rate is generally lower, however, for the foreign workers than for the Swiss; for certain offenses it is slightly higher. One study, for example, reported that although many persons believed that the foreign-born commit more crimes than the native Swiss, they are actually, as a rule, less criminal.[8] One of the best-known studies, done by Jean Graven, found that Italian workers commit fewer crimes than the general population.[9] The overall rate was 441 per 100,000 for the Swiss, as compared to 315 for the foreign workers, but the rate for the Italian workers, who constitute the bulk of them, was even lower. Actually, the differential was much lower, because most foreign workers are young men who are potentially the most criminal. More recently, Komitee Schweiz 80, which has as its primary interest the improvement of relations between foreigners (particularly foreign workers) and the Swiss people, reported that foreign groups, including workers, foreign nonworkers resident for one year or more, and tourists, had been involved in convictions slightly more than the native Swiss (63 percent, as compared with 42 percent).[10] A study was also made in Geneva of Italian workers, whose crime rate, as measured by court records over a ten-year period, was found to be slightly higher than the native Swiss, but was considerably lower when a similar comparison was made with the cantons of Fribourg and Valais.[11]

One cannot be certain, of course, that the foreign workers fully report crimes among themselves that might lead to convictions, and this might influence the validity of statistics based on convictions. Police officials express two points of view on this question. Some feel that many do not report crimes, due to fear of having to deal with the police, fear of possible deportation either for themselves or for the offender, their inability to cope with the language problems involved, or even fear of possible revenge. Others believe that the foreign workers largely do report crimes, because most offenses involve theft, and the loss of any possessions means much to them. Officials holding this view believe that little serious assault occurs among this group; at least, only a few cases of serious assault became known to the authorities. The most definitive solution to these conflicting opinions was the 1973 crime victimization survey made in Zürich that revealed foreign workers to be less likely to be victims of crime than the Swiss and also that they report offenses as frequently as do the Swiss. (Chapter 5.) Jürg Neumann has made the most extensive, and also perhaps the most definitive study of crime among foreign workers.[12] Included in his study were both seasonal and resident Italian workers who had permits to stay (*Aufenthalter*), but he excluded resident workers living in the country for ten or more years, because population data were unavailable. He based his study on official statistics on crime convictions. He concluded that the Italian worker's rate of criminality was no higher than that of the other population and that, in fact, it was surprisingly low, in view of the fact that they came from a country known to have higher rates of crime, that they live in Switzerland under often difficult conditions, and that they are generally separated from their families.[13] The offenses for which they were convicted were less serious than those of the Swiss population at large, as indicated by the methods used to handle them.[14] An average of 43.2 percent of the Italian worker cases — as compared to only 26.4 percent of the remaining Zürich cases — were handled by the prosecuting attorney who customarily deals with petty offenses, rather than by referral to the district court for prosecution.

If Neumann's data are examined by type of offense, considerable differences appear. Rates are much lower for the Italian workers in some cases and much greater than that of the Swiss citizens in others. In 1960 the rate of the foreign workers for crimes "against body and life" were slightly less (34.9 per 100,000, as compared to 35.5), but their involvement in criminal homicide was extremely rare.[15] Their rates for assault, however, were slightly higher. Neumann questioned the actual significance of these data, inasmuch as simple assault is prosecuted on complaint only, and the Swiss are more likely to proceed with criminal charges against an Italian foreign worker than they would against a native Swiss.[16] The overall property offense rates were slightly higher for the Italian worker sample (234.5 per 100,000, as compared with 210.6 for the remaining population). They had a higher larceny rate (187.0, compared to 126.2), but a large proportion of their thefts involved shoplifting.[17] Another study found the shoplifting rate of the foreign worker to be three times as large as that of the native Swiss.[18] The value of the objects stolen, however, was less than that of those stolen by the Swiss. For the native Swiss shoplifter the average value of stolen goods was Sw. F. 12.91; it was Sw. F. 9.62 for the Italian workers and Sw. F. 10.64 for the Spanish.

For sex offenses the male Italian foreign worker's rate was slightly lower than that of the Swiss — 100.4, as compared to 104.3. Nearly three-fourths (71 percent, compared with 67 percent) of all these offenses constituted statutory rape, and there were few cases of forcible rape. Statutory rape involves sexual intercourse with a legally underage female with or without her consent. The high rates of statutory rape by foreign workers were probably due to the differences in the legal and cultural systems of the two countries. In Italy, for example, sexual intercourse with a female under the age of 14 is statutory rape, whereas in Switzerland the upper limit is 16 years of age. The minimum age for marriage in Italy and Switzerland is 14 and 18, respectively. In Italy, moreover, statutory rape prosecution occurs only when the father of the girl brings criminal charges. On the whole, many foreign workers may be unfamiliar with these legal differences, a fact not often taken into account in the courts.[19] Prostitution by women is not a crime in Switzerland, although male prostitution is. It is said that prostitution affords certain advantages, as its availability to the foreign worker diminishes the danger of sexual assaults on Swiss women and children by these unattached males.[20]

Explanation of the low crime rate

The evidence thus indicates that foreign workers generally have no higher total rates of crime than do the Swiss; at the most, their crime rates for some types of crime are only slightly higher. It might be said that this is due to the fact that the very issuance of work permits eliminates persons with a criminal record and that any infraction of the law results in the withdrawal of the permit and subsequent expulsion from Switzerland. Neumann tends to disagree that the Italian workers are a selected noncriminal group, inasmuch as Italian records are not good, criminal registers are not kept up to date, Swiss authorities frequently are not informed of any existing records, and the Swiss courts do not routinely request criminal records in summary cases from the Italian authorities.[21] One possible explanation may have been presented by Hoffmann-Nowotny.[22] He believes that the more general acceptance by the foreign workers of the neofeudalistic discrimination against them shown by the Swiss brings about a reduction in the level of their aspirations. Many simply accept the higher income and the living standards of the Swiss as being distinct from their own, and this tends to diminish their participation in property crime.

A second general explanation of the foreign workers' not having generally higher rates of crime is the nature of the society in which they have come to work. The Swiss social environment generally produces an anticriminal tendency in the foreign worker. Some evidence for this supposition lies in the fact that although the general crime rate of foreign workers is lower than that of the general population in the Federal German Republic, they have a higher rate of murder and assault, the country as a whole having a much higher rate of violence than Switzerland.[23] In Switzerland the foreign worker and his family live in a more law-abiding country, and he is more influenced not to engage in criminal activities than if he were working in a country where crime is more prevalent. The opposite situation has occurred in New York City, where rural migrants from Puerto Rican areas with a low crime rate frequently must reside in high crime rate slum areas and where, consequently, many of the youth become involved in criminal activities.[24] Furthermore, Swiss cities have no slum areas, parts of the city that are generally, in the United States and many other parts of the world, characterized by a slum way of life that involves high rates of crime.[25] This way of life cannot be explained by poverty but by the development, in certain city areas, of a slum culture.[26] Were the migrant worker forced to live in a slum area in order to find cheap housing, he would experience far greater exposure to prevalent illegal norms and behavior patterns than he does in the Swiss cities. In fact, he is presented with only lim-

ited exposure to criminal norms, mostly in the form of prostitution.
Edwin H. Sutherland and Donald R. Cressey have written a major theoretical work in criminology, including available research on situations
similar to this, and they have reached this summary conclusion:

> The extent to which the crime rate of native whites exceeds that of immigrants
> varies with the length of time the immigrants have been in the host country. Both
> immigrants and their sons tend to take on the crime rate of the specific part of the
> community in which they locate. The delinquency rates of the second generation
> are comparatively low when the immigrant group first settles in a community, and
> they increase as contacts with the surrounding culture multiply. The rate remains
> low in those foreign colonies which are comparatively isolated from the surround-
> ing culture.[27]

A recent pilot study carried out by Killias and based on Zürich police
data and Geneva court cases, has shown that the children of foreign-
born workers appear to have a relatively low crime rate, as compared
with Swiss children, until the age of 15.[28] Between the ages of 15 and
18, however, the rate is higher than that of Swiss youth of the same age
group. The crime rate of the second generation, moreover, is higher
than that of their parents. Killias has explained this higher crime rate
on the basis of several Swiss studies which have shown that the children
of immigrants are exposed to great frustrations in school, as the situation in which they are reared differs markedly from that of Swiss children. During their early years the children of the immigrants receive support from their families, but as they become older and participate more
fully in school — and also become integrated into the Swiss labor market — the low status of their families makes it difficult for them to
achieve adequate status positions in Swiss society. Although this interpretation is significant, it does not adequately explain how school frus-
tration itself leads to the acquisition of illegal norms, rather than to
other types of behavior.

Important also in the lower crime rate of the foreign worker is his
relation to Swiss authorities. Each worker recognizes his dependence
upon his permit to enter the country and to continue to live there.
Should he repeat a minor offense, or should he commit a serious one,
he realizes that he can be deported and heavily fined — or imprisoned
— any one of which would mean the loss of his present and future employment, work that has become increasingly lucrative for him. In addition, the Italian worker seems to have great respect for police authority,
a respect no doubt enhanced by his relative lack of familiarity with the

country's customs and with the language. Thus he seeks to avoid contact with the police and with other authorities, a situation that has resulted in the claims advanced by some that prolonged residence in Switzerland tends to make the foreign worker almost overly submissive to authority.[29]

On the other hand, these findings and conclusions are in general accord with those presented in research in the United States and elsewhere, that crime rates among the foreign-born are generally lower than among the native population.[30] Franco Ferracuti reached similar conclusions following his survey for the Council of Europe of all current information available in 1967 on European migration and crime: "The crime rate of European migrants in the host countries, in spite of their greater visibility and probability of stricter reporting, appears to be practically equal or inferior to the rate for the population of the host countries. The high criminality of foreign migrant workers is a xenophobic myth."[31]

Although the matter is still subject to some questioning the likelihood is that Switzerland, as well as other countries, will continue to have low crime rates for its foreign workers. On the other hand, as they become increasingly familiar with their environment and more conscious of their identity, the social controls over them now exercised by the foreign society and by its law enforcement officials may become less important factors. More recently, they have, for example, participated in demonstrations about their treatment in Switzerland, the Federal German Republic, and in France. At the same time, economic developments affecting employment in Switzerland and in other European countries have resulted in a drastic reduction in the immigration of foreign workers. Many foreign workers have been dismissed and have returned to their own countries.

In summary, persons in the lower-class working groups are more vulnerable to higher conventional crime rates. This does not hold true, however, in Switzerland where the foreign worker, who constitutes a large proportion of the lower class, has a crime rate no higher, and usually lower, than the Swiss population. The foreign worker's lower rate of criminal involvement presents a marked contrast with the situation that exists among the lower classes (non-foreign workers) in most countries. This comparatively low involvement in crime among the foreign working class tends to reduce the total crime in the country, as they constitute a large proportion of the population, the largest proportion of any European country. Furthermore, the foreign workers tend to reflect the law-abiding norms of Swiss people in general. Since Sweden also has a considerable proportion of foreign workers, this particular factor obviously is not a crucial variable in the quite different crime situations that exist in the two countries. Also, the Swedish population itself has a high and growing rate of crime, in contrast to the Swiss.

11. Cross-cultural implications of the low Swiss crime rate

From the beginning of this project, several interrelated problems were encountered in trying to establish the hypothesis that Switzerland does have a low crime rate and thus represents an exception to the close relationship between high crime rates and the affluence that results from extensive industrialization and urbanization. First, scientific criminological writings and research are more limited in Switzerland than in any other highly developed Western European nation. There has been only limited interest in criminological research, especially by sociologists, and most of the studies have been in criminal law. Second, the unavailability of statistical data at the federal level, with the exception of convictions, necessitated the collection of other official statistical data, even though serious questions are being raised everywhere today about the validity of official crime statistics. In view of these problems, therefore, it was necessary to conduct a number of independent studies to test the hypothesis of Switzerland's having a low crime rate. The nature and variety of the measures developed for the study represent, in themselves, a contribution to research methodology in comparative criminology.

Studies were made of the degree to which citizens report crimes against them to the police, the degree of governmental concern about crime, public concern about crime in the city of Zürich, the handling of crime news by the newspapers, trends in theft insurance rates and claims, and crime victimization in the city of Zürich. In addition, data on white-collar crime were studied, crime matters were discussed with many informed persons throughout the country, and personal observations were made during a residence of eight months in the country. Wherever possible, efforts were made to compare Swiss crime data with those of the United States and of a number of European countries — particularly Sweden, where the crime problem is serious. Switzerland and Sweden probably have more relevant similarities than differences, as both countries are highly affluent and urbanized, both are democ-

146

racies of approximately the same size population, both have not been engaged in a war for more than a hundred fifty years, and both countries have large proportions of foreign workers. Further comparisons were made with reference to cities. Zürich, for example, was compared with such similarly sized United States cities as Denver, Colorado, and Portland, Oregon, and with Stuttgart in the Federal German Republic.

Findings

Research findings revealed more crime in Switzerland than had been originally anticipated, but the available evidence indicated no serious crime problem. On the whole, ordinary crime presents a far less acute problem than it does in other highly urbanized, affluent countries, and to this extent it may be said to represent an exception to the general pattern of close relationship between crime problems and high degrees of development, urbanization, and affluence. With respect to the hard evidence of Switzerland's low crime rate, findings were sometimes somewhat contradictory, as was also true with regard to trends. At other times the evidence has been somewhat inconclusive. If allowances are made for these occasional inconclusive and contradictory findings, some important and relevant assertions may be made.

1. As determined by several means, no great concern about crime was found in Switzerland. This in itself is markedly different from the situation currently prevailing, for example, in the United States and in Sweden, where both the citizenry and the governments have become alarmingly frightened about crime, particularly in the large cities. Studies of federal government reports and questions raised throughout an eleven-year period in the National Assembly (Federal Parliament), in the Zürich Canton Parliament, and in the Zürich City Council revealed few references to problems of crime. Swiss-German newspapers do not emphasize crime, and were one to use this as one criterion, it might be concluded that crime is not a major problem in the country. This conclusion applies to the amount of space devoted to crime news, the number of stories, and the content of typical crime stories. The Zürich household crime victimization survey indicated that crime ranks low on the list of major civic problems, that citizens do not worry unduly about being alone on city streets at night, and that generally they are not afraid of

crime or of the safety either of their persons or their property. These findings were validated by the general lack of significant differences in attitudes between the Swiss and the foreign-born workers or in groups differing in age, income, or city area. In contrast, Stuttgart residents were more fearful of crime, and Stockholm residents, as well as officials, express great concern about it. Swedish officials state that the Stockholm public is particularly fearful of being assaulted and robbed on the streets at night or in the subways. Far more concern about burglary of apartments and houses is seen in Stockholm, and similar situations exist in many United States cities, as well as elsewhere throughout the world.

2. Studies of police practices, trends in the number of police and relations to the public indicated that official Swiss crime statistics are as adequate as, or perhaps even more reliable than, official statistics in most other countries. Because crime trends were emphazised, some of the problems of using specific rates were minimized. This is an important consideration when cross-national comparisons are involved. In a study of crimes reported to the police in a group of larger cantons and in the larger cities, crime trends, measured by rates, correlations, and regression coefficients, were found either to remain stable or to decline in murder, nonnegligent manslaughter, and in assault. The trend in robbery and auto theft did indicate an increase, but the annual numerical increases were small. Burglary and *Diebstahl* (burglary and theft) have shown substantial increases in rates, but if they are viewed in terms of the amount of numerical increases, the correlations have been minor. Analyses of convictions for crimes against life and limb, property, and morality for the country and for the German-speaking cantons revealed a fairly stable rate — or even one of decline. With respect to trends for specific property offenses, findings were contradictory. In summary, as measured by trends in official statistics, the overall picture was a modest crime problem at the most.

3. When comparisons are made of official crime statistics, the estimated increase in total rates for crimes known to the police (sometimes with adjustments) are found to be lower than those in the United States, Sweden, and the Federal German Republic, as well as a number of other European countries. Attempts to

compare absolute crime rates present problems, but it appears that the absolute rates for Switzerland are generally lower than those of the Federal German Republic. More striking differences in crime data are seen in comparisons with Swedish data. With the exception of auto theft, trend rates were much higher for crimes known to the police in the large Swedish cities than in the Swiss cities. Annual increment increases were much higher in Sweden, even for auto theft. Crime has become a major problem in all categories in Sweden; the number of crimes known to the police increased from 250,000 in 1961 to 550,000 in 1971, with the population remaining about the same. Murder has increased strikingly, and robberies are increasingly common, including armed robberies and bank robberies — both of which had been rare.

4. Switzerland has lower insurance rates for burglary and theft than do similar countries, and the trend was generally lower in the percentage of claims paid to total premium revenues from theft and burglary insurance policies. Auto theft rates are considerably lower than in the surrounding countries and lower than in the United States, on the whole. These findings indicate a generally lower comparable crime rate and a lower trend in crime.

5. Crime victimization rates were generally lower in Zürich than in Stuttgart, a slightly larger city in the southern part of the Federal German Republic where crime rates are generally lower than they are for the country as a whole. Rates for all offenses, with the exception of larceny without contact, were also much lower than in the comparable United States cities of Denver and Portland. In nearly all comparisons, the victimization rates in Zürich were particularly lower for burglary, robbery, and auto theft. Moreover, assault rates were much lower than in Scandinavia, and theft was much lower than in Copenhagen. In general, not only has household and personal theft been lower in Zürich, but the monetary value of most stolen objects has been less than $15. Only rarely are objects of higher value stolen.

6. Informed persons were in complete agreement that Swiss crime rates are considerably lower than those in the Federal German Republic, France, and Italy, countries bordering Switzerland. In agreement with this opinion were such well-informed persons as

professors of criminal law, professors of sociology, police officials, youth and adult prosecutors, and journalists who specialize in crime reporting in the large Swiss cities.

7. Personal observations indicated little need for concern about
the possibility of having a car stolen or broken into anywhere in
the country. Swiss residents appear to take few precautions
against burglary, and they frequently leave articles unattended.
They also carry large sums of cash, and minimal security precautions are in evidence in such places as post offices, where most
money transactions — many of which involve large sums — are customarily carried on. Ticket and vending machines are seldom
broken into. Most surprising of all is the highly effective honor
system used throughout the country for the local tram and bus
transportation systems.

8. In contrast to ordinary crime, crime in business and finance appears to be extensive. This is due primarily to the position of
Switzerland as an international center of business and finance,
to the greater tolerance of these illegal activities by the Swiss
public (as contrasted with their attitude toward ordinary crime),
to the Swiss bank secrecy laws, and to the inability of the cantons to deal effectively with the highly complex nature of white-
collar offenses. Tax violations are extensive, although they do
not generally come under the criminal law.

Explanations

Several explanations may be advanced for this comparative lower incidence of ordinary crime in Switzerland. They include the nature of the
urbanization process, the citizen's relation to government, the accessi-
bility of firearms, together with a low rate of violent crimes, the criminal justice system, the nature of Swiss youth crime, the more open lines
of intergenerational communication, and the low rate of crime among
foreign workers. With reference to urbanization, it was pointed out that
urban growth has been slow, that the Swiss cities have never become
extremely large, and they do not have real slums. Political decentralization of the government is significant, particularly at the cantonal and
communal levels. At these levels, the individual citizen plays an important role in the government, assuming greater responsibility for social
and crime control measures. Contrary to the situation that exists in other European countries, firearms are readily accessible to individuals

throughout the country, either being kept in the home in connection with citizen military service or through legal purchase. The fact that these firearms are not widely used in crimes demonstrates that factors other than availability must be operating, namely, the willingness to use firearms in marital and other personal disputes or in connection with such a crime as robbery. The nature of the Swiss criminal justice system has also helped to reduce ordinary crime. In the German-speaking area, offenders are seldom arrested; citations are usually given instead. No plea bargaining is available for a reduction in the charge, most convictions are suspended, prison sentences are of short duration, and prisons have never been large.

Swiss offenders are older, in general, than are offenders in other countries. If the younger age groups, who commit most conventional crime, do not *proportionately* engage in crime in Switzerland, as they do in other countries, total crime is obviously reduced. Moreover, the rate of increase for youthful offenders is much less than that in Sweden, for example, and little organized gang behavior among the youth is found in the country. In addition, the younger age groups conform to prescribed norms in greater proportions than they do in most West European countries. In conjunction with this conformity, along with more open communication lines between the young and the adult population, youth unrest is less in evidence. This is due, in part, to the greater participation at all age levels — for example, in numerous sports and other activities, as well as the system of national military service that systematically brings men, aged 20 to 55, together at periodic intervals, from the initial induction into the military service until the suspension of service decades later. As these forces have led to more integration in the society, they have also tended to diminish alienation between age groups, a fact of considerable significance in relation to youth crime.

Studies show that Italian and other foreign workers have the same, or even a lower, crime rate than the native-born Swiss — in marked contrast to the situation found among the lower classes (native-born workers) in most countries. If the criminal involvement among the lower class is reduced, the total crime rate in the country is decreased, as the lower class makes up a large proportion of the total criminality. Furthermore, the foreign worker tends to reflect the law-abiding norms of the Swiss people generally. This situation is likely to change, however, with the second generation, which is not large in proportion to the foreign workers as a whole.

Explanation of differences between
Switzerland and Sweden

Marked differences were found between Sweden, where crime is regarded as a serious problem, and Switzerland: Crime trend increases are greater in Sweden, and the rates are much higher, particularly for crimes of violence. In fact, a government study has estimated that Sweden could continue to expect substantial increases in all main categories of crime between 1973 and 1978.[1] The report did not project estimates beyond 1978. Although only minor variations are found in population size and per capita affluence, marked differences exist in the urbanization process itself. Urbanization in Sweden has resulted in far larger cities and a heavier population concentration in a few large metropolitan areas. The urban population of Switzerland, moreover, has largely managed to retain both a physical and a social psychological tie to the cantons and communes from which they come.

Both countries are democracies, but they have developed along different lines.[2] Sweden is a highly integrated country with a strong centralized government — particularly in contrast to Switzerland — and this has tended to inhibit a certain amount of citizen initiative and responsibility for social conditions such as crime. This type of central government existed historically over many centuries of royal rule. Roland Huntsford explains that the twentieth-century technological revolution thus came to a country where there was already "a love of bureaucracy, where the population submitted to a hierarchical order of things and accepted autocratic rule. They were well adapted to a centralized administration and had uniform attitudes controlled by a monolithic educational system. They were steeped in a collective mentality and the individual was at a discount."[3] In fact, the contemporary social welfare state, which began in the 1930s with its all-inclusive programs of control over Swedish life has been built on this historical centralization and the acceptance of authority and decisions from without. The general Swedish attitude today, claims Huntsford, is "the desire not to oppose the necessity of giving the State the appearance of Omnipotence: under Swedish conditions, confrontation in any sphere generates unease everywhere else."[4] The average person tends to accept the decisions of others, the exceptions being primarily those in such elite positions as government, civil service, labor and employer federations, and similar groups. Paul Austin writes about the general paternalistic nature of the system and the Social Democrats: "To sit at dinner with a member of the seemingly eternal Social Democratic government, and hear him talking about what "we" (the Social Democrats) will be doing for "them" (the Swedish nation) in ten years' time, or twenty, or thirty, is to look down a dizzy vista of well-intentioned, enlightened, and yet, even so, dubious values."[5]

"In all things Swedish the expert rules," according to Austin.[6] In contrast, the Swiss frequently use public initiatives and referenda to decide issues, even overruling parliamentary decisions. In Sweden expressions of public opinion are frequently overruled by parliament. A good example of this was the 1957 nationwide plebiscite in which the Swedes voted strongly against the adoption of the general European custom of right-hand driving, only to have the proposal adopted by the government ten years later. Although traditional civil liberties have remained largely intact in Sweden, with complete freedom of the press, free elections, free speech, and freedom of assembly, there has been an ever-growing government encompassing 1.1 million of the country's 4.1 million workers.[7] The Swedish national elections of 1976, in which a coalition of political parties overthrew the Social Democratic Party that had been in power for over forty years, was, in part, a reaction against what had become an overcentralized, bureaucratic government.

The Swedes and the Swiss have taken two different roads. Beginning with the economic problems of the 1930s the Social Democratic government of Sweden has developed comprehensive social welfare measures that cover, as well as control, broad aspects of Swedish life. In fact, in 1976 Olof Palme — at that time the Social Democratic Prime Minister — acknowledged that "society has, to an increasing extent, taken the responsibilities of individuals. Social reforms have required that more and more people must communicate with authorities."[8] Following a different road, the Swiss have largely given only a limited role to the government. As a result, centralized social welfare programs and government controls are more limited in Switzerland, and more reliance has been placed on the individual citizen and the work goal orientation among Swiss youth. Social security is rudimentary in Switzerland and rests on a system of three "pillars": private savings, private insurance programs — although insurance is compulsory in some cantons — and state aid, in this order of importance. A journalist has written, "But social stability seems to be profoundly rooted, and so is the mistrust of government intervention, innovation, or any invasion of communal, family or individual privacy and independence."[9]

In Sweden, where organization is extensive and life is programmed, the youth have become bored, and the boredom with the welfare state has become widespread. Under these conditions crime and other forms of deviant behavior furnish a diversion for some youths who seek excitement. The youth have become more alienated from the controls of an adult society — and at an earlier age — than they are in Switzerland. The social control of the family has become increasingly weakened in Sweden, as has also been true in the United States, due to changes in the society, as well as the extensive government programs. In 1975, 47 percent of the married women were in the Swedish labor force, and 57 percent of those had children under seven years of age. According to Carl-Gunnar Janson, Swedish society has grown "more equalitarian, permissive, humanitarian, and secularized in outlook," with the result that individual opportunities and freedom of choice have increased.[10]

Independence for youth is being encouraged and cultivated, partly through more democratic approaches in the schools, and as a result, both the family and the school in Sweden have become far more permissive than they are in Switzerland. The social welfare program has put great emphasis on the development of youth organizations of various types, and contacts between persons of diverse age groups have diminished. The youth subcultures are pronounced, with differences in dress, interests, and behavior, and, increasingly, youth groups with their pronounced deviant and quasibohemian life styles demonstrate a contempt for the ordinary law-abiding citizen — the square, or *knegare*.[11]

The theft of adult status objects such as autos has become a large part of youth crime. Janson attributes the high rate of delinquency in Sweden to the failure of the socialization process to develop patterns of deferred gratification in the youth, who seek, instead, the complete and immediate gratification of needs.[12]

A final significant difference is related to drug usage: Sweden has a much higher incidence than Switzerland. The consequent need of funds to support a drug habit has undoubtedly had a significant impact and has thus played a significant part in the increasing theft rates. Although this problem is increasing in Switzerland, it is nowhere near as serious a problem there as it is in Sweden.

As these differences seem to indicate, the direction of crime in Switzerland will largely be dependent upon the youth. If they — and particularly those in the younger age groups — become more alienated from adults, as has been the trend in most urbanized and highly developed countries, this alienation will probably be manifested in a search for unconventional forms of excitement and status in the form of criminal activities within a more or less separate peer group or youth culture. In the 1950s the role of youth in Sweden was much like that of the youth in Switzerland today. Obviously, crime in Switzerland will increase, but whether both the rates and the trend remain lower than those of other similar countries will depend on the maintenance of the essential nature of a distinctive Swiss society in the face of accelerated social change. In any event, one should be cautious in interpreting future numerical or percentage increases in crime in Switzerland, for they will generally start from a comparatively small base.

Implications for the United States and other countries

In conclusion, the crime picture presented in Switzerland and the differences between it and Sweden might well provide some guides for crime control that could well be applied to the United States and other Western countries — or even in those countries now in the process of development. The small size of a country need not preclude applicability of the lessons learned to much larger countries. Size is not always an important variable; rather, it is the failure of the larger countries to utilize more adequate preventive and social control measures.

1. Switzerland's lower crime rate cannot be explained by individualistic personality differences. Programs for, and expenditures on, mental health clinics for youth and for psychiatry and psychology, even in prisons, have not been emphasized as much in the Swiss approaches as in Sweden and in the United Sates, for example.
2. The pronounced differences in the extent of crime in these two highly affluent countries indicate that ordinary crime basically is far from being produced by economic disadvantages or poverty.
3. Large urban concentrations can be controlled by the dispersal of industry and the development of satellite cities which would help to decentralize the size and population densities of the large cities. With rare exceptions, optimum maximum city population should not exceed 250,000 to 500,000. Areas of a city

with a slum way of life did not develop in Switzerland, and so subsequent generations of native Swiss, as well as migrants, were spared being infected with criminal and other deviant behavior patterns.

4. Communities or cities that wish to prevent crime should encourage greater political decentralization by developing small governmental units and encouraging citizen responsibility for obedience to the law and crime control. The increased delegation of responsibility for crime control to the police and to governmental agencies, as well as the tendency to blame them for the crime problem, should be reversed. This is particularly true in the large urban areas. In order to stimulate a reversed trend, urban, and particularly slum, areas could well be broken down into semipolitical units of approximately 5,000 persons each, which would be encouraged to assume more active participation in crime control, along with involvement in other acute urban problems.[13] As local leadership is encouraged, as well as greater individual initiative and broader-based citizen organization, a situation could be developed that is more closely parallel to the general local citizen responsibility found in Switzerland.

5. The close relationship between conventional crime and youth demands the development of broader integration of youth and adults in common activities and purposes. The common method of dealing with youth problems by means of special youth programs, rather than through the integration of youth with adult groups, has tended to maximize, rather than to diminish, the alienation of youth from the adult world. Such a goal can be accomplished partly by more interage social and sports groups and by the appointment and election of youth to political office and to national and local boards and committees. The lowering of the voting age from 21 in national and local elections to 18, both in the United States and in several European countries, may gradually result in more youth participation in the general society. Younger persons in the United States have been increasingly elected to local political office. Several states have even granted full adult privileges to those who are eighteen.

6. The German-Swiss criminal justice system of generally not arresting persons should seriously be considered for adoption. Several governmental units in the United States are experiment-

ing with the use of a citation, rather than an arrest, for minor criminal offenses. This practice conforms with the position that the labeling of an offender can have serious consequences for future crime. While plea bargaining for a recommended sentence might be continued, consideration might well be given to the German-Swiss view that a prosecutor cannot bargain for a reduction in the plea. This necessity to prosecute the original charge might result in more justice and greater respect for the criminal justice system. At least, the reduction in charge should be to a related offense. While the readiness in the United States for giving the longest sentences in the world had been presumed to reduce crime, it appears to have had just the opposite result. A recent United States commission has recommended drastic reduction in sentences — though perhaps not as low as the very low sentences in Switzerland.[14] The wide use in Switzerland of suspended sentences has advantages over probation, where an individual's life is often unnecessarily restricted, often with few demonstrable benefits of the supervision. An additional factor of importance in this respect is that of cost, for even though probation is less costly than imprisonment, cost is not a factor in the suspended sentence. Imprisonment should be reduced, but where institutions are needed, attention should be paid to size: They should be much smaller than prisons generally are today.

7. With respect to gun registration and control, and their relation to crimes of violence, it is important to remember the Swiss experience of readily available firearms. This availability, however, is not associated with a general pattern of violence to use them, either in disputes or for robberies. In a country like the United States, where there has been a long history of both personal and collective violence, it is essential that rigid regulations for both registration and control be adopted.[15] Even with rigid controls the basic issue of the use of violence would remain partially unresolved, and other weapons would still be used for assault, homicide, and robbery: This has been the experience in less developed countries, where the criminal homicide rates are the highest.[16] Rigid gun control, as well as the control of other lethal weapons, would constitute at least one important step in resolving the long and complicated problem of violence that results in great injury and death.

8. Finally, the United States might consider the merits of a uniform national criminal code, although it is highly controversial as a constitutional issue. Such a code would have uniform definitions and would set maximum penalties, but the administration of the law would be left to the states. Practically all countries in the world have national criminal codes, and the present United States system is both impractical and confusing as well as unjust, for a highly mobile population. Moreover, the very lengthy sentences in some states constitute cruel and inhuman punishment. If the greatly diverse and extremely independent Swiss cantons realize the necessity for a uniform criminal code, the United States might well do likewise.

Appendixes

Appendix A. *Trends in crimes known to the police for selected cantons and cities, rates per 100,000 population, percentage increase in rates, correlation coefficients, and regression coefficients[a]*

Crime and area	Trend period	Initial rate	End rate	% increase in rate	Correlation coefficient	Regression coefficient
Murder and nonnegligent manslaughter						
Canton						
Zürich	1964–72	.30	1.1	266.7	–.19	–.02
Bern	1962–71	.44	.2	–45.5	–.42	–.03
Basel-Stadt	1968–72	.43	–	–100.0	.48	–.21
City						
Zürich	1962–72	.45	.5	6.7	–.03	.00
Basel	1968–72	.43	–	–100.0	.48	–.21
Bern	1963–72	4.7	–	–100.0	.36	.11
Lausanne	1962–72	3.0	2.9	3.3	–.56	–.25
Assault						
Canton						
Basel-Stadt	1968–72	61.0	117.0	91.8	.94	12.70
City						
Zürich	1962–72	216.0	114.0	–33.3	–.50	–2.89
Basel	1968–72	61.0	117.0	91.8	.94	12.70
Bern	1963–72	75.0	59.0	–21.3	.06	.33
Robbery						
Canton						
Zürich	1963–72	4.4	8.4	90.9	.83	.29
Bern	1962–71	.13	4.7	3515.4	.58	.28

Basel-Stadt	1968–72	10.0	21.0	110.0	.87	2.78
City						
Zürich	1962–72	6.1	16.0	162.5	.65	1.02
Basel	1968–72	10.0	21.0	110.0	.87	2.78
Bern	1963–72	3.6	11.0	217.9	.81	1.16
Lausanne	1967–72	12.0	21.0	75.0	.68	2.02
Burglary						
Canton						
Zürich	1962–71	269.0	368.0	36.8	.81	11.0
City						
Zürich	1962–72	400.0	908.0	127.0	.91	51.8
Burglary and theft (Diebstahl)						
Canton						
Zürich	1962–72	2783.0	2715.0	-2.4	.18	10.5
Bern	1968–72	1131.0	1320.0	16.7	.63	59.0
Basel-Stadt	1968–72	1924.0	2860.0	48.6	1.00	227.3
City						
Zürich	1962–72	3754.0	3827.0	1.9	.42	68.7
Basel	1968–72	1924.0	2860.0	48.6	.63	59.0
Bern	1963–72	2330.0	2725.0	16.9	.70	104.9
Lausanne	1967–72	1402.0	2008.0	43.2	.85	160.5

[a]The data for Basel are repeated under the canton and city. Only arrest data were available for Geneva and are not included.

Appendix B. *Trends in crimes known to the police in Stockholm, Göteborg, Malmö, 1965–72 and Sweden 1962–72, 1965–72[a]*

Crime and area	Differences, rates per 100,000	Correlation coefficient	Regression coefficient
Total violations of penal code			
Sweden, 1962–72	+81.6	+.99	+345.64
Sweden 1965–72	+38.9	+.97	+317.23
Stockholm, 1965–72	+34.8	+.85	+698.26
Göteborg, 1965–72	+8.4	+.61	+184.70
Malmö, 1965–72	+80.2	+.94	+952.22
Murder and non-negligent manslaughter			
Sweden, 1962–72	+84.0	+.77	+.18
Sweden, 1965–72	+43.8	+.74	+.22
Stockholm, 1965–72	+182.6	+.78	+1.46
Göteborg, 1965–72	+93.0	+.80	+.39
Malmö, 1965–72	+177.8	+.37	+.40
Assault			
Sweden, 1962–72	+88.7	+.95	+12.51
Sweden, 1965–72	+42.8	+.87	+10.14
Stockholm, 1965–72	+40.7	+.86	+20.82
Göteborg, 1965–72	+33.5	+.87	+13.17
Malmö, 1965–72	+2.0	+.42	+6.03
Robbery			
Sweden, 1962–72	+238.4	+.98	+1.55
Sweden, 1965–72	+100.0	+.96	+1.56
Stockholm, 1965–72	+126.7	+.98	+7.61
Göteborg, 1965–72	+51.3	+.81	+3.64
Malmö, 1965–72	+218.2	+.79	+4.67
Larceny			
Sweden, 1962–72	+98.8	+.97	+173.78
Sweden, 1965–72	+56.8	+.96	+193.64
Stockholm, 1965–72	+47.2	+.93	+401.12
Göteborg, 1965–72	+1.8	+.25	+34.91
Malmö, 1965–72	+113.8	+.91	+607.72
Burglary			
Sweden, 1962–72	+86.8	+.94	+72.52
Sweden, 1965–72	+47.3	+.90	+82.20

Appendix B (*cont.*)

Crime and area	Differences, rates per 100,000	Correlation coefficient	Regression coefficient
Stockholm, 1965–72	+92.4	+.90	+257.79
Göteborg, 1965–72	+24.3	+.80	+118.52
Malmö, 1965–72	+80.1	+.84	+201.26
Actual and attempted auto theft			
Sweden, 1962–72	+69.1	+.79	+23.04
Sweden, 1965–72	−06.7	+.20	+2.81
Stockholm, 1965–72	−34.2	−.87	−63.53
Göteborg, 1965–72	−26.3	−.10	−4.92
Malmö, 1965–72	+158.2	+.93	+80.99

[a] Data were also secured for Swedish cities for the period 1962–72, but substantial improvements had been made in 1965 in police statistics and procedures. It was advised, therefore, that the trend should be based on the period 1965–72.

Appendix C. *Total criminal convictions, selected offense convictions, rates per 100,000 and correlation and regression coefficients, Switzerland, 1960 and 1971*

Offense	Rate, 1960[a]	Rate, 1971	Rate difference (%)	Correlation coefficient	Regression coefficient
Offense					
Total convictions	412.0	310.0	−24.8	−.84	−9.03
Total life and body	38.0	36.0	−5.3	−.61	−.46
Total property	178.0	180.0	+1.1	+.22	+.45
Total morality	51.0	34.0	−33.3	−.81	−1.44
Major offenses					
Murder and nonnegligent manslaughter	.5	.43	−20.4	−.29	−.01
Assault	13.0	9.3	−28.1	−.60	−.24
Rape	.7	.93	+38.8	+.05	.00
Robbery	1.2	1.5	+25.0	+.28	+.02
Larceny and burglary (*Diebstahl*)	92.0	104.0	+13.0	+.82	+1.61
Petty larceny	1.1	6.8	+518.2	+.82	+.43
Auto theft	24.0	13.0	−45.8	−.91	−1.02
Other offenses					
Receiving stolen property	6.6	6.5	−1.5	+.52	+.09
Embezzlement	17.0	8.5	−50.3	−.96	−.63
Forgery/falsification/counterfeit	8.1	7.1	−12.3	+.04	+.01
Fraud	38.0	24.0	−36.8	−.89	−.95
Vandalism	7.3	6.9	−5.5	−.29	−.07

[a] Rates were based on 1961 for totals, property, larceny because of changes increasing the statistical value of thefts included in the official statistics.

Appendix D. *Trends in criminal convictions in predominantly German-speaking cantons, 1960–71*

	Rate per 100,000			% difference		Correlation coefficient, 1960–71	Regression coefficient, 1960–71
	1960	1961[a]	1971	1960–71	1961–71		
Aargau	575	573	356	−38.1	−37.9	−0.90	−20.45
Appenzell A.R.H.	297	318	195	−34.3	−38.7	−0.71	−9.82
Appenzell I.R.H.	131	108	194	+48.1	+79.6	+0.46	+8.32
Basel-Stadt	671	705	519	−22.7	−26.4	−0.57	−20.44
Basel-Land	301	320	208	−30.9	−35.0	−0.85	−9.93
Bern	449	457	302	−32.7	−33.9	−0.79	−12.46
Glarus	147	345	172	+17.0	+50.1	−0.21	−3.72
Graubünden	390	369	359	−07.9	−2.7	+0.42	+6.63
Luzern	761	718	433	−43.1	−39.7	−0.84	−30.51
Nidwalden	395	214	341	−13.7	+59.4	−0.21	−4.26
Obwalden	474	464	413	−12.9	−11.0	−0.57	−8.89
Schaffhausen	348	414	397	+14.1	−4.1	−0.10	−1.71
Schwyz	352	295	304	−13.6	+3.1	−0.04	−0.40
Solothurn	411	406	308	−25.1	−24.1	−0.72	−8.01
St. Gallen	309	332	299	−03.2	−9.9	−0.27	−2.00
Thurgau	268	261	198	−26.1	−24.1	−0.84	−7.36
Uri	284	236	169	−40.5	−28.4	−0.13	−1.70
Zug	619	474	267	−56.9	−43.7	−0.86	−24.56
Zürich	357	363	294	−17.6	−19.0	−0.81	−6.09
Switzerland	410	412	310	−24.4	−24.8	−0.84	−9.03

[a]Statistics for 1961 were also calculated because of changes increasing the statistical value of thefts included in the official statistics.

Appendix E. *Chi squares, attitudes about crime in Zürich*

	Score	Significance
Number one problem of Zürich by:		
Sex	8.07	NS
Age group	42.68	NS
Education	51.20	NS
Marital status	16.57	NS
Income	76.30	NS
Nationality	36.15	.001
Increase/decrease, by sex, of:		
Theft	7.57	.05
Burglary	3.94	NS
Vehicle theft	2.30	NS
Assault/robbery	8.21	.05
Public fighting	9.12	.05
Murder	7.30	.05
Rape	4.58	NS
Shoplifting	.07	NS
Fraud	2.33	NS
Vandalism	.65	NS
Drugs	1.76	NS
Increase/decrease, by age groups, of:		
Theft	14.66	NS
Burglary	38.63	.00
Vehicle theft	3.10	NS
Assault/robbery	15.23	NS
Public fighting	2.88	NS
Murder	9.93	NS
Rape	12.80	NS
Shoplifting	9.01	NS
Fraud	3.00	NS
Vandalism	2.92	NS
Drugs	1.49	NS
Increase/decrease, by nationality, of:		
Theft	11.81	.01
Burglary	28.21	.00
Vehicle theft	1.43	NS
Assault/robbery	4.29	NS
Public fighting	4.08	NS
Murder	2.44	NS
Rape	19.61	.001
Shoplifting	8.01	.05

	Score	Significance
Fraud	.55	NS
Vandalism	.00	NS
Drugs	.79	NS
Frequency of crime in Switzerland, by:		
Sex	5.67	NS
Age groups	16.29	NS
Respondent	23.74	.05
Nationality	23.47	.00
Concern, by sex, with:		
Robbery	14.12	.01
Burglary	1.01	NS
Theft	3.58	NS
Auto break-in	3.26	NS
Auto theft	8.41	.05
Concern, by age groups, with:		
Robbery	10.88	NS
Burglary	11.14	NS
Theft	17.09	NS
Auto break-in	4.15	NS
Auto theft	6.83	NS
Concern, by education, with:		
Robbery	12.26	NS
Burglary	6.95	NS
Theft	7.23	NS
Auto break-in	6.92	NS
Auto theft	7.57	NS
Concern, by nationality, with:		
Robbery	3.86	NS
Burglary	1.90	NS
Theft	3.86	NS
Auto break-in	.21	NS
Auto theft	10.99	.05
Frequency of neighborhood crime, by:		
Sex	2.61	NS
Age	12.20	NS
Nationality	3.99	NS
Urban district	6.29	NS
Education	11.32	NS
Respondent	27.79	.01

Appendix E (*cont.*)

	Score	Significance
Who commits neighborhood crime, by:		
Sex	.60	NS
Age	21.14	.01
Nationality	30.04	.000
Perceived safety of neighborhood, by:		
Urban district	18.09	NS
Sex	104.24	.000
Age groups	23.34	NS
Nationality	.04	NS
Education	15.49	NS
Marital status	24.30	.01
Respondent	14.19	NS
Perceived safety of Zürich by:		
Respondent	25.36	.01
Sex	49.57	.000
Age	33.49	.0001
Nationality	2.87	NS
Marital status	24.36	.0001
Areas viewed as unsafe, by:		
Respondent	13.13	NS
Sex	19.53	.01
Age	19.73	NS
Nationality	8.12	NS
Marital status	6.06	NS
Why feel unsafe in certain Zürich areas, by:		
Respondent	11.90	NS
Sex	1.76	NS
Age	15.68	NS
Nationality	21.55	.001
Marital status	9.43	NS
Known victim of crime, by:		
Sex	.39	NS
Age	5.11	NS
Income	7.68	NS
Buying power	10.34	.05
Nationality	11.31	.0001

The goal of the survey was the selection of a final representative sample of approximately five hundred households that would also include, as well as possible, the foreign worker population, which is generally conceded to be about 17 percent of the Zürich population. Although a representative sample of individuals could have been secured easily from directory lists, the selection of households presented serious difficulties. No representative sample of Zürich households is publicly available, nor does any survey organization have such data. The city government believes that the availability of such data might result in the subjection of households to possible harassment by commercial researchers or enterprises. In fact, the representative household sample finally drawn for this particular study had to be returned to the census files by Publitest, the Swiss public opinion organization which conducted the actual survey, and no record could be kept of the names and addresses of the household heads used. An alternative method would have been to draw a random sample from the city directory, but because there would have been no way to determine the composition of the households or the heads of the household, this was not considered feasible.

Before a representative household sample could be drawn, access files had to be obtained from Census authorities. Because permission for this access could not be granted to the survey organization, it had to be obtained through Professor Peter Heintz, director of the Sociological Institute of the University of Zürich, who, through sponsorship of the research project, enabled the researcher to have access to the Zürich census files and thus made available to Publitest. (This permission was granted by Dr. Ulrich Zwingli of the Zürich Statistical Bureau, whose cooperation in this survey was important and is much appreciated.) On December 1, 1970, these census files contained information in packets arranged by private households (*Bogens*), a total of approximately 170,000 households in Zürich. It was necessary to go through this entire file to obtain 700 households randomly (500, plus a 200 oversample), or every 240

169

packets, in order to secure one sample household. (The selection of each household required about five minutes, a total of about 60 hours of work, all of which was done by the University of Zürich students.) This particular method "lost" the so-called institutional households, about one-half of one percent of all households, which included some foreign workers living in barracks-type housing. Although it was estimated that these households totaled only 7 percent of the city's foreign worker population, it did mean that seasonal workers were largely excluded from the sample. Furthermore, the date on which the census was conducted fell during a time period when the foreign workers were likely to have been at a lower figure for the year.

From these census packets were recorded the addresses and telephone numbers of each household head, the names of all household members aged 14 and over, the nationality of each member, and the urban district in which the household was located. These data were then processed as follows: (1) households were classified by type (married couples, single households, widow or widower with children, and mixed households); (2) telephone calls were made to determine the degree of homogeneity of the mixed households, that is, if several persons were living at one address, and, where necessary, a change in household category was made (e.g., two unmarried couples living separately at the same address were considered as two households); (3) the sample was again reduced to 700 households by random selection; and (4) as husband-and-wife households were divided by type, a random selection was made with respect to which person to interview among the married couples, in order that the sex of the respondents would be about equal. The only possible means of checking the reliability of the sample with the total population was the marital status of the sample in the groups aged 20 and above. Of the 1970 Zürich population 58.7 percent in this age group were married; the proportion was 58.3 percent in the total sample.

The necessity of using three-year-old addresses in the interviewing presented some unanticipated problems, as the assumption had been made that residential stability in the city was high. Nearly 1 out of 10 of the original sample of 700, however, could not be located, largely because of change in adresses since the 1970 census, as well as changes like deaths, demolition of the building, and so on. The interviewers were permitted to make substitutions if the household could not be located, but only at the *same addresses.* In some cases, however, it was not possible to determine the exact flat, particularly in large blocks of flats where the addresses were the same but where people hardly knew each other. The majority of the mixed households contained foreign workers and some youths; in most cases their residences were temporary and replacements could not be found. In cases where the designated person could not be located at the same address, the new resident might speak neither German nor Italian, the two languages used in the interviewing. In other cases it was found that some of the younger persons no longer lived with the parents. In these cases Publitest decided not to substitute new selections, as this would then have permitted the free selection of alternates by the interviewers. It was concluded that it would be better to lose some cases, rather than to accept a certain degree of uncontrollability on the part of the interviewer that might have produced a major distortion of the original random sample. Randomly designated persons, therefore, were not used as substitutes. There remained, for possible interviews, 636 households, 90.1 percent of the original sample, and of this total, 24.2 percent could not be completed. (Almost no differences were found, for example, in the proportion of household victimization. The major differences were in the mixed households, and it was felt that the weighted measures should be applied, in order to make the sample more representative when the independent variables were anlyzed.) There were 67 refusals, 43 unsuccessful third visits, 30 absences during the time period for interviewing, and 14 for other reasons.

Weights were then applied to the final sample in order to make it conform to the original sample, as the distribution by household type differed somewhat from the 700 originally sampled. Only slight differences were generally found, however, between the weighted and unweighted figures. There is no reason to assume that the individuals in the original sample differed from those in the weighted sample — that is, that individuals who may have set up independent households since the census, for example, differed from those who had not. The use of the weighted sample was thought to provide greater accuracy, in spite of the fact that only minor differences were found, generally. The weights assigned by household type, as well as a comparison of weighted and unweighted numbers and distributions, is seen in Appendix G.

A special sampling problem was presented by the Zürich foreign workers. Their exclusion would have resulted in an unrepresentative sample of the city population, as they constitute about 17 percent of it. Italian workers make up, by far, the largest group among them, and they were the only ones included in the sample, largely because Italian was the only language, other than German, in which most of the interviewers were sufficiently fluent to conduct interviews. The final sample consisted of 57 foreign households, or 11.8 percent. This percentage was later raised, in data analysis, to 12.4 percent (60) of the mixed households through the application of corrective weights. The foreign worker sample tended to consist of a disproportionate number of the more long-term workers, some of whom are married, largely because some of the others are only temporary residents of the city, have no permanent addresses, or live in joint households.

Prior to the actual interviewing, letters were sent to each potential household respondent informing the resident that an interviewer would soon contact the household to ask their "opinions about certain urban problems in Zürich" in a special study being conducted under the auspices of the Sociological Institute of the University of Zürich, whose director, Professor Heintz, signed it. It was felt to be important that each respondent know that the study was being sponsored by the Institute. Without such sponsorship it might have been difficult to "legitimate" the study and to avoid a higher refusal rate, particularly as it dealt with crime problems. While crime was not mentioned in the letter, which in itself might have increased the refusal rate, the interviewers were instructed to state at the outset of each interview that the primary interest of the survey was to seek information and attitudes about crime.

Questions relating to attitudes toward crime were incorporated into the victimization survey: Attitude questions were asked of 517 persons, and in addition to the 482 representative household heads, 35 younger respondents, aged 20 and over and living in the household, were included. This additional group provided a better age balance, the assumption being that household heads were somewhat older. If one were to obtain a representative sample of individual opinions, a sample representative of the total Zürich population would have had to be drawn. It was not possible to do this type of survey, as research funds were concentrated on the household victimization survey. (See Chapter 5.)

Due to a loss in interview responses in the original sample of respondents in the attitude survey, a series of weights were applied to the final sample in order to bring it more into line with the population composition of the originally drawn sample. (See Appendix H.) No claim can be made that the final sample was representative of individual opinions of the Zürich population as a whole; rather, it represents opinions of household respondents who came from a representative sample of Zürich households. In spite of this differentiation, the attitude responses can be regarded as a fairly reasonable, but by no means perfect, sample of the opinions of Zürich residents aged 20 and over. It does represent a more valid sample than simply the opinions of 517 persons living in the city.

Due to the high costs of face-to-face interviewing in the survey, a telephone survey was originally planned, with a letter sent in advance. For a number of reasons this plan was dropped. (See Charles A. Ibsen and John A. Ballweg, "Telephone Interviews in Social Research: Some Methodological Considerations," *Quality and Quantity*, 8 [1974], 181−192.) In the first place, this method has not been used elsewhere, except in a few pilot studies in the United States − and then only as a follow-up on original interviews. Such data would not therefore be useful for comparative purposes. Second, it was not recommended by informed persons who felt that the Swiss do not react favorably to impersonal telephone interviews, due to their wishes to maintain privacy about personal family matters. Third, telephone interviewing has stricter time limitations. The LEAA has not found mail questionnaires satisfactory in United States victimization surveys; a high degree of underreporting was found, particularly in assault, robbery, and burglary. (See Anthony G. Turner, "Methodological Issues in the Development of the National Crime Survey Panel: Partial Findings," Statistics Division, LEAA, December, 1972 [mimeo].) A recent Texas study, however, used a mail survey with reportedly good results. (See *The Texas Crime Trend Survey*. Advance Report on a Mail Survey of the General Public by Alfred St. Louis, Statistical Management Analyst, Statistical Analysis Center, Texas Department of Public Safety, Austin, Texas, August, 1976.)

Appendix G. *Percentage distribution of original Zürich sample and the number and proportion of unweighted and weighted completed 482 household interviews*

Household type	Distribution of original sample (%)	Unweighted completed interviews		Weighted interviews		Weight
		Number	%	Number	%	
Married couple households						
Husbands	28.2	134	27.8	136	28.2	1.02
Wives	28.1	163	33.8	135	28.0	0.83
Single persons	30.6	130	27.0	148	30.7	1.13
Widow(er) and children	4.6	27	5.6	22	4.6	0.82
Mixed households	8.5	28	5.8	41	8.5	1.47

Appendix H. *Distribution of original sample and conversion to weighted sample in Zürich attitude survey*

| | Distribution of original sample (%) | Weighted sample | | Weights |
		Number	%	
Spouses	53.5	297	57.4	0.98
Single persons	15.3	130	25.2	0.61
Widow(ers) and children	2.3	27	5.2	0.44
Persons in mixed households	14.7	28	5.4	2.72
Juveniles living with parents and widow(er)	11.6	35	6.8	1.71
Totals	100.0	517	100.0	

Appendix I. *Zürich household victimization rates per 1,000 households, by characteristics of victimized households and type of victimization*[a]

	Number of house-holds	Burglary	Household larceny	Vandalism	Others
Nationality of head of household					
Swiss	422	91	118	61	20
Foreign	60	50	102	55	
Age of head of household					
14–19					
20–34	81	55	131	41	
35–49	151	110	204	91	38
50–64	143	66	61	37	20
65+	107	99	53	63	
Number of persons in household					
1	149	74	68	38	
2–3	229	89	86	59	20
4–5	99	100	263	92	41
6+	5			184	
Income (Sw. F.)					
501–1,000	17	64			
1,001–2,000	125	54	95	48	
2,001–3,000	130	97	115	41	16
3,001–4,500	87	116	168	110	64
4,500+	29	162	187	92	
No income	13		167	88	
Don't know	81	73	85	54	13
Urban district[b]					
Old Town	16	226	89	69	62
Higher income areas	127	100	74	57	45
Salaried employee areas	289	57	142	68	6
Working-class areas	50	167	80	23	
Respondent					
Husband	136	75	158	75	45
Wife	135	74	129	61	18
Single	148	92	84	46	

Appendix I (*cont.*)

	Number of house-holds	Burglary	Household larceny	Vandalism	Others
Div./widow	22	74	74	37	
Mixed	41	143	71	71	
Total	482	83	116	60	18

[a] Auto theft rate of 10 per 1000 households. Number too small to analyze by characteristics.

[b] Based on predominant income and occupational status of residents in area. Many areas were quite mixed so that this is only an approximate measure. Categories are combinations of the 12 Zürich political districts: Old Town (District 11), higher income residential areas (2, 6, 7), salaried employees (3, 8, 9, 10, 11, 12), workers (4, 5).

Appendix J. *Victimization rate per 1,000 for persons aged 14 and over, by characteristics of victim and type of victimization*[a]

Characteristics	Number of persons	Assault			Larceny		
		Total	Aggra-vated	Attempted	Total	With contact	Without contact
Sex							
Male	412	32	22	10	67	27	40
Female	502	20	12	9	54	17	37
Not known	26						
Age							
14–19	70	47	32	15	94	68	27
20–34	228	15	15		91	25	66
35–49	267	25	9	17	61	15	46
50–64	230				35	15	20
65+	145	20	10	10	21	14	8
Nationality							
Swiss	839	28	18	10	57	21	36
Foreign-born	101				66	21	45
Urban district							
Old Town	28				37		37
Higher income areas	238	16	16		55	31	25
Salaried-employee areas	584	32	17	15	66	20	46
Working-class areas	90	13	13		21	9	11

Income (Sw. F.)

	N						
501–1,000	20						
1,001–2,000	206	43	22	21	32	15	18
2,001–3,000	266	14	7	7	75	18	58
3,001–4,500	197	55	55		96	39	57
4,501+	74				39	25	14
No income	16	193	124	69			
Don't know							
No response	161	22	13	9	39	15	24
Respondent							
Husband	329	28	25	3	62	28	34
Wife	333	8	3	5	55	25	30
Single	162	49	21	28	84	14	70
Div./widowed	44	19	19		56		56
Mixed	72	41	20	20			
Total	940	25	16	9	58	21	37

[a]For robbery cases (11) and auto theft (2)-cases, the numbers were too small to analyze by characteristics.

Notes

1. Crime and Switzerland

1 The rapidly industrializing Socialist countries repeatedly maintain that the generalization of increasing crime rates does not apply to them. However, they offer no hard data to support this contention. See, for example, the reports of the various United Nations congresses on the Prevention of Crime and the Treatment of Offenders.

2 Karl O. Cristiansen, "Industrialization and Urbanization in Relation to Crime and Delinquency," *International Review of Criminal Policy* 18 (October 1960), 8.

3 See Manuel López-Rey, *Crime: An Analytical Appraisal* (New York: Praeger, 1970), p. 2.

4 Marshall B. Clinard and Daniel J. Abbott, *Crime in Developing Countries: A Comparative Perspective* (New York: Wiley, 1973), p. 254.

5 Wolfgang Schmidt, "The Prevalence of Alcoholism and Drug Addiction in Canada," *Addictions* 15 (1968), 1–13. Also see Von P. Wüthrich, "Quantitative und qualitative Dimensionen des Alkoholproblems in der Schweiz," *Bulletin des Eidg. Gesundheitsamtes*, February, 1975, 1–11; and F. Welti, *Der Verbrauch alkoholischer Getränke in den Jahren 1966–1970 und früheren Zeitabschnitten* (Bern: 1973).

The shorter term Federal German Republic is used in this book instead of the longer official name, Federal Republic of Germany. This was considered to be more correct than West Germany which is not an official title in any way.

6 Welti, *Der Verbrauch*. Part of the high per capita consumption is due to the numerous tourists.

7 *Demographic Yearbook 1971* (New York: The United Nations, 1972), Table 33.

8 Prior to conducting this study I had had many conversations about this problem with various foreign criminologists. As an example of popular belief, the widely read book *Switzerland* (New York: Time, Inc., 1964) mentioned the low murder, robbery, and burglary rates in the country. Various advertisements of Swissair in various magazines and their own travel literature refer to Zürich as a city with little crime. For example, one Swissair advertisement in the *New Yorker* stated that Zürich is a city where a woman walking alone and at night can feel safe.

9 See *International Exchange of Information on Current Criminological Research Projects in Member States* (Strasbourg: The Council of Europe, 1969), Vols. 7 and 8. Also see *Current Trends in Criminological Research* (Strasbourg: Council of Europe, 1970), Vol. 6 of the collected studies in criminological research, consisting of reports presented to the Seventh Conference of Directors of Criminological Research Institutes. The European Committee on Crime Problems of The Council of Europe published its first volume in 1966.

10 Jörg M. Frey, *Die Kriminalität in Zeiten des Wohlstandes: Eine Untersuchung der schweizerischen Kriminalität von 1951–1964* (Zürich: Verlag Schulthess & Co., 1968), p. 75. A major earlier work on criminality in Switzerland was written by Ervin Hacker, *Die Kriminalität des Kantons Zürich* (Miskolc, Hungary: Buchdrukerei Stephan Ludvig, 1939).

11 Hans Schultz is Professor of Law, University of Bern. His annual analyses of published statistics on criminal convictions appear in *Schweizerische Zeitschrift für Strafrecht/Revue pénale Suisse*.

180

12 The President's Commission on Law Enforcement and Administration of Justice, *Task Force Report: Crime and Its Impact — an Assessment* (Washington, D.C.: U.S. Government Printing Office, 1967), p. 39. Also included in *The Challenge of Crime in a Free Society: A Report by the President's Commission on Law Enforcement and Administration of Justice* (New York: Avon Books, 1968).

13 *Demographic Year Book 1971* (New York: United Nations, 1972).

14 According to 1975 reports issued by the World Bank, two small, nonindustrialized, oil-rich Arab countries had the highest per capita gross national product (GNP): United Arab Emirates ($13,500) and Kuwait ($11,640). Saudi Arabia, with the world's richest oil reserves, ranked well down, with $2,080 per capita. The World Bank based its conclusions on each nation's 1974 GNP. Reported in a UPI Washington news story and appearing in the *Wisconsin State Journal* on December 21, 1975.

15 Peter Tonge, "Switzerland Working Well," *The Christian Science Monitor*, reprinted in the *Wisconsin State Journal*, March 29, 1976, Section 5, p. 1.

16 Walter Sorell, *The Swiss: A Cultural Panorama of Switzerland* (New York: Bobbs-Merrill, 1972), p. 55.

17 Peter Heintz (with the collaboration of Suzanne Heintz), *The Future of Development*, (Bern: Hans Huber, 1973), p. 124, and Michel Bassand, *Urbanisation et Pouvoir Politique: Le Cas de la Suisse* (Geneva: Georg-Librairie de l'Université-Genève, 1974), p. 3.

18 *Demographic Year Book 1971* (New York: United Nations, 1972).

19 For a discussion of other types of communes, see chapter 8.

20 Jürg Steiner, *Amicable Agreement versus Majority Rule: Conflict Resolution in Switzerland*, rev. ed. (Chapel Hill: University of North Carolina Press, 1974). Also see Chester L. Hunt and Lewis Walker, *Ethnic Dynamics: Patterns of Intergroup Relations in Various Societies* (Homewood, Ill.: Dorsey 1974).

21 For information on Swedish crime, Paul C. Friday: "Delinquency and Crime in Sweden," unpublished M.A. thesis, University of Wisconsin, 1966; "Differential Opportunity and Differential Association in Sweden: A Study of Youth Crime," unpublished Ph.D. dissertation, University of Wisconsin, 1970; and "Research on Youth Crime in Sweden: Some Problems in Methodology," *Scandinavian Studies* 46 (Winter 1974), pp. 20–30. See also Knut Sveri, "Brott och Brottslingar," in Knut Sveri, Gösta Rylander, Torsten Eriksson and Åke Asp, *Kriminaliteten och Samhället* (Stockholm: Aldus/Bonniers, 1966), p. 10. I was a Fulbright Research Professor studying crime in Sweden in 1954–55, and I have returned there several times, last in 1973, to gather additional material for this study.

2. Swiss concern about crime

1 *Bericht des Bundesrates an die Bundesversammlung über seine Geschäftsführung* (Annual Report of the Federal Council to the Parliament).

2 *Bericht des Bundesrates über die Richtlinien der Regierungspolitik der Legislaturperiode* (Report of the Federal Council: Main Topics of Government Policy During the Legislative Period).

3 See *Schweizerisches Strafgesetzbuch* (Bern: Schweizerische Bundeskanzlei, 1972)/*Code pénal suisse* (Berne: Chancellerie fédérale, 1972).

4 This commission has worked on abortion laws, crimes involving homicide and assault, sex crimes, and crimes against the family. By 1977 it had submitted its proposals to the government, and it expects to continue its work on crimes of violence.

5 Switzerland has no special legal code for delinquency: all such rules are incorporated into the general Swiss Penal Code.

6 The laws governing parliamentary affairs outline the methods of handling these questions as follows: (1) A "motion" is a question combined with the instruction that the Bundesrat must make a specific proposition to the Parliament concerning the question raised. The

Bundesrat is obliged to follow the instruction only if a majority of both chambers, Nationalrat and Ständerat, agrees with the instruction. (2) A "postulate" is a question combined with the invitation to the Bundesrat (Federal Council) to examine the questioned matter and to report to the parliament or to make specific propositions. The Bundesrat is not bound by the postulate. The postulate must be agreed upon by a majority of the chamber in which it has been raised. (3) An "interpellation" is a question raised by a certain number of MPs asking the Bundesrat for information on a certain matter. (4) "Kleine Anfrage" ("a short question") may be raised by one MP asking the Bundesrat for information on a certain matter. The short question is permitted only in the Nationalrat.

7 In the 1950—60 period, seventeen such questions were raised; seventeen were raised in the 1961—70 period; and eighteen in the 1971—72 period.

8 This unpublished Swedish study was arranged by Professor Knut Sveri, director of the Criminological Institute, University of Stockholm. The questions were "enkla frogor" (simple questions), those given directly to a cabinet minister, who may or may not choose to answer them, and "interpellationer" (interpolations), those given to a parliamentary committee and which may be discussed in Parliament. These differences must be regarded, however, in terms of the fundamental differences in the governmental structures of the governments.

9 Roland Huntsford, "'Law and Order' Issue Hot as Swedish Voting Nears," an article in The London *Observer* Service, reprinted in *The Milwaukee Journal*, September 9, 1973.

10 Swedish Information Service, *News from Sweden* (New York: Swedish Consulate General, 1973), p. 2.

11 From a 1975 letter from Martin Killias, who was an assistant in this research project.

12 One-third of the attitude questions asked were especially constructed for this survey; the remainder were actual or derived questions used in the LEAA—U.S. Census survey conducted in the United States in 1973. (See Appendix F.)

13 The Stuttgart survey did not include foreign workers, due to their resistance to being interviewed. The Zürich survey, however, showed that the attitudes of the foreign workers were not markedly different, on the whole, from those of the Swiss. Unfortunately, results of the LEAA—U.S. Census 1973 survey of attitudes toward crime were not yet available for comparison at the time of the writing of this book. The Stuttgart survey was based largely on the questionnaires used in the Zürich survey and was carried out under the general direction of Professor Günther Kaiser, director of the Criminological Institute, University of Freiburg. The results were later published in Egon Stephan, *Die Stuttgarter Opferbefragung: Eine kriminologischviktimologische Analyse zur Erforschung des Dunkelfeldes unter besonderer Berücksichtigung der Einstellung der Bevölkerung zur Kriminalität*, BKA Forschungsreihe Bd. 3 (Wiesbaden, 1976).

14 George Gallup, "Crime is Rated Worst Urban Problem," *The Washington Post*, January 16, 1973, p. A-3. Also see "Poll Finds Added Worry on Crime and Its Control," *The New York Times*, October 29, 1974, pp. 1 and 26.

15 A 1970 study of a representative sample of the population of Baltimore, Maryland, found great fear of being a victim of personal or property crime. See Steward Leland and Wentworth Clark, *Priorities for the 70's — Crime* (New York: John Day, 1971), pp. 1—25. Also see Louis Harris, "Changing Public Opinion Toward Crime and Corrections," *Federal Probation* 33 (March, 1969), 9—16 and Frank Furstenburg, Jr., "Public Reaction to Crime in the Streets," *The American Scholar* 40 (August, 1971) 601—10.

16 Originally, this question also was asked with reference to daytime safety, following the United States survey question, but the Swiss response on the pretest was one of such amused ridicule that the question was dropped.

17 American Institute of Public Opinion study, cited in Michael J. Hindelang, "Public Opinion Regarding Crime, Criminal Justice, and Related Topics," *Journal of Research in Crime and Delinquency* 11:2 (July, 1974), 103.

18 "Poll Finds Added Worry on Crime and Its Control," *The New York Times*, October 29, 1974, pp. 1 and 26. Crime was the most important of eight problems mentioned by those living in the Harlem area of New York City 1974 survey. Over one-half of the persons interviewed in Harlem gave crime as the most important concern, outranking, for example, housing, unemployment, inflation, education, etc. See *The New York Times*, November 21, 1974, pp. 1 ff.

19 Thomas Held and René Levy, *Die Stellung der Frau in Familie und Gesellschaft* (Frauenfeld Stuttgart: Verlag Huber, 1974).

20 *Media-Informationen (Tages Anzeiger)*. Circulation data from a 1973 media study of Swiss-German newspapers.

21 Leif Lenke, "Criminal Policy and Public Opinion Towards Crimes of Violence," preliminary report to the Council of Europe, 1973 (mimeo). The period studied was May 24—9, 1971.

22 Cherie Kay Hurlbut, "A Content Analysis of German and American Popular and Quality Newspapers," thesis in partial fulfillment of B.A. degree in journalism, University of Wisconsin, 1974.

23 Ibid.

24 Paul J. Deutschmann, *News-page Content of Twelve Metropolitan Dailies* (Cincinnati: Scripps-Howard Research, 1959). Deutschmann was then a professor at Michigan State University.

25 Crime news customarily is assigned to certain pages: in *Tages Anzeiger*, for example, certain pages are assigned to city crime, and others to canton crimes.

26 Lenke, "Criminal Policy."

3. Trends in official crime statistics

1 Günther Kaiser, "The Volume, Development, and Structure of Registered Criminality in Regard to Switzerland," unpublished lectures, the University of Freiburg and the University of Basel, 1973 (English translation).

2 Part of the greater increase in crime in the Federal German Republic, as compared with Switzerland, however, can be explained by the more likely increases in the police registration of small thefts in the criminal statistics (crimes known to the police) in the former, as compared to the latter.

3 *Die Strafurteile in der Schweiz/Les Condamnations pénales en Suisse 1972* (Bern: Eidgenössisches Statistisches Amt, 1973).

4 Arrests for murder in Geneva (1968—72) averaged only two per year.

5 *Uniform Crime Reports, 1972* (Washington, D.C.: U.S. Government Printing Office, 1973), p. 102.

6 Calculated from 1965—72 *Uniform Crime Reports,* published in Washington annually by the U.S. Government Printing Office.

7 The Zürich crime victimization figures also included purse-snatching, and this inflated the figure. Legally, the taking of money from a person without a weapon, or without the use of force and violence, is not considered robbery in Switzerland and is not included in official statistics as such. It is regarded as a form of theft.

8 In Zürich in 1977 a thief ran into a bank located in the center of the city, leaped onto a teller's counter, snatched Sw. F. 52,000 from an open drawer, and ran outside — all in a few seconds.

9 *News From Sweden*, Swedish Information Service, (New York: Swedish Consulate General, March, 1976), p. 3.

10 *Time*, July 19, 1976, p. 32.

11 Data for property crime were supplied to me by officials in the cantons of Zürich and Bern, but they were considered chiefly as burglaries and thefts.

12 Kaiser, "Volume, Development, and Structure." Kaiser also estimates that the chances of a shoplifter's being apprehended, at least in the Federal German Republic are about one in twenty.

13 Rolf Stephani, "Die Wegnahme von Waren in Selbstbedienungsgeschäften durch Kunden, Eine kriminologische Untersuchung von 1481 Tätern," *Berner kriminologische Untersuchungen*, Hans Schultz, ed. (Bern and Stuttgart: Verlag Paul Haupt, 1968), Vol. 5. Also see Rolf Stephani, "La Soustraction de Marchandises par les Clients des grands Magasins," *International Exchange* 4 (1968), 284.

14 Stephani's study involved 1,481 apprehended offenders, but he estimated that approximately 90 percent of all shoplifters go undetected.

15 Between 1972 and 1975, auto thefts for Switzerland (except for the Canton of Aargau) increased 5 percent, but there was a decrease of 4 percent in Zürich canton during this same period — probably due to the safety locks for steering wheels — according to the Zürich police. See "Statistik des Fahrzeugfahndungsdienstes von Kantons und Stadtpolizei, Zürich, 1964—1975," unpublished, Zürich Kantonpolizei.

16 The eight were Zürich, Bern, Basel-Stadt, Basel-Land, Geneva, Solothurn, Vaud, and Ticino.

17 Data furnished to me by the Office of the Bundesanswalt (Federal Attorney-General). Of the 1973 cases, 41 percent involved traffic in drugs.

18 Ingemar Rexed and Nils Wickberg, "Domar I Narkotikamal" (mimeo), Riksåklagåren, 1973.

19 See Harald Olav Siegrist, "Drug Abuse in Switzerland," *The International Journal of the Addictions* 7 (1972), 170. Only 720 persons, or 20.3 percent were investigated for the use of opiates. As measured by police investigations, the movement to the use of hard drugs appears to be increasing: Heroin investigations in the city of Zürich, for example, increased from 6 in 1970 to 154 in 1973. *Tages Anzeiger Magazin,* May 5, 1974

20 H. Solms, M. Burmer, and H. Feldman, *Jeunesse, Drogue, Société en Suisse, 1970—1972* (Lausanne: Payot, 1972). Also see M. Weidmann, D. Ladewig, V. Faust, M. Gastpar, H. Heise, V. Hobi, Sybille Mayer-Boss, and P. Wyss, "Drogengebrauch von Basler Schülern — ein Beitrag zur Epidemiologie," *Schweizerische Medizinische Wochenschrift* 103 (January, 1973), 121—6.

21 R. Battegay, R. Mühlemann, R. Zehnder, and A. Dillinger, "Konsumverhalten einer repräsentativen Stichprobe von 4082 gesunden 20-jährigen Schweizer Männern in bezug auf Alkohol, Drogen und Rauchwaren," *Schweizerische Medizinische Wochenschrift* 105 (1975), 180—7.

22 From 1946 to 1968, statistics have been published in *Schweizerische Kriminalstatistik, Statistique de la Criminalité en Suisse,* and from 1969 onward they appeared in *Die Strafurteile in der Schweiz, Les Condamnations Pénales en Suisse,* edited by Eidgenössisches Statistisches Amt, Bern. For many years Professor Hans Schultz, Faculty of Law, University of Bern, has made an annual analysis of these statistics. They have been published in *Schweizerische Zeitschrift für Kriminologie und Strafrechtsreform.* What has been used here has been a longer time span and the application of more sophisticated statistical techniques.

23 This limitation to criminal statistics accounts for differences in some other analyses of *total convictions* in Switzerland that have included traffic offenses.

24 Until 1961 each fine of at least Sw. F. 50 for petty offenses was included in the statistics. Thereafter, only petty offenses involving deprivation of liberty or a fine of Sw. F. 100 were included. Our analysis covers the period 1960—71, except in *rates* for total convictions, property convictions, and larceny, where the 1961 figure is used as the base. The statistical tabulation method changes between 1960 and 1961 were discovered too late to affect the other analyses. The trend analysis covers an eleven-year period; however, the correlations and the regression coefficients were not materially affected. Only small rate changes occurred in using 1960, rather than 1961, data.

25 Roger Hood and Richard Sparks, *Key Issues in Criminology* (New York: World University Library, 1970), p. 44.

26 Kaiser, "Volume, Development, and Structure," p. 68.

27 Ibid.

28 Ibid.

29 Hans Schultz's studies show that the Swiss crime rate, as measured by convictions, has recently been showing a small general increase in total convictions but a decrease in some types of crime.

30 Donald J. Newman, *Conviction: The Determination of Guilt or Innocence Without Trial* (Boston: Little, Brown, 1966).

31 Unfortunately, it was discovered too late that the value of thefts included in the statistics had been increased from Sw. F. 50 to Sw. F. 100 in 1961. This did not materially affect the correlation and regression coefficients, however, between 1960 and 1971. (See Appendix C.)

32 Hans Schultz, "Schweiz Kriminalstatistik 1966," *Zeitschrift für Schweizerische Strafrecht* 83 (1968), 220.

33 *Die Strafurteile der Schweiz*, 1972 Bern: Federal Statistics Bureau, 1974, p. 30.

34 "2 Arrestations à Nice," *La Suisse* May 5, 1977, pp. 1 and 23.

35 In 1972, 1,268 persons entered the cantonal prison in Bellinzona, Canton of Ticino, most of them prisoners awaiting trial: There were 241 from Ticino; 149 from other Swiss cantons; and 703 from Italy. In addition, there were 49 Germans, 31 Yugoslavs, 18 Spaniards, 13 Frenchmen, 11 Austrians; 13 East Europeans, 4 Greeks, 4 Belgians, 4 Scandinavians, 2 British, 1 Portuguese, and 25 nationals of other countries.

4. The Swiss police and crime reporting

1 Clarence Schrag, *Crime and Justice: American Style* (Rockville, Md.: National Institute of Mental Health, 1971), p. 147. Also see Elmer H. Johnson, 3rd ed., *Crime, Correction, and Society* (Homewood, Ill.: Dorsey, 1974), Chapter 13, p. 333.

2 As plebiscites in several cantons have rejected such proposals, it is likely to be a long time before such intercantonal police cooperation will cover all of Switzerland.

3 Statistics were furnished by Major Dr. P. Grob, Commander of the Zürich canton police, although they were gathered by the St. Gallen cantonal police. Statistics consisted of the number of police in various categories; the analysis here is limited to the effective police force. In the case of a few cantons civilian employees have been included, as it was not possible to exclude them. Most cantonal police forces constitute all the police, but in some cantons city forces had to be combined with the cantonal forces. For example, the total for Zürich and Bern include the forces of the cantons plus the cities; this was not the case in Basel and Geneva, as in these two cases, the cantons and cities are virtually identical.

4 *Crime in the United States, 1972*, Uniform Crime Reports for the United States, Federal Bureau of Investigation, U.S. Department of Justice (Washington, D.C.: Superintendent of Documents, 1973), p. 163.

5 Egon Stephan, *Die Stuttgarter Opferbefragung: Eine kriminologischviktimologische Analyse zur Erforschung des Dunkelfeldes unter besonderer Berücksichtigung der Einstellung der Bevölkerung zur Kriminalität*, BKA Forschungsreihe Bd. 3 (Wiesbaden, 1976), p. 325.

6 Louis Harris and Associates Survey, 1970, reported in Michael J. Hindelang, *Public Opinion Regarding Crime* (Washington, D.C.: Law Enforcement Assistance Administration, Department of Justice, 1975).

7 For a discussion of some of these issues, see Richard Sparks, Hazel G. Genn, and David J. Dodd, *Surveying Victims: A Study of the Measurement of Criminal Victimization, Perceptions of Crime, and Attitudes to Criminal Justice* (London: Wiley, 1977).

8 In Zürich 71 percent of victims for all offenses reported them themselves, 14 percent were reported by another household member, 12 percent by someone else, and 2 percent involved cases where the police were present when the crime was committed.

9 Law Enforcement Assistance Administration, *Crime in Eight American Cities* (Washington, D.C.: U.S. Government Printing Office, 1974), p. 8. These cities were similar in size to Zürich. For a detailed analysis of victimization studies, see Michael J. Hindelang, *Criminal Victimization in Eight American Cities* (Cambridge, Mass.: Ballinger Publishing Co., 1976).

10 Ragnar Hauge and Preben Wolf, "Violence in Three Scandinavian Countries," *Scandinavian Studies in Criminology*, 5 (1974), 25. A follow-up study of assault was made in 1974. The results, available only for Denmark, indicated that only 13.5 percent were reported. See Preben Wolf, "Victimization Research and Means Other than Crime Statistics to Provide Data on Criminality," a report presented at the Second Criminological Colloquium, Council of Europe, Strasbourg, August 20, 1975 (mimeo), p. 17.

5. Crime victimization in Zürich

1 It has often been charged in the United States, and in some other countries, that the police themselves do not always record crimes, either those reported to them or discovered themselves, until they have been "cleared" by arrest, as they fear they might be subject to criticism for lack of efficiency by the public, the press, or by higher authorities. See, for example, Edwin H. Sutherland and Donald R. Cressey, *Criminology*, 9th ed. (Philadelphia: Lippincott, 1974), p. 28.

2 Philip H. Ennis, *Criminal Victimization in the United States: A Report of a National Survey*, the President's Commission on Law Enforcement and Administration of Justice, Field Surveys II (Washington, D.C.: U.S. Government Printing Office, May 1976), and Albert D. Biderman et al., *Report on a Pilot Study in the District of Columbia on Victimization and Attitudes Toward Law Enforcement*, the President's Commission, Field Surveys I (Washington, D.C.: U.S. Government Printing Office, 1967), and Albert J. Reiss, Jr., *Studies in Crime and Law Enforcement in the Major Metropolitan Areas*, the President's Commission on Law Enforcement and Administration of Justice, Field Surveys III, Vol. 1 (Washington, D.C.: U.S. Government Printing Office, 1967).

3 *Crime in the Nation's Largest Cities.* National Crime Panel Surveys of Chicago, Detroit, Los Angeles, New York, and Philadelphia. U.S. Department of Justice, Law Enforcement Assistance Administration, National Criminal Justice Information and Statistics Service (Washington, D.C., April, 1974). Law Enforcement Assistance Administration, *Crime in Eight Cities* (Washington, D.C.: U.S. Government Printing Office, 1974). See also *Criminal Victimization in the United States, A Comparison of 1973 and 1974 Findings*, A National Crime Panel Survey Report, U.S. Department of Justice, Law Enforcement Assistance Administration, National Criminal Justice Information and Statistics Service (Washington, D.C.: U.S. Government Printing Office, May 1976). For a discussion of the advantages and problems of United States victimization studies, see Daniel Glaser, *Strategic Criminal Justice Planning* (Rockville, Md.: National Institute of Mental Health Center for Studies of Crime and Delinquency, 1975), pp. 195–9. Also see Marie G. Argana, "Development of a National Victimization Survey," in Israel Drapkin and Emilio Viano, eds., *Victimology: A New Focus* (Lexington, Mass.: Heath, 1973), Vol. III, *Crimes, Victims, and Justice*, pp. 171–9. Also see Wesley G. Skogan, "Victimization Surveys and Criminal Justice Planning," *University of Cincinnati Law Review* 45 (1976) 167–206, and Michael J. Hindelang, *Criminal Victimization in Eight American Cities* (Cambridge, Mass.: Ballinger, 1976).

4 Ragnar Hauge and Preben Wolf, "Violence in Three Scandinavian Countries," *Scandinavian Studies in Criminology*, 5 (1974).

5 Richard Sparks, Hazel G. Genn, and David J. Dodd, *Surveying Victims: A Study of the Measurement of Criminal Victimization, Perceptions of Crime, and Attitudes to Criminal Justice* (London: Wiley, 1977).

6 Egon Stephan, *Die Stuttgarter Opferbefragung: Eine kriminologischvictimologische Analyse zur Erforschung des Dunkelfeldes unter besonderer Berücksichtigung der Einstellung der Bevölkerung zur Kriminalität*, BKA Forschungsreihe 3 (Wiesbaden, 1976) and Egon Stephan, "Die Ergebnisse der Stuttgarter Opferbefragung unter Berücksichtigung vergleichbarer amerikanischer Daten," *Kriminalistik* 5 (May 1975), 201—6. These surveys were carried out under the general direction of Professor Günther Kaiser who is director of the Institute of Criminology, University of Freiburg.

7 Hans Dieter Schwind, Wilfried Ahlborn, Hans Jürgen Eger, Ulrich Jany, Volker Pudel, and Rüdiger Weiss, *Dunkelfeldforschung in Göttingen, 1973—1974. Eine Opferbefragung zur Aufhellung des Dunkelfeldes und zur Erforschung der Bestimmungsgründe für die Unterlassung von Strafanzeigen* (Wiesbaden: Bundesdruckerei, 1975).

8 W. Buikhusen, *Geregistreerde en niet-geregistreerde Kriminaliteit* (The Hague: Ministry of Justice, 1975).

9 Yves Brillon, "Justice Pénale Moderne et Traditionnelle en Côte d'Ivoire," *Internationale Journal de Criminologie et de Police Technique* 27 (1975). Brillon has another publication in press.

10 See Anthony G. Turner, "Victimization Surveying — Its History, Uses and Limitations," prepared for the Report of the National Advisory Commission on Criminal Justice Standards and Goals, Statistics Division, LEAA, Washington, D.C., 1972. Also see Marshall B. Clinard, "Comparative Crime Victimization Surveys: Some Problems and Results," *International Journal of Criminology and Penology* (to be published in Autumn 1978).

11 A well-known survey that tested the two methods of response, for example, used simply a "household respondent," rather than limiting the household repondent to the household head. See *Crimes and Victims: A Report on the Dayton—San Jose Pilot Survey of Victimization* (Washington, D.C.: U.S. Department of Justice, Law Enforcement Assistance Administration, June, 1974).

12 Complete coverage would have necessitated interviewing each household member over the age of 14, totaling 940 interviews, instead of the 482 household heads. With the estimated cost of about $20 per head, funds were simply not available for doubling the number of interviews.

13 Thomas Held and Réne Levy, *Die Stellung der Frau in Familie und Gesellschaft* (Frauenfeld and Stuttgart: Verlag Huber, 1974).

14 The fact that household respondents surveyed in some U.S. cities did not know of as many as half of the robberies or attempted robberies of other household members shows the unique situation that prevails in U.S. urban areas with high crime rates. See *Crimes and Victims*.

15 Surveys of assault and attempted assault in San Jose, California, and Dayton, Ohio, indicated a 75-percent error in replies of household respondents, generally. (See *Crimes and Victims*, p. 36.) This high percentage error was considered far too high for the Swiss data. Consequently, an adjustment was made by increasing the 23 reported assaults by 50 percent, or 3.5 percent of the households, on the assumption that one-half of them would have occurred in households not reporting the offenses. Small thefts or acts of vandalism were regarded as offenses in which the cash value of items such as clothing, vehicle parts, and unspecific household items was known to be less than Sw. F. 50 ($15). This amounted to 78 out of 119 cases, or 66 percent, and thus the total of 119 larcenies was increased 66 percent, making a total of 197 larcenies. It was assumed, moreover, that one-half of the adjusted increase involved additional victimized households, or 39. No corrections were made on robbery or attempted robbery, as they are most uncommon offenses throughout

Switzerland and would thus have been more obvious topics of general household knowledge and interest.

16　The translation was done by Thomas Held of the Sociological Institute of the University of Zürich, who acted as a research assistant on the study.

17　For a discussion of some of the problems of definitions, see Sparks, *Surveying Victims.* Also see James P. Levine, "The Potential for Crime Overreporting in Criminal Victimization Surveys," *Criminology* 14 (November 1976), 307—30.

18　Clinard, "Comparative Crime Victimization Surveys."

19　*Crime in Eight American Cities.*

20　This involved the same basic questionnaire and similar sampling procedures. See Stephan, *Die Stuttgarter Opferbefragung.* The Stuttgart survey, unfortunately, did not include foreign workers, as had been done in Zürich, due to the fact that it was found to be too difficult to obtain responses from them. The effect was probably minimal, inasmuch as few differences were found between the Swiss and the foreign-born workers in Zürich. For this reason, as well as some differences in tabulation procedures, the comparative conclusions must be regarded as only approximate comparisons.

21　*Kriminalitätsatlas der Bundesrepublik Deutschland und West Berlins* (Wiesbaden: Bundeskriminalamt, 1972), p. 43.

22　Preben Wolf, "Vold i Danmark og Finland 1970—1971: En Samnenligning af Voldsofre" (mimeo), Criminological Institute, University of Copenhagen, April 30, 1972.

23　Preben Wolf, "Individuelle ofre for Ejendomsforbrydelser i Danmark 1971/1972" (mimeo), Criminological Institute, University of Copenhagen, August 7, 1974.

24　Sparks et al., *Surveying Victims.*

25　In fact, the number of reported crimes was extremely small in some cases: only six auto thefts, ten robberies, including attempts, and two attempted rapes were reported. Where such small frequencies occur, some questions may be raised about the reliability of the data. They can be answered as follows: (1) Had the frequency of crimes been as high as it is in most United States cities, the number of incidents would probably have been adequate, even though the original sample was no larger; (2) because analysis is focused on the frequency of crime incidents, and not as much on comparisons of incidents by characteristics of the persons, small frequencies are not a major handicap. If frequencies were very small, no analysis was attempted; (3) finally, due to limited funds, it was not possible to draw a sample large enough to give a greater, and consequently a more significant, number of incidents.

26　Household respondents were asked if they personally had ever been victimized during their entire lifetimes; in both Zürich and Stuttgart two-thirds of the samples reported no previous victimization. This finding is important, in spite of obvious problems of recall. Zürich respondents generally reported only one incident, although one in ten said they had been victimized more than once. No differences were found by sex, but those in higher economic levels reported more lifetime victimizations, a finding contrary to expectations.

27　The twelve Zürich political districts were grouped into the Old City (mixed area of stores, houses, and apartments), working-class areas, salaried employee areas, and higher-income residential areas.) Because of the mixed class and occupational residence of most areas, the urban district in which the household was located was only partially useful and represents only a rough approximation of the predominant type. The average income of the Swiss worker is high, and thus income differentials are not as great as they are in some countries.

28　The U.S. Census—LEAA survey uses people aged 12 and over, one of the several reasons being that they are victims of theft of bicycles and are robbed; paper boys are often subjected to robbery of their collections or assaulted. Even the age of 14 would be considered to be too low by many Swiss, and 16 perhaps would have been a more realistic figure.

The Stuttgart survey also was based on age 14 and over. Even with a change in age groups, however, there probably would have been little rate differences. No assaults, robberies, rapes, or sexual threats were reported in the age group 14—19, and only 9.4 percent of this group were reported to have had anything stolen from them. Even with some errors in the respondents' reporting, the general crime picture for this younger age group probably would not have been affected.

29 There were only two cases, both reported attempted rapes of males — presumably homosexual rapes. The number was too small for analysis.

30 Individuals victimized in Zürich generally did not know or recognize the offenders. Only 6 percent recognized all of the offenders, 3 percent recognized some of them, and 87 percent recognized none. The percentage was about the same in the Stuttgart study for those who recognized none (89 percent). (Four percent did not know.) Surprisingly, slightly more perpetrators of property offenses were recognized than of personal crimes: In nine out of ten cases of personal crimes the offender was unknown to the victim, a much higher figure than is found in similar United States studies. For property crime, 85 percent recognized none of the offenders, 6 percent recognized all, 4 percent some, and 5 percent did not know. A somewhat reversed situation was found in Stuttgart, where 75 percent were unknown in personal offenses and 92 percent in property offenses.

31 A similar position was adopted in crime research carried out in Kampala, Uganda, in 1969. See Marshall B. Clinard and Daniel J. Abbott, *Crime in Developing Countries* (New York: Wiley, 1973). Since 1975 the larceny-theft statistics in the *Uniform Crime Reports* in the United States no longer are restricted to the value of the stolen object, which previously had been $50 or more.

32 For a discussion of the wide market for nearly any type of stolen used goods in the developing countries see Clinard and Abbott, *Crime in Developing Countries*, pp. 37—8.

6. Measuring crimes by theft insurance

1 *The New York Times*, May 6, 1974.

2 *Society* 12 (November/December 1974), 10—11.

3 Estimates were furnished by Rhodes-Gallagher and Associates, Inc., Madison, Wisconsin, representatives for Aetna Insurance Company.

4 In some cantons, where household theft coverage is obligatory, "simple theft" insurance can be excluded if one desires a lower rate.

5 The foreign quotations given here have been translated into dollars, using the rate of exchange in early 1973 of approximately three Swiss francs to the dollar.

6 These United States data were furnished by Aetna Casualty and Surety Company, one of the country's largest companies. Their assistance in providing these data is gratefully acknowledged.

7 These figures do not include such administrative costs as appraisals and the like. Figures reported here are the totals of all Swiss companies, furnished by Schweizerische Mobiliar.

8 The Swedish insurance data were secured directly from the companies by Leif Persson, Research Associate, Department of Sociology, University of Stockholm, in 1973. I should like to acknowledge his assistance.

7. White-collar crime and tax violations

1 Richard Quinney, *The Social Reality of Crime* (Boston: Little, Brown, 1970), pp. 3—25.

2 Edwin H. Sutherland, *White Collar Crime* (New York: Holt, Rinehart & Winston, 1949). While Sutherland's use of the term has been criticized as being too broad in scope, it be-

came the accepted term for such illegal behavior. A more useful distinction is (1) occupational crime, or crimes committed in the course of any legitimate occupation, whether white collar or not, and (2) crime committed by large organizational units, companies, corporations or their officers, either to further the corporation or their own objectives. A term currently in use for both occupational and corporate business crime is "economic crime." See Marshall B. Clinard and Richard Quinney, *Criminal Behavior Systems: A Typology,* 2nd ed. (New York: Holt, Rinehart and Winston, 1973), Chapters 7 and 8, "Occupational Criminal Behavior," and "Corporate Criminal Behavior." Following Sutherland, "white-collar crime" includes violations of administrative, civil, and criminal laws of the political state. To do otherwise would make it difficult to compare their illegal behavior with that of ordinary offenders who are dealt with only by the criminal law.

3   Gilbert Geis, "Avocational Crime," in Daniel Glaser, ed., *Handbook of Criminology* (Chicago: Rand McNally, 1974), p. 273. Also see Gilbert Geis and Robert F. Meier, eds., *White-Collar Crime,* rev. ed. (New York: The Free Press, 1977).

4   Marshall B. Clinard, "White Collar Crime," *International Encyclopedia of the Social Sciences* (New York: Macmillan and Free Press, 1968), pp. 483—90.

5   John C. Spencer, "A Study of Incarcerated White-Collar Offenders," in Gilbert Geis, ed., *White-Collar Criminal: The Offender in Business and the Professions* (New York: Atherton, 1968), p. 342.

6   See Niklaus Schmid, "Probleme der Untersuchungsführung," *Monatszeitschrift des Gottlieb Duttweiler-Institut* 11/12 (1970), 32—5.

7   Bernhard R. Rimann, *Wirtschaftskriminalität: Die Untersuchung bei Wirtschaftsdelikten* (Zürich: Schulthess Polygraphischer Verlag, 1973), pp. 54—5. This opinion was also expressed by several informed persons, such as Alfred Messerli, a leading Swiss journalist of *Tages Anzeiger* who has studied white-collar offenses in Switzerland. He wrote a series of newspaper articles on the subject and a special journal article. See *Tages Anzeiger,* June 28, July 5, July 12, July 19, July 26, and August 2, 1969. Also see Alfred Messerli, "Möglichkeiten der Presse zur Vorbeugung," *Monatszeitschrift des Gottlieb Duttweiler-Institut* 11/12 (1970), 42—6. This special issue of the well-recognized *Monatszeitschrift des Gottlieb Duttweiler-Institut* was devoted to white-collar crime, indicating an increased concern about these offenses.

8   Rimann, *Wirtschaftskriminalität.*

9   Willy Ulrich, "Wie können Wirtschaftsdelikte verhindert werden?" *Monatszeitschrift des Gottlieb Duttweiler-Institut* 11/12 (1970), 36—41.

10   The President's Commission on Law Enforcement and Administration of Justice, *The Challenge of Crime in a Free Society* (New York: Avon, 1968), p. 158. A study of 100 white-collar crime court cases in the canton of Zürich between 1960 and 1974, for example, found that they were mostly Swiss, about 40 years of age, and with above-average educational status. See Niklaus Schmid, "Der Wirtschaftstäter. Ergebnisse einer Züricher Untersuchung. Folgerungen für Prävention und Repression der Wirtschaftsdelikte" *Schweizerische Zeitschrift für Strafrecht* 92 (1976), 51—97.

11   Quinney, *Social Reality,* p. 18.

12   Erwin Zimmerli, "Kommt dem Begriff der Wirtschaftskriminalität wirklich nur kriminaltaktische Bedeutung zu?" *Schweizerische Zeitschrift für Strafrecht* 91 (1975), 305—20.

13   Schmid, "Probleme der Untersuchungsführung," 32.

14   Rimann, *Wirtschaftskriminalität.*

15   Wilhelm Aubert, "White Collar Crime and Social Structure," *American Journal of Sociology* 58 (1952), 263—71.

16   Whitney North Seymour, Jr., *Fighting White Collar Crime: A Handbook on How to Combat Crime in the Business World* (New York: Office of the United States Attorney for the Southern District of New York, December, 1972), p. 16.

17 Sutherland, *White Collar Crime*. Also see Marshall B. Clinard, *The Black Market: A Study of White Collar Crime* (New York: Holt, Rinehart and Winston, 1952; reprinted by Patterson Smith, paperback, 1972) and Robert E. Lane, "Why Business Men Violate the Law," *Journal of Criminal Law, Criminology, and Police Science*, 44 (1953), 151—65.

18 See Clinard, *The Black Market*, pp. 333—40.

19 Sutherland, *White Collar Crime*, p. 220.

20 Ulrich, "Wie können."

21 The first example is from Messerli, "Möglichkeiten."

22 T. R. Fehrenbach, *The Gnomes of Zürich* (London: Leslie Frewin, 1974). For a history of the development of Swiss banking, see pages 32—117. The first edition of Fehrenbach's book appeared in 1966. Also see Ray Vicker, *Those Swiss Money Men* (New York: Scribners, 1973).

23 Fehrenbach, *Gnomes*, pp. 44—5.

24 Ibid., p. 131.

25 For a discussion of these complex international banking operations, see Jean Ziegler, *Une Suisse au-dessus de tout Soupçon* (Paris: Editions du Seuil, 1976). For a reply to Ziegler, see Victor Lassere, *Une Suisse insoupçonnée; Lettre ouverte à Jean Ziegler* (Paris: Editions Buchet, 1977).

26 Fehrenbach, *Gnomes*, pp. 25—6.

27 Ibid., p. 13.

28 Thurston Clarke and John Tigue, Jr., *Dirty Money: Swiss Banks, the Mafia, Money Laundering and White Collar Crime* (London: Millington Books, 1976), p. 110.

29 Ibid., p. 111.

30 Ibid.

31 Clifford Irving (with Richard Suskind), *Clifford Irving: What Really Happened; His Untold Story of the Hughes Affair* (New York: Grove Press, 1972).

32 Clarke and Tigue, *Dirty Money*, p. 29.

33 Ibid.

34 Ibid., p. 30.

35 Peter-Dieter Klingenberg, "Schützt das schweizerische Bankgeheimnis den Wirtschaftstäter?" *Monatszeitschrift des Gottlieb Duttweiler-Institut* 11/12 (1970), 46—50.

36 Fehrenbach, *Gnomes*, p. 75.

37 Hans Schultz, *Banking Secrecy and the Swiss-American Treaty on Legal Assistance in Criminal Matters* (Zürich: Swiss Bank Corporation, 1977), p. 7. This was originally published in French as *Le Secret bancaire et le Traité d'entraide judiciare en Matière pénale conclu entre la Suisse et les Etats-Unis d'Amérique* (Zürich: Société de Banque Suisse, 1976). See, particularly, pp. 8—13 in the English version.

38 Schultz, *Banking Secrecy and the Swiss-American Treaty*, pp. 6—7.

39 Ibid., particularly pp. 8—12.

40 Ibid., pp. 21—30.

41 This poll was conducted by Isopublic Institute of Zürich for the Swiss Credit Bank (Crédit Suisse).

42 Hans J. Mast, "Swiss Bank Secrecy: Its Rules and Limits," *Gazette*, September 17, 1975, p. 8. *Gazette* is a Swissair publication. Hans J. Mast is Executive Vice-President, Swiss Credit Bank.

43 F. Zuppinger, "Der Steuerbetrug unter Berücksichtigung des züricherischen Rechts," *"Schweizerische Zeitschrift für Strafrecht* 91 (1975), 113—81.

44 There are a few exceptions. Zürich canton, for example, made fraud on direct taxes a crime in 1951. The only federal law making tax fraud a crime was enacted in 1974.

45 Report of the Federal Government to the Members of the Federal Parliament Concerning the Success of the Tax-Amnesty of 1969 (June 1, 1972).

8. Political decentralization and the criminal justice system

1 Marshall B. Clinard, "The Relation of Urbanization and Urbanism to Criminal Behavior," in Ernest W. Burgess and Donald J. Bogue, eds., *Contributions to Urban Sociology* (Chicago: University of Chicago Press, 1965), pp. 541—58; Denis Szabo, *Crimes et Villes* (Louvain, France: Catholic University of Louvain, 1960); Denis Szabo, *Criminologie* (Montreal: University of Montreal Press, 1965); and Denis Szabo, "Urbanisation et Criminalité," *Revue de Sociologie* 1 (1963), 38—52.

2 Marshall B. Clinard and Daniel J. Abbott, *Crime in Developing Countries: A Comparative Perspective* (New York: Wiley, 1973).

3 U.S. Department of Justice, *Uniform Crime Reports 1975* (Washington, D.C.: U.S. Government Printing Office, 1976), pp. 160—1.

4 Law Enforcement Assistance Administration, *Criminal Victimization in the United States 1973* (Washington, D.C.: U.S. Department of Justice, December, 1976), pp. 80—1.

5 Michel Bassand, "Urbanisation et Politique: Quelques Aspects du Problème en Suisse," *Transactions of the Sixth World Congress of Sociology* (International Sociological Association) 4 (1970), 413—33.

6 E. A. Gutkind, *Urban Development in the Alpine and Scandinavian Countries,* Vol. II (New York: The Free Press, 1965), p. 180. Sweden has also had a slow growth of urbanization, from 21.5 percent in 1900, to 29.5 percent in 1920, to 51.2 percent in 1960.

7 Ibid.

8 C. B. Arwed Emminghaus, *Die Schweizerische Volkswirtschaft* (Leipzig: G. Mayer, 1860).

9 For a discussion of the slum and the slum "way of life," see Marshall B. Clinard, *Slums and Community Development: Experiments in Self-Help* (New York: The Free Press, 1966; paperback, 1970), pp. 3—23.

10 Anne-Marie Conza and Danielle Simonet, "La Déliquance Juvénile: Enquête faite sur 100 Dossiers de Garçons ayant passé devant la Chambre Pénale de l'Enfance à Genève, 1965—1966," Institut d'Etudes Sociales, Genève (mimeo, 1971).

11 Madeleine Droz, "Enquête sur 70 Jeunes Délinquants habitant en Ville et dans les grands Ensembles de Genève," Institut d'Etudes Sociales, Genève (mimeo, 1971).

12 Werner Sutter, "Die Kriminalität im Kanton Basel-Stadt: Querschnittsuntersuchung zur Soziologie der Delinquenz," thesis written at the Faculty of Philosophy, University of Basel, 1970.

13 Kathrin Preiswerk-Gysin, "Jugenddelinquenz und Armut," Institut d'Etudes Sociales, Genève (mimeo, 1971).

14 Benjamin R. Barber, "Switzerland: Progress Against the Communes," *Society* 8 (February 1971), 30.

15 T. R. Fehrenbach, *The Gnomes of Zürich* (London: Leslie Frewin, 1974), pp; 19—20.

16 Walter Sorell, *The Swiss: A Cultural Panorama of Switzerland* (New York: Bobbs-Merrill, 1972), p. 24.

17 Barber, "Switzerland," p. 50.

18 Ibid.

19 Hektor Ammann and Karl Schib, eds., *Historischer Atlas der Schweiz,* 2nd ed. (Aarau: 1968), maps 41—67, which show the genesis of all the cantons. I am indebted to Alfred Neukom of the University of Zürich for his valuable research help on the historical development of Switzerland.

20 William E. Rappard, "Du Renouvellement des Pactes Confédéraux, 1351—1798," *Zeitschrift für Schweizerische Geschichte* (Zürich and Leipzig, 1944), Supplement No. 2, pp. 21—46, and Karl Mommsen, "Eidgenossen, Kaiser und Reich, Studien zur Stellung der Eidgenossenschaft innerhalb des Heiligen Römischen Reiches," *Basler Beiträge zur Geschichtswissenschaft* 72 (1958), 237—41.

21 F. Fleiner and G. Giacometti, *Schweizerisches Bundesstaatsrecht* (Zürich: 1949), pp. 1—20. Also see Ammann and Schib, *Historischer Atlas,* map 33, and Paul Klaüi and Eduard Imhof, *Atlas zur Geschichte des Kantons Zürich* (Zürich: 1951), maps 5—8 concerning Zürich canton.

22 For example, most of the rural districts in the canton of Graubünden contintue to elect representatives to the canton parliament in their Landsgemeinde.

23 Georg Thürer, *Free and Swiss: The Story of Switzerland* (London: Oswald Wolff, 1970), p. 175.

24 Ibid., p. 173.

25 I had a number of personal experiences of this type. On one occasion in Bern when I stopped on the street to clean the windshield of my car, several persons told me that I should not stop in that particular place. On one cold day when I left the motor on while I was waiting in a parking lot, a woman passing with a young child asked me to turn off the motor, as it was polluting the air. If autos are left unattended for several days they are frequently reported to the police. I was once told that a Geneva car owner whose license had expired was reported to the police by persons living in his apartment building.

26 Peter Tonge, "Switzerland Working Well," *Christian Science Monitor,* as reprinted in *The Wisconsin State Journal,* March 29, 1976, section 5, p. 1.

27 At the time of this research the only other honor system known to me is that of Amsterdam, the only city where it is used in the Netherlands. During a brief stay there I was checked on three different occasions. Although there are unattended coin boxes, particularly in Socialist countries, into which fares are dropped at the rear of the vehicle, this is not the same system as that used in Switzerland, as others can see if one drops in coins in a vehicle farebox, whereas one is often unobserved at bus stops, and passengers do not know if others have either bought tickets or had a coupon stamped in the machines. Experiments in the use of a similar honor system on railroads were being conducted in the Bern area in 1976, thus largely eliminating a regular conductor on certain lines.

28 *Neue Zürcher Zeitung,* March 14, 1975, p. 50.

29 The original canton concordat on the traffic in firearms was established in 1944. The new concordat of 1969 is binding on all but five cantons, but they are still bound by the 1944 agreement.

30 Marvin E. Wolfgang and Franco Ferracuti, *The Subculture of Violence: Toward an Integrated Theory in Criminology* (London: Tavistock Publications, 1967) and Marvin E. Wolfgang, *Patterns in Criminal Homicide* (Philadelphia: The University of Pennsylvania Press, 1958).

31 See George D. Newton and Franklin E. Zimring, *Firearms and Violence in American Life: A Staff Report to the National Commission on the Causes and Prevention of Violence* (Washington, D.C.: U.S. Government Printing Office, 1970). The number of handguns is estimated to be increasing by 2 million a year. See report of the United States Conference of Mayors, *Hand Gun Control: Issues and Alternatives* (Washington, D.C., 1975).

32 Newton and Zimring, *Firearms,* p. 6.

33 Arrests are usually made only in homicides and in cases of serious violence, or when the officer believes that the person may flee the country.

34 These figures and those that follow come from the annual *Die Strafurteile in der Schweiz/ Les Condamnations pénales en Suisse,* edited in Bern by the Federal Statistics Bureau.

35 The use of the suspended sentence for juveniles between 1968 and 1972 also increased by 31.5 percent, and there was a 20.8 percent decrease in detention use.

36 Hans Schultz, "Der bedingte Strafvollzug," *Schweizerische Zeitschrift für Strafrecht* 89 (1973), 53. Schultz included all traffic offenses.

37 Swiss law provides three types of confinement facilities: a penitentiary (*Zuchthaus*), a prison (*Gefängnis*), or jail (*Haftstrafe*). Since 1971 there has been no differentiation in the

treatment of offenders sentenced to the penitentiary and prisons, and they are here regarded as the same. The only separation now in Swiss prisons is between first offenders and recidivists. See Hans Schultz, "Zuchthaus, Gefängnis, Einheitsstrafe," *Monatsschrift für Kriminologie und Strafrechtsreform* 51 (1968), 297–310.

38 Jerzy Jasiński, "Punitywnośc Systemów Karnych" (The Punitiveness of Penal Systems), *Polska Akademia Nauk, Instytut Nauk Prawnych, Studia Prawnicze* (Polish Academy of Science, Institute for Legal Science, Studies of Law) 35 (1973).

39 *The Correctional System, 1972* (Stockholm: The National Correctional Administration, 1973), p. 11.

40 Jasiński, "Punitywnośc."

41 *The Correctional System, 1972.*

42 Jasiński, "Punitywnośc."

43 Ibid. His analysis does not deal with the length of sentence for specific crimes. The variations by countries could be due, in part, to the fact that the different prison populations vary in the distribution of offenses.

44 Marshall B. Clinard and Richard Quinney, *Criminal Behavior Systems: A Typology,* 2nd ed. (New York: Holt, Rinehart and Winston, 1973), pp. 131–53. Also see Edwin M. Lemert, *Human Deviance, Social Problems, and Social Control,* 2nd ed. (Englewood Cliffs, N.J.: Prentice-Hall, 1972), pp. 62–92.

45 *Die Strafurteile in der Schweiz, 1971,* pp. 72–3.

46 According to a letter from Professor Günther Stratenwerth, University of Basel, who has conducted a study of Swiss prisons.

47 The only previous complete study of Swiss prison populations was made by a Basel prison chaplain in 1954 and revised in 1957. This study, however, concerned only capacity, and not the average number of inmates. See Martin Schwarz, *Verzeichnis der Anstalten in der Schweiz des Straf- und Massnahmevollzugs und der Untersuchungsgefangenschaft,* 2nd ed. (Basel: mimeo, 1959).

48 Two small institutions for administrative detention are not included.

49 The problem of security detention is less a legislative than an administrative one in Switzerland. It is governed by cantonal criminal procedure laws and by prison regulations. Some follow the French system, where the judge enjoys extensive discretionary authority in imposing security detention. Others follow the German system, which tends to circumscribe the powers of the judge, limiting detention to certain specified cases. The more recent codes provide additional safeguards for detained suspects' personal freedom. The imposition of security detention depends upon the gravity of the offense, serious indications of legal responsibility for it, need of investigation, probability of escape, and imminent social danger. Several cantons provide for the possibility of appeal or for indemnity in case of unjustified security detention. See François Clerc, "La Détention Préventive," *Schweizerische Zeitschrift für Strafrecht* 84:2 (1968), 149–73.

50 In a letter from Professor Günther Stratenwerth, February 20, 1974.

51 Ibid.

52 From *The Correctional System, 1972.*

53 Paul C. Friday, "Sanctioning in Sweden: An Over-view," *Federal Probation* 40 (1976), 48–55.

9. Youth and Swiss society

1 For studies see Edwin H. Sutherland and Donald R. Cressey, *Criminology,* 9th ed. (Philadelphia: Lippincott, 1974), pp. 71–93 and 187–97; Marshall B. Clinard, *Sociology of Deviant Behavior,* 4th ed. (New York: Holt, Rinehart and Winston, 1974), pp. 275–87;

and Marshall B. Clinard and Richard Quinney, *Criminal Behavior Systems*, 2nd ed. (New York: Holt, Rinehart and Winston, 1973), pp. 131–53.

2 Günther Kaiser, "The Volume, Development, and Structure of Registered Criminality in Regard to Switzerland," unpublished lectures, the University of Freiburg and the University of Basel, 1973.

3 Sveri reports a similar finding for Sweden. See Knut Sveri, "Brott och Brottslingar," in Knut Sveri, Gösta Rylander, Torsten Eriksson, and Åke Asp, *Kriminaliteten och Samhället* (Stockholm: Aldus-Bonniers, 1966), pp. 1–24. Swiss offenders are similar in age to those in developing countries – that is, 18 to 20 years old, the age at which young migrants usually leave the village for the city. See Marshall B. Clinard and Daniel J. Abbott, *Crime in Developing Countries* (New York: Wiley, 1973), p. 208.

4 J. Jürzinger, "Entwicklungstendenzen der Kriminalität," *Vorgänge* 12: (1973), 55–67.

5 Werner Sutter, *Die Kriminalität im Kanton Basel-Stadt: Querschnittsuntersuchung zur Soziologie der Delinquenz* (Basel: Birkhäuser A.G., 1970).

6 *Kriminalitätsatlas der Bundesrepublik Deutschland und West Berlin* (Wiesbaden: Bundeskriminalamt, 1972), p. 344.

7 Günther Kaiser, *Kriminologie: Eine Einführung in die Grundlagen* (Karlsruhe: Verlag C. F. Müller, 1971), Vol. 2, p. 133. Also see Joachim Schneider, *Kriminologie: Standpunkte und Probleme* (Berlin: Walter de Gruyter, 1974).

8 Kaiser, *Kriminologie*, p. 137.

9 Carl-Gunnar Janson, "Juvenile Delinquency in Sweden," *Youth and Society* (1970), 207–31. Also see Sven Rengby, "Uppgifter anförda i Betändet," *Ungdomsbrottslighet* (Stockholm: Statens offentliga utredningar, 1969), pp. 99–101.

10 *Crime in the United States, 1972* (Washington, D.C.: United States Government Printing Office, 1973), p. 126. The Uniform Crime Reports are issued each year by the Federal Bureau of Investigation of the U.S. Department of Justice.

11 *Crime in the United States, 1972*, p. 126. Although the Swiss figures are for convictions, the differences are so great that they are significant.

12 This Swiss research will be published as John Casparis and Edmund W. Vaz, *Swiss Society and Youth* (Leiden: E. J. Brill, 1978). The self-report questionnaires used by Casparis and Vaz covered various aspects of Zürich youth society, particularly the youth culture. From the original sample, responses were received from 997 persons (707 males, 290 females) in the age group 15–20. The sample was fairly broad-based, and 48.8 percent were from the working class, as measured by the father's occupation.

13 Robert Blancpain and Erich Häuselmann, *Zur Unrast der Jugend. Eine soziologische Untersuchung über Einstellungen, politische Verhaltensweisen und ihre gesellschaftlichen Determinanten (Reihe Soziologie in der Schweiz, Vol. 2)* (Frauenfeld and Stuttgart: Verlag Huber, 1974), p. 261. This interdepartmental project at the University of Zürich was initiated by a commission of Zürich city and sponsored by the canton of Zürich, the city of Zürich, and the Swiss National Foundation. Professor Peter Heintz supervised the sociological aspects of the project.

14 Two factors may be significant in this low profile of vandalism, from the point of view of official statistics. First, under the Swiss penal code, a person can be convicted for vandalism (Sachbeschädigung) only if the person affected by the action requests it. In other words, there must be a complaining victim. Second, any vandalism in connection with an offense such as burglary is generally recorded only as a burglary. See Clinard, *Sociology of Deviant Behavior*, pp. 306–8. Vandalism is rare in developing countries, where the destruction, rather than the theft of property, is often almost inconceivable. See Clinard and Abbott, *Crime in Developing Countries*, p. 44.

15 See Madeleine Droz, "Enquête sur 70 Jeunes Délinquants habitant en Ville et dans les

grands Ensembles de Genève," mimeo, Institut d'Etudes Sociales, Ecole de Service Social, Genève, May, 1971.

16 See Peter Bosshard, *Bildung als kriminologischer Faktor, Untersuchungen über kriminalsoziologische Zusammenhänge zwischen Bildungsgrad und kriminellem Verhalten Jugendlicher* (Zürich: Verlag Schulthess, 1968), p. 118.

17 See Sylvia Staub, *Ursachen und Erscheinungsformen bei der Bildung jugendlicher Banden* (Zürich: Verlag Schulthess, 1965), p. 16.

18 See Dick Blomberg, *Den Svenska ungdomsbrottsligheten* (Falun: Falu Nya Boktryckeri, 1960), p. 49. Also see Marshall B. Clinard's Swedish study, "The relation of Urbanization and Urbanism to Criminal Behavior," in Ernest W. Burgess and Donald J. Bogue, eds., *Contributions to Urban Sociology* (Chicago: University of Chicage Press, 1965), pp. 541–58. On the other hand, Hood and Sparks concluded from their survey of European studies that less evidence of much gang activity of a cohesive nature is found outside of the United States. See Roger Hood and Richard Sparks, *Key Issues in Criminology* (New York: McGraw-Hill, 1970), p. 94, and David M. Downes, *The Delinquent Solution* (London: Routledge, Kegan Paul, 1966), p. 199.

19 Staub, *Ursachen,* Chapter 11, "Jugendliche Banden in der Schweiz," pp. 118–23.

20 Staub, *Ursachen,* Chapter 12, "Jugendliche Banden in der Stadt Zürich," pp. 124–33.

21 *Tages Anzeiger,* January 11, 1974.

22 Anne-Marie Conza and Danielle Simonet, "La Délinquance Juvénile, Enquête faite sur 100 Dossiers de garçons ayant passé devant la Chambre Pénale d l'enfance à Genève, 1965/ 1966" (mimeo), Institut d'Etudes Sociales, Genève, 1971, p. 97. A forensic psychiatrist who works with youth in connection with his clinic at the University of Geneva told me in 1973 that no *formal* youth gangs existed in all of Geneva. He stated that the groups that did exist were loosely organized, had no self-identity as a group, no set philosophy, and no leaders, all of which constitute a situation quite different from that found in cities in France, for example. See Philippe Parrott and Monique Gueneau, *Les Gangs d'Adolescents* (Paris: Presses Universitaires de France, 1959), and Philippe Robert and Pierre Lascoumes, *Les Bandes d'Adolescents: Une Théorie de la Ségrégation* (Paris: Les Editions Ouvrières, 1974).

23 Hans Jürgen Wolter, "Phänomene und Behandlung des Rockertums," *Kriminalistik* 27:2 (July 1973).

24 In the Federal German Republic these groups also engaged in robbery of persons such as homosexuals and drug addicts. See Wolter, "Phänomene."

25 Bernhard Meili, "Familie, Schule, Freunde und Jugenddelinquenz" (mimeo), Sociologisches Institut der Universität Zürich, 1975. This study involved four hundred boys aged 15 to 16.

26 Pierre Arnold, Michel Bassand, Bernard Crettaz, and Jean Kellerhals, *Jeunesse et Société* (Lausanne: Payot, 1971), particularly chapter 8.

27 Ibid., p. 86 (translated from the French).

28 H. P. Müller and G. Lotmar, *Der Bunker von Zürich: Jugend zwischen Rückzug and Revolte, Ein Modellfall* (Olten: Walter Verlag, 1972).

29 Arnold et al., *Jeunesse,* pp. 86–7. One still commonly sees, in the larger cities, young persons give up their seats on trams and buses to adult women and to older persons.

30 In a 1973 study of a representative sample of 2,260 youths aged 15 to 30 in Zürich canton, for example, they generally were found to be optimistic about employment and professional development. See Blancpain and Häuselmann, *Zur Unrast,* pp. 164–5.

31 Thomas Held and René Levy, *Die Stellung der Frau in Familie und Gesellschaft* (Frauenfeld and Stuttgart: Verlag Huber, 1974), p. 81. The following data come from page 71 and page 81.

32 Edmund W. Vaz and John Casparis, "A Comparative Study of Youth Culture and Delin-

quency: Upper Middle-Class Canadian and Swiss Boys," *International Journal of Comparative Sociology* 12:1 (March, 1971), 7. Their research concentrated on youth culture peer orientation and self-reported delinquency of middle-class youth in both countries. Unfortunately, however, the Canadian study was carried out primarily in four suburban communities adjacent to cities of 100,000 to 250,000 people, while that in Switzerland was carried out in Chur, a city of 25,000 in the canton of Graubünden, one of the least industrialized and urbanized cantons. Although this failure to control for urbanization and the concentration on upper-middle-class youth in Canada makes the comparative findings less useful than they otherwise might have been, they still show significant differences.

33 Blancpain and Häuselmann, *Zur Unrast.* Chapter 3.

34 Casparis and Vaz, *Swiss Society.* In their earlier study of Graubünden they had tried to place it on an urban—industrial continuum with Canadian urban youth, but they have now dropped this comparison. See Vaz and Casparis, "A Comparative Study."

35 Blancpain and Häuselmann, *Zur Unrast,* p. 54.

36 Claudio Casparis, *Zur Unrast der Jugend: Eine sozialpsychologische Untersuchung der Beziehungen zwischen Erwachsenen und Jugendlichen in Familie, Bildung und Beruf (Reihe Soziologie in der Schweiz,* Vol. 3) (Frauenfeld and Stuttgart: Verlag Huber, 1975). Somewhat over 10 percent indicated as a first priority "to satisfy my parents," and 52 percent ranked first "to develop my personality and live according to my interests." Another study, done, however, on a very young group of boys *and* girls found them to be more peer-oriented than Americans of the same age. Since their age was thirteen, the finding is of significance as it indicates a trend for the potential criminal age groups discussed here. K. Lüscher, "Dreizehnjährige Schweizer zwischen Peers und Erwachsenen im interkulturellen Vergleich," *Schweizerische Zeitschrift für Psychologie* 30:3 (1971), 219—29.

37 Blancpain and Häuselmann, *Zur Unrast.*

38 Arnold et al., *Jeunesse et Société,* p. 87.

39 Blancpain and Häuselmann, *Zur Unrast* p. 283 (Summary in English).

40 Ibid., p. 177. This is perhaps a somewhat biased sample, because today generally approximately 40 percent of the 20-year-olds are declared unfit for military service, and the figure is even larger in the cities. What this percentage was in 1964 is not known, but it was probably less.

41 Even though service is compulsory, in actuality four out of ten of those subject to military service are considered either physically unfit or are exempt from it for other reasons. *Neue Zürcher Zeitung,* January, 1975. Proposals have been made for non-military service as a substitute, primarily because of increasing opposition to military service among some youth. A 1977 national referendum rejected an amendment to the constitution that would have exempted conscientious objectors from military service.

42 See Eidgenössisches Militärdepartement, "Stab der Gruppe für Ausbildung, Statistik der Offiziersschüler 1975," Tables 8a and 8c.

10. Crime and the foreign worker

1 See Jean Graven, "Le Problème des Travailleurs étrangers délinquants en Suisse," *Revue Internationale de Criminologie et de Police Technique* 19 (July—September 1965), 265—90. Also see Hans Joachim Hoffmann-Nowotny, *Soziologie des Fremdarbeiterproblems* (Stuttgart: Enke, 1973);

2 For a discussion of the foreign worker in other countries, see Edward R. F. Sheehand, "Europe's Hired Poor," *The New York Times Magazine,* December 9, 1973, pp. 36 ff.

3 According to Professor H. J. Hoffmann-Nowotny, University of Zürich, an informed authority in this area, the percentage of Italians among the entire Swiss foreign population is slightly less, 53.6 percent.

4 In October, 1974, Swiss citizens voted on a referendum to deport one-half of the foreign workers, but it lost, 66 percent to 34 percent. One of the principal arguments against the proposal was that Swiss citizens would be forced to perform many of the menial tasks now being done by the foreigners if they were forced to leave. See "Swiss Vote to Let Foreigners Stay," *The New York Times*, October 21, 1974, pp. 1 and 5.

5 Hoffman-Nowotny, *Soziologie*.

6 Ibid., pp. 2—3.

7 Ibid., p. 4

8 Hans-Rudolf Emmenegger, "Erscheinungsformen der Kriminalität bei Schweizern und Ausländern," *Kriminalistik* 21 (1967), 647—9.

9 Graven, "Le Problème."

10 "Komitee Schweiz 80," *Handbuch zur Ausländerpolitik*, 1974, p. 17. Figures are based on *Statistisches Jahrbuch der Schweiz und Statistisches Quellenwerk der Schweiz*, No. 487, 1972.

11 Pierre Pradervand and Laura Cardia, "Quelques Aspects de la Délinquance Italienne à Genève, une Enquête Sociologique," *Revue Internationale de Criminologie et de Police Technique* 20 (1966), 43—58.

12 Jürg Neumann, *Die Kriminalität der italienischen Arbeitskräfte im Kanton Zürich* (Zürich: Juris-Verlag, 1963). Neumann's study of the Italian workers in the canton of Zürich was done in 1963, but conversations with well-informed persons indicated that the situation has not greatly changed. He based his research on 415 cases handled in the Zürich courts in 1949, 1954, 1955, and 1960. He selected 1949 because it was the first year for which data were available, 1954 and 1955 because it was during the 1950s that the foreign workers had become predominantly male, rather than female domestics, and 1960 because the latest available data were available then for his study. In calculating rates he used an average population figure, because the foreign worker population is larger in summer than in winter.

13 Neumann, *Die Kriminalität*, p. 53.

14 If a convicted foreign worker receives a suspended sentence, he is regularly deported and is not permitted to reenter Switzerland for several years.

15 Neumann, *Die Kriminalität*, p. 81.

16 Ibid., p. 83.

17 Ibid., p. 95.

18 Rolf Stephani, "Die Wegnahme von Waren in Selbstbedienungsläden durch Kunden, Eine kriminologische Untersuchung von 1481 Tätern," *Berner kriminologische Untersuchungen*, Hans Schultz, ed. (Bern: Paul Haupt, 1968), Vol 5.

19 Neumann, *Die Kriminalität*, p. 118.

20 Hans Witschi, "Probleme der Prostitution," *Kriminalistik* 20 (1966), 500—3.

21 Neumann, *Die Kriminalität*, pp. 71—2.

22 Hoffmann-Nowotny, *Soziologie*.

23 See *Kriminalitätsatlas der Bundesrepublik Deutschland und West Berlin* (Wiesbaden: Bundeskriminalamt, 1972).

24 Patricia Cayo Sexton, *Spanish Harlem: Anatomy of Poverty* (New York: Harper & Row, 1965).

25 The President's Commission on Law Enforcement and Administration of Justice, *Task Force Report: Crime and Its Impact — an Assessment* (Washington, D.C.: U.S. Government Printing Office, 1967), p. 35. Also see *The Challenge of Crime in a Free Society: A Report by the President's Commission on Law Enforcement and Administration of Justice* (New York: Avon Books, 1968); and Marshall B. Clinard, *Slums and Community Development: Experiments in Self-Help* (New York: The Free Press/Macmillan, 1966), pp. 9—11.

26 Clinard, *Slums and Community Development,* pp. 11—17, and pages 108—12; and Marshall B. Clinard, *Sociology of Deviant Behavior,* 4th ed. (New York: Holt, Rinehart and Winston, 1974), pp. 61—93.

27 Edwin H. Sutherland and Donald R. Cressey, *Criminology,* 9th ed. (Philadelphia: Lippincott, 1974), p. 147.

28 Martin Killias, "Kriminelle Fremdarbeiterkinder? Strukturelle Determinanten der Delinquenz bei Fremdarbeitern unter besonderer Berücksichtigung der zweiten Generation, Eine explorative Studie am Beispiel der Städte Zürich und Genf," *Schweizerische Zeitschrift für Soziologie* 3:2 (June 1977), 3—33. Killias also suggests theoretically that the criminality of foreign workers increases according to the time spent in Switzerland. Workers who have resided in the country for a long time tend more to be individuals who still have high aspirational levels, although they increasingly perceive these goals as being non-realizeable. (See Hoffmann-Nowotny, *Soziologie,* p. 232.)

29 The Zürich crime victimization survey showed that both the Swiss and foreign-born generally approve highly of the work of the police.

30 Sutherland and Cressey, *Criminology,* pp. 142—9.

31 Franco Ferracuti, "European Migration and Crime," Paper presented at the Fifth European Conference of Directors of Criminological Research Institutes, Strasbourg, October 25, 1967 (Strasbourg: Council of Europe, 1967), p. 26.

11. Cross-cultural implications of the low Swiss crime rate

1 See *Brottsutvecklinger 1973—1978.* Rapport avgiven av Arbetsgruppen für Kriminalitetsprognoser, Justitiedepartmentet (mimeo), July 16, 1973.

2 Some of the conclusions presented here have been reached with reluctance because of the author's liberal political views and those once enthusiastically held while he was a visiting professor at the University of Stockholm for a year.

3 Roland Huntsford, *The New Totalitarians* (New York: Stein and Day, 1971), p. 125.

4 Ibid., p. 126.

5 Paul Britten Austin, *On Being Swedish* (Coral Gables, Fla.: University of Miami Press, 1968), 89—90.

6 Ibid., p. 37.

7 "Something Souring in Utopia," *Time,* July 19, 1976, p. 35.

8 Swedish Information Office, *News from Sweden* (New York: Swedish Consulate General, August, 1976).

9 Flora Lewis, "Swiss, Stable and Affluent, Facing Problems from Too Much Success," *The New York Times,* September 7, 1976, section C, p. 6.

10 Carl-Gunnar Janson, "Juvenile Delinquency in Sweden," *Youth and Society* (December 1970), 207—31. Janson is one of the leading Swedish sociologists.

11 Ibid., 214. For Swedish literature on peer orientation, see the following: Birgitta Olofsson, *Vad Var Det Vi Så!* (Stockholm: Utbildningsförlaget, 1971). See, especially, pp. 145 ff; Skolöverstyrelsen, *Tonåringar och Normer* (Stockholm: Utbildningsförlaget, 1973): Birgitta Olofsson, ed., *Unga Lagöverträdare III* (Stockholm: Statens Offentliga Utredningar, 1973), especially pp. 138—47; and Åke Daun, Bengt Börjesen, and Stig Ahs, *Samhällsförändringar och Brottslighet* (Stockholm: Tidens Förlag, 1974), especially section 2.

12 Janson, "Juvenile Delinquency," p. 221.

13 Marshall B. Clinard, *Slums and Community Development: Experiments in Self-Help* (New York: The Free Press/Macmillan, 1966; paperback, 1970).

14 National Advisory Commission on Criminal Justice, Standards, and Goals, *Corrections* (Washington, D.C.: U.S. Department of Justice, 1973).

15 See, for example, the proposals of the United States Conference of Mayors, *Hand Gun Control: Issues and Alternatives* (Washington, D.C.: U.S. Government Printing Office, 1975).
16 See *United Nations Demographic Year Book, 1970.*

Index

201

Blancpain, Robert, 131, 132, 195 n13
Blick (newspaper), 28, 29, 31
Blomberg, Dick, 196 n18
Bogue, Donald J., 192 n1, 196 n18
bonds, regulation of, 89
border cantons, crime rates in, 51
Börjesen, Bengt, 199 n11
Bosshard, Peter, 196 n16
Boston, crime victimization survey in, 61
Brandenberger, W., xvi
Brillon, Yves, 187 n9
Britain, *see* England and Wales
Buikhusen, W., 187 n8
Bundesrat, *see* Federal Council
Bundesversammlung, *see* Federal Assembly
Bureau of the Census (U.S.), *see* Census Bureau (U.S.) - LEAA
Burgess, Ernest W., 192 n1, 196 n18
burglary: attitudes toward increases in, 21, 148; insurance rates and, 77, 78, 79; by juveniles, 124, 125; rates of, 39—40, 47, 150; reporting of, 59, 68—9; urbanization and, 104
Burkhard, Heidi, xvi
Burmer, M., 184 n20
business, laws regulating, 89

Calvinist ethic, 93
Cambridge University, Institute of Criminology of, 62
Canada: firearms in, 114; juvenile crime in, 123; schools in, 131
cantons: border, crime in, 51; crime control and, 17, 86; criminal law and, 7; politics and, 6, 108—9, 110
capital en fuite, 93
capital punishment, 7, 46
Cardia, Laura, 198 n11
cartels, 88
Casparis, John, 124, 125, 131, 195 n12, 196 n32, 197 n34, 197 n36
Census Bureau (U.S.) - LEAA, 62, 64, 65, 66, 70, 73
Centraf AG, 89
checking accounts, *see* post office accounts
Chicago: crime victimization survey in, 61; insurance rates in, 75, 76, 77
Christiansen, Karl O., 180 n2
citizenship: communes and, 106, 109; foreign workers and, 137
Clark, Wentworth, 182 n15
Clarke, Thurston, 95, 191 n28, 191 n32
class: criminal definition and, 85—6; foreign workers and, 136; juvenile delinquency and, 124, 129
Clerc, François, 194 n49
Clinard, Marshall B., 180 n4, 187 n10, 188 n18, 189 n31, 189 n32, 190 n2, 190 n3, 191 n17, 191 n18, 192 n1, 192 n2, 192

n9, 194 n44, 194 n1, 195 n1, 195 n3, 195 n14, 196 n18, 198 n25, 199 n26, 199 n13
communes, 106, 108—9, 111
communication(s): intergenerational, 103, 122, 130, 131, 132, 133—5, 150; within Switzerland, 110
commuters, 106
COMP, *see* Council on Municipal Performance
competition, white-collar crime and, 88
Conservative Party (Swedish), crime control and, 16
convictions, rates of, 3, 46—9, 52, 164—5
Conza, Anne-Marie, 192 n10, 196 n22
Copenhagen (Denmark): crime victimization survey in, 66, 70, 149; population of, 105
Cornfeld, Bernard, 91
Council of Europe, 2
Council of Municipal Performance (COMP), 73
Council of States (Ständerat), *see* Federal Assembly
courts, 108: attitudes toward, 56—7; foreign workers and, 142
Crédit Mobilier, 92
Crédit Suisse Bank, 90, 91, 92, 98
Cressey, Donald, R., 143, 186 n1, 194 n1, 199 n27, 199 n30
Crettaz, Bernhard, 196 n26
crime, *see entries for individual criminal acts*
crime rates: of assault, 38, 51, 141, 142, 148; of burglary, 39—40, 47, 150; comparative statistics of, 3, 34—5, 162—3; crime victimiztion survey and, 61, 62; for foreign workers, 139—41, 151; of homicide, 1, 37—8, 47, 52, 114, 148; for juveniles, 27, 43, 107, 122—3, 154; of robbery, 38—9, 47, 48, 51, 67, 114, 148; in Switzerland, 2, 36—7, 160—1, 164, 165; of theft (*Diebstahl*), 41—3, 47, 148
crime statistics: police and, 53—4, 55—6, 61; politics and, 34; theft insurance and, 73—4; unavailability of, 34, 146
crime victimization survey, 3, 41, 147, 149, 169—73, 178—9: assumptions of, 63; comparisons of, 62, 65—7; crimes against households and, 68—9, 176—7; crimes against persons and, 69—71; development of, 61; foreign workers and, 140; interview schedules of, 64—5; reports to police and, 57—8; urbanization and, 104
Criminal Code (Swiss), 7, 13, 15, 36, 46, 86, 116, 121, 127
criminal justice system: political decentralization and, 108; Swiss, 1, 103, 115—21, 150, 151; white-collar crime and, 86
criminal law procedures, changes in, 13

183 n1, 184 n12, 184 n25, 187 n6, 195 n2, 195 n7, 195 n8
Keller, W., xvi
Kellerhals, Jean, 196 n26
Killias, Martin, xv, 143, 182 n11
Klaüi, Paul, 193 n21
Klingenberg, Peter-Dieter, 191 n35
Komitee Schweiz 80, 139, 198 n10
Kurier (Vienna), 29, 31

labor, in Switzerland, 8—9: *see also* foreign workers
Ladewig, D., 184 n20
Lane, Robert E., 191 n17
language: distribution of, 7; politics and, 8
larceny: crime victimization survey and, 68, 69, 70—71; by foreign workers, 141; increases in rates of, 41, 47; insurance claims for, 78; by juveniles, 124; urbanization and, 104
Lascoumes, Pierre, 196 n22
Lassere, Victor, 191 n25
Lausanne: crime rates in, 36, 41; population of, 5
Law Enforcement Administration (LEAA), *see* Census Bureau (U.S.) - LEAA
Lehman, Walter, xvi
Leland, Steward, 182 n15
Lemert, Edwin M., 194 n44
Lenke, Leif, 183 n21, 183 n26
Le Soir (Paris), 29, 31
letters to editors, crime attitudes and, 31—2
Levine, James P., 188 n17
Levy, René, 130, 183 n19, 187 n13, 196 n31
Lewis, Flora, 199 n9
loans, fraudulent, 89
Lomecky, Zdenek, xvi
London, crime victimization survey in, 62, 66
López—Rey, Manuel, 180 n3
Lotmar, G., 196 n28
Lugano: banks in, 88; foreign visitor crime in, 50
Luvini, Mario, xvi
Luxemburg, crime rates in, 35

McGraw-Hill Company, 94
Malmö (Sweden): crime rates in, 36; crime victimization survey in, 70; drug arrests in, 45; population of, 10
manslaughter (nonnegligent), *see* homicide
marijuana, *see* drugs
marriage age, 130—1, 141
mass media, criminal stereotypes in, 84
Mast, Hans, J. 97—8, 191 n42
Mayer, Kurt, xv
Mayer-Boss, Sybille, 184 n42
Meier, Erick, xv
Meier, J., xvi

Meier, Robert F., 190 n3
Meili, Bernhard, 196 n25
Messerli, Alfred, xv, 190 n7
migration: crime and, 144; cultural diversity and, 105; rural to urban, 104, 107
military criminal code, 46
Miller, H. P., 196 n28
mineral resources, 8
Minnesota, auto theft insurance in, 77
Mobiliar, *see* Schweizerische Mobiliar
mobility (geographic), limits of, 105, 107
mobility (occupational), of foreign workers, 138
Mommsen, Karl, 192 n20
monetary speculation, 86
morality: conviction rates and, 49, 52; crimes against, 47
motorcycles: insurance claims for theft of, 78; juvenile delinquency and, 127
Mühlemann, R., 184 n21
murder, *see* homicide

National Assembly, *see* Federal Assembly
National Council (Nationalrat), *see* Federal Assembly
National Crime Panel (U.S.), 62
National Opinion Research Center, 61
National Science Foundation, 3
naturalization, 109
Nazi Germany, bank secrecy law and, 96
neighborhoods: attitudes toward crime and, 21; crime rates and, 106; crime victimization survey and, 69; safety in, 24—6
Netherlands, the: crime rates in, 35; imprisonment in, 116, 117; population in, 105
Neue Zürcher Zeitung, 18, 28, 29, 30, 31
Neukom, Alfred, 192 n19
Neumann, Jürg, 140, 142, 198 n12, 198 n13, 198 n15, 198 n19, 198 n21
Newman, Donald J., 185 n30
newspapers, 3, 18, 28—32, 33, 136, 147
Newton, George D., 193 n31, 193 n32
New York City: auto insurance rates in, 77; fear of crime in, 25; insurance rates in, 75, 76; Puerto Rican workers in, 142
New York Daily News, The, 29
New York Journal American, 29
New York Stock Exchange, 87
New York Times, The, 28, 29
Noll, Peter, xv
Norway: conviction rates in, 46; crime rates in, 35; crime reporting in, 59; imprisonment in, 116, 117; insurance claims in, 80, 81

Ohio, insurance rates in, 77
Olofsson, Birgitta, 199 n11
organized crime, attitudes toward, 27

206

sexual offenses, 15, 132, 141
Seymour, Whitney North, Jr., 190 n16
Sheehand, Edward R. F., 197 n2
shoplifting: by foreign workers, 141; increases in, 21, 42—3; by juveniles, 127
Siegrist, Harald Olav, xvi, 184 n19
Simonet, Danielle, 192 n10, 196 n22
Skogan, Wesley G., 186 n3
slums: absence of, in Switzerland, 103, 106; crime rates and, 142, 156
Social Democratic party (Swedish), 16, 153
socialist countries, 180 n1
social problems, ranking of, compared, 22, 23
social security benefits, 138, 153
Solms, H., 184 n20
Sorell, Walter, 5, 108, 181 n16, 192 n16
Spain, insurance claims in, 79, 80
Sparks, Richard, xvi, 185 n25, 185 n7, 187 n5, 188 n17, 188 n24, 196 n18
sports, 133, 134, 151
Staub, Sylvia, 127, 196 n17, 196 n19, 196 n20
Steiner, Jürg, 181 n20
Stephan, Egon, 182 n13, 185 n5, 187 n6, 188 n20
Stephani, Rolf, 42, 184 n13, 198 n18
stock exchange (black market), 92
Stockholm (Sweden): crime rates in, 36, 40, 148; crime victimization survey in, 66, 70; drug arrests in, 45; population of, 10, 105
Stratenwerth, Günther, xv, 119, 194 n46, 194 n50
Stuttgart (F.G.R.): attitudes toward crime in, 19, 21, 22, 148; attitudes toward police in, 56—7; concern about crime in 24; crime rates in, 38; crime reporting in, 58—9, 60; crime victimization survey in, 62, 66—7, 69, 70, 71, 182 n13; neighborhoods in, 25—6; population of, 19
suffrage, see franchise
suicide, rates of, in Switzerland, 2
Suskind, Richard, 191 n31
Sutherland, Edwin H., 88, 143, 186 n1, 189 n2, 190 n17, 191 n19, 194 n1, 199 n27, 199 n30
Sutter, Werner, 192 n12, 195 n5
Sveri, Knut, xvi, 181 n21, 182 n8, 195 n3
Sweden: crime control in, 16; crime rates in, 35, 36, 38, 39, 40, 43, 51, 52, 149; crime reporting in, 59; drug use in, 45; economy of, 10; firearms in, 115; foreign workers in, 137, 145; imprisonment in, 116, 117; insurance rates in, 78; juvenile crime in, 123, 126, 154, 181 n21; newspapers in, 30; political structure of, 10—11, 107, 108, 152—3; population of, 9—10, 105; welfare in, 115

Swiss army: drug use in, 45; membership in, 114, 133—4, 151; police and, 54
Swiss Bankers Association, 94, 98
Swiss Banking Commission, 95
Swiss Bank Secrecy law, 87, 93—8, 150
Swiss Credit Bank, see Crédit Suisse Bank
Swiss National Bank, 91, 98
Swiss Reinsurance Company, 74
Szabo, Denis, 192 n1

Tages Anzeiger, 19, 29, 30, 31
taxation: amnesty in, 99—101; bank secrecy law and, 98; forms of, in Switzerland, 98—9; violations of, 46, 86, 89, 150
terrorism, 32
Texon Finanzanstalt, 90
theft: attitudes toward increases in, 21; rates of, by insurance claims, 79
Thürer, Georg, 193 n23
Ticino: attitudes toward crime in, 27; foreign visitor crime in, 49, 50, 51,
Tigue, John, Jr., 95, 191 n28, 191 n32
Time magazine, 40
Tonge, Peter, 181 n15, 193 n26
tourism: crime victimization and, 71—2, 78; Swiss economy and, 5
trade associations, 88
trade, restraint of, 88
Trechsel, Stefan, xvi
Tuchschmid, Axel, xvi
Turner, Anthony G., xvi, 173, 187 n10

Ulrich, Willy, 190 n9, 191 n20
Uniform Criminal Code (Swiss), 7, 13, 15, 36, 46, 86; 116, 121, 127
United Nations Congress on the Prevention of Crime, 62
United States: crime rates in, compared, 37, 38, 39, 40, 43, 51, 52, 104; crime victimization surveys in, 61—2; drug use in, compared, 45; firearms in, 114—15; guidelines for, 155—8; imprisonment in, 117, 121; insurance in, compared, 74—6, 77, 79, 80, 81; juvenile crime in, 123, 124, 125, 126; police forces of, compared, 55; shoplifting in, 42; see also entries for individual cities and states
universities, 105
University of Freiburg, 19, 62
University of Zürich, 63, 169
urbanization: crime rates and, 102, 103—4; in Sweden, 10, 152; in Switzerland, 5, 104—5, 107, 150; see also industrialization

value conflicts, white-collar crime and, 87—8
vandalism, 67: crime victimization survey and, 68, 69; decrease in rates of, 47; juvenile crime and, 125—6

Vaz, Edmund W., 124, 125, 131, 195 n12, 196 n32, 197 n34
Vesco, Robert, 91
Viano, Emilio, 186 n3
violence, crimes of, 3, 14, 27, 30, 51, 67, 114
vote, *see* franchise

wages, *see* income(s)
Walker, Lewis, 181 n20
Warynski, Jean-Robert, xvi
Washington, D.C., crime victimization survey in, 61
Watergate investigations, 29
weapons: federal control of, 14; foreign workers and, 17; juveniles and, 125; *see also* firearms
Weidmann, M., 184 n20
Weiland, H., xvi
Weiss, Rüdiger, 187 n7
welfare (relief): communes and, 109; self-reliance and, 112
Welti, F., 180 n5, 180 n6
white-collar crime, 32: in banking, 92—8; extent of, 84—5, 102, 150; increases in, 18, 101; political system and, 85—7, 108; self-concept and, 83—4; types of, 89—92; value conflicts and, 87—8; *see also* banks and banking
Wickberg, Nils, 184 n18
Winsborough, Halliman, xvii
Wisconsin, insurance rates in, 74, 77
Witschi, Hans, 198 n20
Wolf, Preben, xvi, 186 n10, 186 n4, 188 n22, 188 n23
Wolfgang, Marvin E., 193 n30

Wolter, Hans Jürgen, 196 n23
women: attitudes toward crime of, 20, 21; crime victimization survey and, 63—4; among foreign workers, 137; in labor force, 154; political rights of, 8, 131; prisons for, 119; status of, in Switzerland, 25, 130
workmen's compensation, 138
World Bank Atlas, The, 4
World War II, bank secrecy laws and, 97
Wüthrich, Von P., 180 n5
Wyss, P., 184 n20

youth, *see* juveniles and juvenile delinquency

Zehnder, R., 184 n21
Ziegler, Jean, 191 n25
Zimmerli, Erwin, 190 n12
Zimring, Franklin E., 193 n31, 193 n32
Zuppinger, F., 191 n43
Zürich: attitudes toward crime in, 20—1, 22; attitudes toward drug use in, 44; attitudes toward police in, 56, 57; crime rate in, 36, 37, 38, 40, 41; crime reporting in, 58—9; crime victimization survey in, 62—3, 65—71, 169—75; foreign visitor crime in, 49, 50; homicide in, 114; household sampling in, 18—19; juvenile crime in, 127, 128, 132; neighborhoods in, 24—6; police forces in, 55, 56, 57; population of, 5, 105; white-collar crime in, 91
Zürich City Council (Gemeinderat), 17: crime control and, 18
Zürich Parliament (Kantonsrat), 17—18
Zwingli, Ulrich, xvi, 169